A Wordsmith's Work

THREE DECADES OF WRITING
TO PERSUADE, INFORM, AND AMUSE

Mark R. Weaver

Central Ohio

Mark R. Weaver, Esq.
Isaac, Wiles, Burkholder & Teetor
Two Miranova, #700
Columbus, Ohio 43215
www.AWordsmithsWork.com

Ordering Information:
This book is available on several online book marketplaces.

A Wordsmith's Work/ Mark R. Weaver —3rd ed.
ISBN 978-1544912592

Contents

Ghostwriting

Speeches

Book Reviews

Writing for grief

A wordsmith's toolbox

Dedication

This book is dedicated to the memory of my mother, Joanne Mateer Weaver Stroh. With love and unusual patience, she taught me to read and write, laying a firm foundation so this wordsmith could eventually help others communicate better.

Acknowledgements

I simply could not have written this book without the generous support and encouragement of my cherished wife Lori and our two beloved children, Jamieson and Robbie. Every moment spent writing the works in this book was a moment away from this family I love and treasure beyond any earthly measure. Their understanding of those absences was more gracious than I deserve.

Thank you to Matt Dole and Michael Shearer, who helped edit this book. They offered insightful advice and certainly helped improve this wordsmith's work. I am also grateful to my friend U.S. Congressman Bill Johnson for his very generous words of praise in the Foreword.

The book's cover was designed by a talented artist who freelances after a day's work at a major ad agency. The work is anonymous and the artist politely declined my offer of a published thank you. This well-crafted and thoroughly innovative design may well encourage casual observers to actually judge a book by its cover. One can hope.

In the ideas presented and the words chosen, any errors of form or substance are mine alone. Any good work that I may have achieved along the way is best credited to the selfless dedication, fervent hopes, and patient guidance of my mother, Joanne Mateer Weaver Stroh.

And, most importantly, all glory to God.

Mark R. Weaver
April 2017

Foreword

I first met Mark Weaver in 2007, when officials in my area suggested I run for a seat in the United States House of Representatives. Realizing my 26 years in the U.S. Air Force and 10 years as a businessman hadn't given me even the most basic knowledge of mounting a national-level campaign, I immediately sought help. Friends in Ohio directed me to a training course, where Mark Weaver happened to be the keynote speaker. Over the course of just a few hours, he skillfully captivated the crowd, explaining the complex issues surrounding media and messaging.

Amazed by the way he presented such complicated communications principles in terms that even a political novice like me could understand, it was clear he knew his stuff. On a break from class, I phoned my wife. "Honey," I said, "if we're ever going to consider running for public office, we must have someone like Mark Weaver to help us." I introduced myself to Mark on the next break, and that began a relationship that has matured into not only a professional partnership, but a lasting friendship based on mutual respect and shared values.

Over the next two years, Mark led me through the intricate process of putting together a grassroots movement. Mark knew we needed to inform people in my community about my background and raise my profile. We started by telling my story to the citizens of Ohio, through a narrative that emphasized my leadership and business experience. Mark helped me build a statewide effort to reform sales tax laws to keep millions of sales tax dollars in Ohio and create or protect thousands of retail jobs. State legislators eventually supported the idea, passed a new law, and implemented a sales tax holiday, which helps working families purchase the supplies they need to send their children to school.

In 2010, we turned our attention to running for Congress, and once again Mark put his messaging skills to good work. At the outset, no one even noticed us. Party officials at the national level paid little attention. We were up against an entrenched, well-liked incumbent congressman, and few thought we had a prayer of achieving victory. Despite the long odds, Mark led the strategic and communications effort with gusto. Our funds were limited, and communicating in a district with eight major media markets was expensive. Mark knew we had to make every message, indeed, every word, count.

With Mark at the center of our outreach, he systematically delivered hard-hitting, focused media that told my story and differentiated me from my opponent. He understood the dynamic of reaching people in a cluttered media environment, and he knew what messages would change minds and open hearts. Mark's themes hit home, deep in the soul of the hardworking people of eastern Ohio. On election night, many were stunned when we won by a nearly five-point margin. Since then, Mark has led my communications efforts and we've been more and more successful with each new challenge.

Along the way, Mark has used his powerful writing skills to help me compose community speeches, newspaper op-eds, and even some of the addresses I give from the floor of the U.S. Congress. He understands my voice, knows my values, and consistently drafts eloquent language that helps me do my job as a national leader.

There's no more apt term to describe Mark Weaver than what's reflected in the title of this book — he is truly a "wordsmith." He's a master at understanding the cultural, societal, and media influences of the day. He takes that knowledge and crafts a message that cuts through the confusion, so people see the clear truth.

I can't think of anyone more committed to the values upon which our great nation was founded, and his writing and communications work serve to remind all Americans just how precious those ideals remain today. When I learned that Mark once wrote for, and worked one-on-one with, former President Ronald Reagan, I was more than impressed. I was excited to collaborate with Mark in a similar vein.

I'm proud to be a member of the United States Congress. And I can say without any hesitation that I simply wouldn't be where I am today had I not met Mark Weaver and harnessed his powerful communications skills.

You'll be glad you read this book. The examples and tips Mark provides in these pages can help just about anyone be a better writer and communicator. It's my hope that you'll use this knowledge as I have, to help make a difference in the greatest nation the world has known — the United States of America.

Please enjoy *A Wordsmith's Work*. I know I have.

Bill Johnson
Member of Congress

Preface

My first attempts at writing involved wielding a crayon like the proverbial blunt instrument. The remnants of that work survive in crumpled form, dismissed into odd corners of boxes otherwise groaning with the detritus of my childhood. It is best left undisturbed.

Later, despite my very best effort at being unnoticeable in class behind an open copy of *The Hockey News*, my eighth-grade English teacher (an avid Philadelphia Flyers fan himself) saw something in my writing. He asked me to serve as the editor of our school newspaper. Anyone who knew me well back then was as surprised as I was. My contributions to the Abington Junior High School *Informer* were pedestrian and as unmemorable as an hour of detention. Perhaps the sole exception was my internationally-acclaimed work as the newspaper's anonymous advice columnist "Dear Gabby." Such brilliance of composition would not go unnoticed.

In high school, few people would have pegged me as much of a writer, particularly since I could neither type well nor handwrite legibly. The advent of computers and word processing software helped that along and, by the time I finished graduate school and law school, my ability to write in a format for mass distribution was supported and enhanced by technology.

Early on, my writing was almost always on behalf of others. While I'd written a few letters to the editor in my own name (the first being published in the now-defunct *Philadelphia Bulletin* daily newspaper when I was 16), I was mostly a ghostwriter for public officials and politicians. Word got around that I was available to write news releases, opinion columns, and speeches and I soon cobbled together a small income from it.

Even while going to law school at night, which requires a significant amount of writing in itself, I shunted leisure pursuits aside and made time to tackle several writing projects every week. The prose was workmanlike and passable for the tasks assigned. Some projects were fun to write. Others felt like ten miles of bad road. For example, while I was glad to cash the checks, I was not particularly enamored of my toil doing technical writing for a ball bearing manufacturer. Did you know that a chromium steel shielded ball bearing can help protect against leaks? Of course, you didn't. But I had to. And so, I wrote.

Years later, after a stint as a national spokesman for the United States Department of Justice, I worked as a communications and media consultant in Washington, D.C., where instead of writing for state legislators, commissioners, and judges, I found myself drafting work for congressmen, senators, and governors. During those five years, the highlight was writing, directing, and producing a television special that was hosted by former president Ronald Reagan. That media project, which including spending a morning with Mr. Reagan helping him with his television delivery, remains the stellar highlight of my communications career. I penned the script in the best Reaganesqe style I could manage, and I was proud to see President Reagan's own copy of my script underlined, highlighted, and dog-eared. A previously-published firsthand account of that session is featured here in this book.

Later, when I moved to Ohio in 1995 to become the state's Deputy Attorney General, I found the kind of work I do much in demand. Legal drafting, composing high-profile editorial work, and persuasive writing in the policy arena became my daily tasks. Many days, I wrote as much as a working journalist would. Other days, I spent hours editing the work of my staff and colleagues.

Once, I was discussing my daily writing routine with a handyman working in my home. When he learned that I often spend several hours looking at the same document, massaging the words and coaxing out the highest clarity of thought, the man remarked that he wouldn't have the patience to do that. I pointed out that I get frustrated after about five minutes with a screwdriver, so we were probably both well suited to our respective callings.

I've taught law school and graduate school for more than two decades and I lecture around the country. I'm also regularly interviewed on TV and radio public affairs programs, engaging in the nerve-rattling thrust and parry of political debate. While there's a certain intoxication of involvement that comes along with standing in front of hundreds of industry leaders and endeavoring to impart wisdom or instantly crafting a retort to an interviewer's aggressive inquiry, more often, I'm magnetically drawn to the quieter pursuit of writing. Public speaking — particularly speaking extemporaneously, my most common enterprise — can be an exertion. Writing, in the hush of reflection, is restorative.

The title of this book stems from a comment I've heard countless times in my career. Advising hundreds of clients in 26 states, I often found myself in a meeting where a group of intense and intelligent people were debating what messages their organization wanted to convey. After exhausting the conversation, someone would typically look over at me and say, "we all agree on the basics of what we want to say, now let's just let Mark wordsmith it."

Wordsmith as a verb. Hmm.

We all know the noun "smith." The most common use is someone who fashions metal using heat, resulting in a blackened patina—hence, a blacksmith. The "smith" part of the word could mean the verb "to strike" (the Old English variation) or it could mean a skilled worker (the German origin). But whether as a noun or a verb, where did we get the expression "wordsmith?"

My research suggests the first known use of the word in a published setting arose in 1915, in a book by newspaperman and art critic James Huneker, entitled *New Cosmopolis*. He uses the term in passing, pointing out that, after taking an excursion and then returning to work, he headed "back to the newspaper forge, there to resume my old job of *wordsmith*." Like me, Huneker was born in Philadelphia and enjoyed wrestling with words. I'm sure he would have joined me in rooting for the Philadelphia Flyers, if the team had only existed at the time.

Huneker's analogy of his writing desk as a forge is apt. Shaping the right words from the raw material of idea requires great effort and the intense heat of mental focus. Selecting words that work is an exacting process. The American wordsmith Mark Twain may have put it best:

"The difference between the almost right word and the right word is really a large matter—it's the difference between the lightning bug and the lightning."

Writing giants like Twain, Herman Wouk, C. S. Lewis, Frank McCourt, Andrew Peterson, and Peggy Noonan are much more deserving of the title wordsmith than me. Yet each time a notion pesters me into action and I finally sit down to square off against a menacing blank screen and toothy keyboard, I boldly aspire yet again to the calling. This book chronicles those journeys of composition.

———

A Wordsmith's Work is a compilation of my best writing over three decades. Most of it was published in my own name. A few pieces never saw publication. I've also included those ghostwriting projects of which I am proudest. The clients for whom I wrote have always been open about my work for them. Where the words were written for someone else, typically the ideas belonged to them and the expression of those ideas came from me (with their edits).

Some chapters in this book are from a crisis communications blog I once created called *Unsolicited Advice*. A few chapters, notably the eulogies I wrote and delivered upon the deaths of my parents and a letter I wrote to console friends whose young daughter died of a heroin overdose, are included largely to add diversity to the material and exemplify a more personal style of writing.

Across all this work, where needed and appropriate, I've made style edits and excised sections that are out of date or unimportant to the overall substance of the piece.

I've also included several tips on how others can sharpen their writing skills in the settings often used for business and media. My goal is to provide guidance to those who want to hone their craft and so I offer exhortation and exemplar in tandem.

As this book was going to print, my other personal writing efforts were divided between a novel and a business book. With luck and God willing, you'll see those titles available in the future. Keep up to date by following me on Twitter: @MarkRWeaver.

Crisis Communications

Amid a news media crisis, those less traveled in that treacherous terrain will often seek refuge in the infamous phrase, "no comment." This is a recipe for a rockslide into more trouble. The only way out is to share correct and largely unchangeable information quickly. The chapters that follow look at crisis communications in general and as they relate to two industries I often advise – health care and law enforcement. There are tips and takeaways, however, that are applicable to any industry.

CHAPTER 1

Reducing "crisis" in your communications takes planning

I t's as certain as the sun rising every morning. Sooner or later, your business or organization will face a moment where a crisis will force its leaders to offer a response that could shape and define public perception of your reputation for years to come.

Unfortunately, too many companies and organizations struggle at these critical moments by failing to respond quickly and adequately enough to make a difference. That's why I spend a significant amount of my time training leaders to work more effectively with the news media and preparing for the inevitable day when a crisis communications plan will be taken off the shelf and put to use.

While this complex topic could fill a book of its own, here are some key elements you need to consider no matter the size or scope of your business or organization.

Always comment quickly

To the initial dismay of some clients hoping I can bury their bad news, I always recommend making an initial comment to reporters and putting out statements on social media to directly reach the public. Even when all the facts remain unknown, it's smart to at least explain that you're working on the problem and want to resolve it.

Giving your side before an opponent can offer a more critical perspective can help you gain and protect credibility throughout the incident. This is the concept of primacy — whatever an otherwise unbiased observer hears first is seen as more credible than information received later.

The need for this approach is best illustrated by what happens when siblings fight.

We've all been there. One sibling usually runs to a mom or dad crying or calls out that "Joey hit me." The response of most harried parents, likely would be to assume that the information is correct and then ask "Joey, why did you hit your brother?"

Acting on the only information available, this parent just accused Joey, based on the word of another child. Joey may have been provoked, responding to his brother taking a toy from him, or an innocent angel guilty only of minding his own business. Regardless of the facts, Joey is presumed to be in the wrong.

Sound familiar?

The same thing happens in the court of public opinion when your organization comes under news media scrutiny. What the public hears first will largely shape its opinion unless there's a compelling and well-argued counterpoint that finds its way into the news stories as quickly as possible.

Many otherwise intelligent leaders presume that an early response is imprudent because they hope the problem will go away or because many facts are still unknown. When the press calls, they offer up "no comment" as their magic mantra.

But most people automatically translate a "no comment" into "guilty as charged," a decision that can harm confidence in your organization. Even worse, refusing to return calls from professional reporters comes off as rude and suggests you have something to hide, which often leads journalists to dig harder for dirt.

Ideally, it's best to get in front of headlines by releasing the news on your timetable with your carefully planned talking points leading the way. If that's not possible, it's imperative to respond as quickly as possible, especially in today's digital age where news, especially videos, can go viral without warning.

Consider the 2016 scandal involving Wells Fargo, which exploded in the media when federal regulators fined the company $185 million for opening millions of accounts without customers' knowledge. The company's failure to get in front of the story cost it much more, including expensive image advertising.

Remember, the longer you wait, the more likely public opinion will become harder to change or shape.

Carefully craft crisis messages

When you're ready to make a comment, it's imperative to understand what messages are most likely to work.

It's best to plan ahead by creating a series of responses that could come in handy for your business or organization's likely crisis scenarios. This will allow you to respond quickly and more thoughtfully during a stressful moment. Having a "we're aware of the situation and are working on it" holding statement ready to send out when an incident occurs also can buy you time to collect facts and determine the best strategy.

Now, before you write anything, think about what you're trying to accomplish.

Imagine you're trying to swim your story to shore in an ocean directly against an outflowing riptide which keeps you from advancing while exhausting your energy. If you keep fighting the current (the bad news), you could easily drown. If you go with the current, you're taken out to sea and the news is presumed to be true. If you swim to the side — neither challenging hardened public opinion nor agreeing with it, and messaging on an issue the public will believe, and that will help you - you can escape the danger.

That's what needs to happen during most crisis communication events. Messaging against preconceived notions (the riptide) presents many obstacles that can derail your story. By messaging sideways, you can share key facts without directly disputing what people believe to be true.

While you can't change the fact that you've been sued for harassment, but you can tell people all about your organization does to protect employees and follow the law.

I recommend organizing all information about the situation into three categories.

- **Red light:** This is information you must not talk about for legal, ethical, or professional reasons. You can't defame someone or release information that is confidential by law, for example. Despite your belief that doing so might help you look better, discussing red light information is likely to make the situation worse.

- **Yellow light:** This describes facts or information you'd rather not talk about because it's less important or distracting from the message. Avoid answering hypothetical questions, sharing personal opinions and talking about processes and procedures. This doesn't mean a reporter won't ask about a yellow-light topic or that you won't answer the question, but yellow-light information won't help you advance your message.

- **Green light:** These are the points that help show the public that you're doing the right thing. It's information you want to talk about to spread the desired message. Normally, I recommend selecting the three most important points. This might include examples of hard work or a good effort, reiterating your mission, and showing why the problem at issue is important to your organization. For each green-light point, try to develop three anecdotes, three memorable statistics, and three punchlines.

Going back to our harassment lawsuit example, a green light point could look like this: "All of our employees are trained on equal employment laws and encouraged to report discrimination."

A supporting anecdote might state: "One of the women who conducts our annual training is an expert witness for the U.S. Justice Department on how to protect employees from sexual discrimination."

A memorable statistic might include: "Over the last decade, we've held more training in this area than any other type of training."

And a punchline might say: "We train all of our team members to treat people fairly and follow the law."

While your spokesperson may not share every point during an interview, they will be well prepared to make a statement and answer questions.

If you have evidence refuting the allegations, share it quickly. You could note the plaintiff has sued her last five employers and lost every case, for example. Or that the plaintiff and the person she is accusing never worked together in the same office or on the same projects.

Sharing this information could flip headlines in your favor, putting you ahead in the battle for public favor. Waiting even a few hours can lead to unfavorable headlines that never go away.

Being concise matters

Framing the facts in your favor requires some practice and paying close attention to how the media will use your comments.

It's highly unlikely TV reporters and their editors will give your spokesman more than one or two short sound bites of 8 to 10 seconds. Newspaper reporters will probably be limited to 400 or 500 words, of which your side may get a few paragraphs.

It's important to keep your points concise, use power words that convey clear meaning and stick to your message. Your vocabulary should be understandable by eighth-graders as not everyone can or will understand more complex words or industry jargon.

It helps to avoid using pejorative words offered by the opposition or reporters. Remember, the question asked is rarely in the story. Imagine that, following a scandal, you plan on staying in your job and helping your organization recover. A reporter might ask "will you resign?" Notice the word "resign" comes from the reporter. If you use it in your answer, by saying, "I will not resign," you have given credence to the possibility of resignation and you've used a word that you wouldn't have used on your own. It would be better to say "I'll continue to lead this effort."

In short, when you want to rebuff, you don't repeat. Imagine if former President Nixon had said "I'm a trustworthy person" instead of "I am not a crook." His phrase would have been a lot less memorable.

Involve attorneys in responses

While commenting in some form or fashion is always the right choice, there can be legitimate legal concerns complicating your public message.

Volkswagen couldn't just admit to tampering with its engines to ensure new cars passed environmental tests without creating even more liability issues. That would not help the company.

At the same time, there are attorneys who can create unnecessary reputational risks by refusing to make any comments or instructing you to do so. This is where I use my legal background to help clients communicate in a way that will protect their reputation without hurting (and maybe even helping) their legal position.

It's critical to understand attorneys think much differently than people who are not "J.D. impaired." We're trained to be defensive and protect clients from legal exposure at all costs. Some lawyers are so focused on winning over one judge in a court of law months from now, they risk allowing their client to lose bigger in the court of public opinion right away.

I've taught hundreds of future attorneys in my class at The Ohio State University Moritz School of Law. My focus was preparing them to speak with reporters in a way that's both ethical and effective. I remind people that I'm bilingual — I speak lawyer as well as plain English.

When a crisis occurs, it's critical to sit down with your legal counsel and hammer out what can be said as soon as possible. Responses can't waste words with meaningless dribble such as "we'll have a lot more to say in court as we aggressively defend this case." Nor can they can create more legal issues by accusing plaintiffs of wrongdoing.

Yes, there are some risks to answering questions in the media. But a carefully crafted statement always beats hiding behind a "no comment."

Understand the role of reporters

Like any profession, there are good and bad reporters, although in my experience I've encountered far more ethical journalists striving to get stories correct.

Anyone working in crisis communications must learn about how the media operate and build professional relationships with reporters and editors who routinely cover their industry. Journalists who know you and key players on your team are more likely extend professional courtesies in their reporting. Being respectful of their deadlines and needs can go a long way to helping your organization thrive during a crisis. Being combative can backfire quickly.

Reporters are trained to tell all sides of a story, meaning even if you share strong facts supporting your side, they're obligated to share the other side. They're also under near constant deadline pressure to update stories for online and social media readers, meaning they don't always wait until the end of the day or the next broadcast to publish or air a story. Yes, they will update articles with fresh facts, but that doesn't automatically mean headlines will be updated, too.

It's also important to understand the different mediums.

While the power of newspapers is shrinking, print media still play a large role in shaping public opinion, especially with older folks.

Print reporters, who also write online stories and take videos these days, tend to be the most accurate and complete in their work, benefitting from more space and time to tell their stories. Visuals are increasingly important to print reporters and their editors, who are heavily focused on growing their digital audience. Reporters work for editors, who often write or edit the headlines and control the flow of news to print and online. Having a relationship with a reporter and their editor is recommended.

While ethical reporters are careful to avoid sharing their opinions publicly, some newspapers also employ columnists and editorial writers who are expected to share their opinions on op-ed pages, making them important opinion leaders in the community.

Radio reporters always need short sound clips, which can be recorded over the phone, if necessary. I prefer to dictate a higher quality audio statement into a smartphone, which can be shared with the radio news staff by email or a cloud service. It's important to speak clearly, talk in self-contained sound bites and remember that your voice's inflection and emotion matter. You don't want to sound uncaring.

Some of the same rules apply for television news reports, which tend to carry the most impact with the public while being the least accurate. Ratings drive many coverage decisions, but the extreme brevity of reports, juggling of many new stories every day, and wide geographic coverage areas makes it challenging for reporters to deliver a complete story. Television reporters rarely have defined beats like their print counterparts, meaning you could be interviewed by a different reporter every time. These journalists also need video to go with their story, so they prefer on-camera interviews even if only a few seconds ever gets used.

When conducting TV interviews, make sure you dress appropriately and always look at the interviewer, not the camera, when speaking. Engage the reporter before going on camera to build some rapport and comfort. For taped interviews, it's OK to stop after a mistake and start over. Answer in those same short self-contained sound bites and never address the interviewer by name.

When news breaks

Several of my clients are universities, so I took note of a strong crisis communications effort by The Ohio State University, during a terrorist attack on campus in late 2016.

There are good lessons here for any organization that might need to quickly inform employees or others of a threat, which inspired me to create a simple preparation checklist to summarize this chapter.

On that morning, Ohio State students and employees were alerted to an attacker on campus by both text messages and social media with the same "Run Hide Fight" message.

The university's new alert system sent the pre-written messages with the simple push of a button, eliminating any notification delay. As the crisis unfolded, subsequent updates were distributed in the same manner, keeping students, parents, faculty, and media updated at the same time.

Unfortunately, not every campus is as prepared.

Not long ago, one of my higher education clients was holding a senior staff meeting, when someone interrupted with a report of a shooter on campus. As police and news helicopters descended, the team quickly decided to send out a campus-wide alert. Their only available method to send the message was an app on a staffer's iPhone. Yet, the phone's battery was nearly out of juice. As the team wondered if they were in mortal danger and worried about how to alert students and faculty, the president left the meeting to find a charging cord.

Moments later, the apparent shooter called to say he was just fooling around with an airsoft gun. So, the danger was somewhat imagined. But the flaw in the crisis communications response was real.

Ten things every crisis communications plan should consider.

1. Every organization needs a clear chain of command for issuing alerts or news information at all hours. If the normal decision maker is out of town, who's in charge?

2. Your system for sending alerts and releases needs to be ready 24/7/365. Dying iPhones don't cut it if lives are at stake. Portable chargers should be ready and accessible.

3. Depending on your organization's mission, you may want to have pre-written messages for everything from robberies to active shooters and tornadoes.

4. Those messages should include holding statements, which buy you time while alerting people to danger. For example: "Report of dangerous criminal activity on site. Please take necessary caution until we get more information to you."

5. Alerts clearly need to be sent out as text messages, but don't neglect Twitter. Tweets can be shared and don't get comments attached, which protects the original message.

6. Tell people all updates will come from your Twitter feed. Followers, especially media, can amplify it from there.

7. We don't recommend using Facebook for immediate messages, although it can't be ignored. User comments can confuse your communication, which also can be missed due to Facebook's content algorithms. Create a Facebook post linking to your Twitter or an alerts page online.

8. Your crisis plan, including all phone numbers and pre-written messages, must be stored in the cloud somewhere. Don't count on your computer system to be working. Your data should be accessible from any device anywhere.

9.   Have someone on your staff monitor social media for rumors that need squashed. Never repeat rumors. Simply state: "There's misinformation out there. The facts are..."

10. Practice your plan routinely.

By the way, no. 10 may be the most important.

CHAPTER 2

Crisis Communications in Health Care

E very industry and profession can face a crisis on any given day. But those who've dedicated their careers to healing have a unique and daunting challenge in that their crises typically have much higher stakes. A factory or office building is as likely to experience an active shooter as a hospital or medical practice, yet the healing arts uniquely face issues of life and death in many other ways. These are the most difficult crises, replete with some of the most unnerving and heart-thumping news media encounters.

My years of work with hospitals, doctors, and industry associations that represent medical professionals have given me some insight into these formidable issues. I'm no subject matter expert on medical care, but I have learned what works when it comes to using strategic communications to avoid the reputational snares that await around every hospital corner.

Every day, reporters must make decisions about which stories to cover. They have many topics to choose from, and stories involving health care or injury, illness, and death have a strong human-interest element. This makes subjects that arise from the work of medical professionals much more newsworthy. When you're seeking positive press, this is good news. But when bad things happen in your world, this newsworthy formula will work against you. Expect coverage when things go wrong.

TRAINING

Just as doctors, physician assistants, and nurses must spend years in school before they can become successful dealing with illness and injury, so too must leaders in hospitals and medical facilities undergo significant media training before they can become successful in communicating in the wake of catastrophe and calamity. These skills don't come naturally.

I teach seminars on this topic. Much like med school classes, we study theories, practice the techniques, and then apply them to real-life situations. When necessary, we even conduct post-mortems. When providing this sort of training, I stress the need for leaders to surround themselves with at least three kinds of professionals to form an effective crisis communications team. Each of these team members plays a vital role. After all, even the best surgeons don't operate alone – they lead an interdisciplinary team.

Attorney. After the decision maker is in place, the first seat at this leader's table should be filled by the attorney who regularly advises the hospital or medical team. This is often someone on staff serving as general counsel or assistant general counsel. If the organization's legal representation comes from a local law firm, preference should be given to an attorney who respects and understands the need for robust external communications in a crisis. All too often, attorneys (incorrectly and without good legal basis) advise clients to say "no comment" or otherwise rebuff news media inquiries. These attorneys rightly worry about public comment becoming possible admissions in potential litigation but, done properly, leaders can conduct detailed news media interviews without increasing legal liability.

For two decades, I taught a course at The Ohio State University College of Law that showed law students how to legally and ethically conduct media interviews during crises, investigations, and litigation. Sadly, there are very few law schools that offer similar training. As a result, the vast majority of practicing attorneys focus exclusively on winning cases in the court of law and often advocate a barely-there media strategy that might result in a damaging loss in the court of public opinion.

Medical leaders should insist on being represented by attorneys who understand and agree that an effective communications strategy is as elemental to a successful crisis response as effective patient communication is to successful medical outcomes.

Public relations advisor. This person is typically already employed by a hospital, but not usually found on staff anywhere other than larger medical practices. If there's no one employed fulltime to fill this role, it's a good idea to develop a working relationship with a local public relations firm. Be sure that the company regularly provides crisis communications consulting as part of their services. While not every qualified firm can be found in any one website, you can start your search at *tinyurl.com/FindPRfirm*.

There are a few things to keep in mind as you assess potential public relations firms. First, review the company's client list to see if they've previously advised hospitals or medical professionals. A firm flush with clients in fashion might be a good pick if you're rolling out a new set of designer scrubs, but it won't be a good choice to help explain the complex circumstances surrounding the death of a child from an apparent mistake made during an arterial switch procedure.

Once you've identified a few firms with the relevant experience, take a strong and long look at their web presence and social media outreach. Does their communications philosophy align with yours? Do they regularly work with the news media in your area? In particular, look at their Twitter feed. Is it current, up to the same week you're reviewing it? Are they using Twitter to regularly engage with reporters? Given that Twitter is one of the most effective tools available to communicate in a fast-moving crisis, a firm that claims crisis expertise but fails to regularly use this social media tool may not be a good option.

After this review, conduct a meeting with the PR professionals who want to serve your account. Ask them to provide case studies or real examples of their work in this area. See if they regularly speak at conferences on this topic. And, notice whether you have rapport with them. Someone who can't make a connection with you may also be ineffective at working with reporters.

Subject Matter Expert. Even though a hospital or medical practice leader is often a doctor, no one can be an expert in every aspect of medicine. That's why, when a crisis emerges, the team that will be crafting the media response must include someone who understands both the details of the topic at issue and the facts behind what happened.

If a hospital is being sued for gender discrimination, the director of human resources might be a key subject matter expert. Depending on the facts, the team may need to expand the planning group to also include the aggrieved employee's direct supervisor.

If the crisis involves an ongoing threat such as a serious MRSA outbreak among patients of a surgical center, the crisis team should include the staff member directly responsible for resolving the problem. Given that a continuing crisis is likely to include a cascade of new facts and issues, this person can directly consult with the crisis communications team throughout.

Subject matter experts may not be media savvy, but that's not necessarily a required qualification. They are at the crisis communications table to provide facts, context, and answer questions about the intricacies of what happened and what's next. They will play a key role in briefing the spokesperson.

FREQUENCY OF TRAINING

Once the crisis team members are identified, organizations should schedule crisis communications training on at least an annual basis. Best practices dictate some form of skill-building and practice every quarter, but a full hands-on training should occur every year. These sessions should be a mix of learning best practices and then practicing them on scenarios that are squarely relevant to the organization's work.

Larger organizations, like a hospital or regional medical center, should also do a tabletop exercise in conjunction with local law enforcement or emergency response officials. These sessions usually last a full day and will allow participants to build relationships with their partner agencies as well as learn the issues and challenges of those offices.

MESSAGE

Once you have a communications team and they understand the structure and timing of a response to an incoming crisis, the foremost goal must be to determine the message to be delivered. Messages may differ slightly, depending on whether the audience is internal or external. The message may also vary based on who needs to know what about the situation. But all messages surrounding a health care crisis should have a few essential elements.

First, given that the main mission of the medical field is to heal and prevent illness and injury, the message must stress that the organization's first priority is to care for and protect its patients. This theme can be included in nearly every crisis communication sequence, even when patients are not directly at risk. For example, when a hospital is being accused of allowing a senior executive to remain on staff despite allegations of Medicaid fraud, the essence of the reputational threat to the hospital does not involve patient safety. Nonetheless, including the message of protecting patients as a core value in the press statements about the alleged fraud would be effective.

The message must be acceptable to all the team members on the crisis communications decision group. The attorney must confirm that the statement and fact points will not add to the organization's liability, the subject matter expert must approve the accuracy of the information, and the public relations professional must ensure that it will help persuade stakeholders in the organization's favor.

A good way to begin organizing the message and fact points is to start with information that is factual and confirmed. Discussing unverified information is risky. Advancing rumors is irresponsible. And speculating is a precarious practice.

If it's certain that three people died following a series of tainted blood transfusions, include that number in your statement. Privacy laws and the logistics of notifying family may prevent naming the people who died, but releasing the facts surrounding the number of people early will show transparency and would not violate the law. Because it would likely be too soon to assure the public that no one else will be affected by the bad blood, offering conjecture that no one else is likely to die could be reckless.

Example: *"Here at Anytown Hospital, we're committed to saving lives and doing our best to heal our patients. That's why we're deeply sad to announce that a batch of blood used in transfusions over the last 24 hours appears to have been tainted in some way. Three people who were given the blood have since died."*

You'll note that the above example is not a complete statement. There are many other factors that may need to be included in that release, or in subsequent information releases. This could include statements about the procedures in place to guard against these dangers, what's being done to find out what might have happened, and who is on the team working to get a final resolution. None of that information involves releasing HIPAA information or any individual patient details. But any combination of it is a much better response than "no comment" or a news report that says, "officials from Anytown Hospital did not return phone calls seeking comment."

When reporters are pushing hard for more details about a crisis, acknowledge their concern and address it directly. One way to do this would be to say, "we know the public wants to know more about what happened. That's why we're working so hard to gather accurate information. When we have that, we will release it quickly. We want to be responsible and only give out information that's correct."

If there's a public health risk involved in the crisis, such as an outbreak of meningitis at a local nursing college, your message ought to include tips on what potentially affected people can do to stay safe. These tips already exist in the literature and standard of care manuals and your fact points can be taken directly from these trusted sources.

Early on in a crisis, you may prefer to only release statements and not field questions. If you decide this approach is suitable for your situation, it's best to do it in the form of a video statement, perhaps one that is released on social media. Limiting your statement to a written release makes it unlikely to be used by TV or radio news outlets, which means fewer people in your community will know about it. In a news conference setting, if you attempt to give a statement and then refuse to take questions, it would give the appearance that you're hiding something and being unresponsive.

As soon as possible, you should transition to press encounters that do allow for questions. Your answers should remain very close to the points approved for release by your crisis communications team. Whenever you're asked a question that might reveal confidential information, explain that limitation as part of your answer and shift the answer back to the information your crisis communications team has already approved. This interview technique is called "bridging" and your annual media training should include that as part of the material discussed.

If you choose to discuss information beyond your control, try to avoid speculation. When there's a possibility that information could change, say so. Imagine a medical practice responding to reporters covering the criminal charges filed against one of the practice's physicians. Police say the doctor inappropriately touched patients. Your records indicate that no patient ever filed a complaint about this doctor. It might be effective to point that out (to alleviate concerns that the practice ignored warning signs) but it's possible that complaints were made directly to staff no long employed there. If you decide you want to advance this point as part of your media response, rather than say, "no one ever complained about Dr. X," a better option would be, "we've checked our records and we can find no evidence that anyone ever complained about Dr. X."

There's always a temptation to over-reassure the public or other stakeholders. Be very careful not to do this. You may want to say, "we're sure this will never happen again" or "no one else is at risk from this outbreak" but, unless you can completely guarantee those statements (and it would be very difficult to do so), it's prudent to avoid them. Over-reassurance followed by media coverage proving the statements wrong is a classic formula for reputational damage and loss of institutional credibility.

MESSENGERS

Once the crisis communications team has determined the message, you'll need to identify a spokesperson. Many hospital staffers presume that this must be their president. Others just presume that the public relations person is the one to speak to the media. Yet the most effective approach is to select a spokesperson who has the competence, credibility, and compassion to advance the message persuasively. This formula is based on the time-honored guidance of Aristotle, who counseled that effective persuasion is a mix of logos (competence), ethos (credibility), and pathos (compassion).

Competence means the spokesperson has enough knowledge of the circumstances and the approved fact points to discuss the matter and answer questions. With the right briefing and enough time, nearly anyone can be made competent to do media interviews. When I was Spokesman for the United States Department of Justice in Washington, D.C., I fielded as many as 50 press calls a day. For most of them, I knew nothing of the topic or case when I took the call. It was only my legal training, combined with the discussion with the internal subject matter expert (usually the attorney handling the case) that allowed me to respond to press questions effectively.

Credibility refers to the position the spokesperson holds, as well as that person's demeanor in an interview. A nursing assistant with only one month on the job might be able to be made competent for an interview, but that person would not be seen as a credible spokesperson for a large medical practice.

Further, the owner of that practice could potentially be a credible spokesperson, but if he or she had very nervous mannerisms, it could diminish credibility and detract from the message. Particularly in a TV news interview, the appearance of a medical spokesperson relates directly to credibility. If the chosen representative is a doctor, pharmacist, or nurse, the person should wear a white coat and/or scrubs during the interview. A stethoscope around the neck or in the pocket is optional.

Finally, compassion is a required qualification to speak to the press and in health care, it becomes paramount. Whenever the news media is covering a medical crisis, there's always a human element involved. Our spokesperson must be able to discuss the matter in a way that gives stakeholders and the general public a genuine sense that the medical professionals involved care about what happened and the people who might be affected.

In addition to selecting internal messengers, it may be prudent to recruit third parties to speak on behalf of your organization. If they are willing to coordinate message strategy with your team, there's a strong likelihood that their independent position will add strength to your persuasiveness. Examples of third party messengers include the local health department, the state medical board, local law enforcement, or industry groups such as local chapters of the American Medical Association, the American Nurses Association, or the American Hospital Association. There are many other options beyond these.

OTHER KEY POINTS

The other information discussed throughout this book will also be helpful to medical professionals responding to media inquiries about a crisis situation. But there are a few other medical-related lessons to remember for crisis communications.

Avoid jargon. The medical field is littered with words known only to medical professionals. It might be common for a doctor to say to a colleague, "the patient presented with a high fever," but the average person is unaccustomed to hearing the word "presented" used that way. Better to say, "this person came to us with a high fever."

I once had a friendly dispute with a doctor in one of my crisis communications seminars. He was role-playing as a spokesperson in a news media interview and used the word (spoken rather quickly) "C.D.C." I certainly know that this is an acronym for the Centers for Disease Control and I even know a little about what that federal agency does. Yet the doctor looked stunned when I informed him that most people in the general public wouldn't know all that. In fact, when I tell that story to non-medical audiences, I sometimes get a knowing laugh from the class, indicating that many people think medical professionals unnecessarily use medical shorthand that confuses laypeople.

Use personal examples. Trying to make a point with statistics can be ineffective. Tell it more like a story, with a hypothetical person. Rather than saying, "More than 75 million Americans have hypertension," say "think of three adults you know – it's likely that at least one of them has high blood pressure." Specific examples should not disclose personal information. It violates no privacy laws to say to the media, "years ago, I treated a woman with the worst kinds of burns over half her body. Yet she fully recovered. largely because of the anti-infection medicine that we developed here in our lab."

Keep professional distance. There may be a few rare occasions when a medical professional will break down and cry during a news interview, but it presents a serious risk of loss of credibility. The public expects doctors, nurses, and other leaders in medicine to be people who can maintain composure and offer insight and solace. Certainly, your spokesperson should show human emotion when discussing topics that involve suffering and loss, but not to the point where professionalism could be undermined.

Be a teacher. Reporters and the general public don't know a lot about medicine. You do. Use the media response around a crisis to teach what you already know. It may seem rather basic to point out that the lungs and heart work together to distribute oxygenated blood throughout the body, but many (perhaps most) people don't really know or understand that. The same way a good physician's assistant or nurse practitioner will use color diagrams or life size models of the heart and arteries to explain a stent procedure to the family members of someone undergoing a catherization, a spokesperson can brief the press. You may even want to distribute high quality JPG documents to the press and encourage them to use them for the TV graphics around the story or in the newspaper charts appearing next to a story.

CHAPTER 3

Crisis Communications for Law Enforcement

W hen danger erupts, first responders run toward it. These are valiant men and women who deserve our support. Yet when a crisis engulfs police agencies, the same people who are experts at defending others from violent attacks often fail to effectively defend themselves from verbal attacks. This chapter is devoted to helping them.

Most months, I teach 5-10 different classes in crisis communications and more than half of these sessions are for police, prosecutors, and other public safety professionals. I feel a kinship with these good people. One of my earliest jobs – while I went to grad school and law school at night – was working as the Public Information Officer (PIO) for my hometown police department. In that role, I learned a lot about working with the news media on issues surrounding law enforcement. I also came to understand and appreciate "cop humor!" This police experience was helpful to me a few years later, when I was appointed as a Spokesman for the United States Department of Justice in Washington, D.C.

At Main Justice (as we called it), I fielded an average of 50 press calls a day and worked closely with FBI agents and federal prosecutors from around the country. Our cases ranged from murder to arson and a wide variety of other crimes. We took on some of the most high-profile issues imaginable. Not every matter involved a crisis, but I saw enough of it that I began to learn what can and should be said in a law enforcement setting when reporters circle like irate hornets.

More recently, my work with the national Fraternal Order of Police and many city and county governments across the nation has exposed me to numerous cases of officer-involved shootings. These can be tense and intimidating crisis communications situations. They're all factually different from each other, but they share at least one common element – the overarching need for calm, effective and credible public communications. Poor or unfocused press communications can lead to anger, mistrust, and even deadly riots. Done properly, public statements can save lives and preserve precious police credibility.

With the proper mindset, planning, and thoughtful messaging, law enforcement professionals can communicate in a crisis in ways that prove the right people are in charge. While there are several different effective approaches, I've honed a particular way of doing this that has yielded excellent results. It starts with knowing when and where reputational risk is likely to occur.

The Danger Signs

People who are savvy about the press can spot a growing media crisis the same way a sun-wizened sailor can sense a sea squall before it starts. In the world of public safety, some cases or incidents are much more likely to draw the attention of reporters looking for a story.

The obvious example of this is when a law enforcement officer is forced to use deadly force against someone who is found later to be unarmed. There's one modern American incident that generated more media coverage than nearly any other with these facts. In 2014, Michael Brown tried to grab the gun[*] of Ferguson, Missouri police officer

---

[*] Page 14, U.S. Department of Justice Report Regarding the Criminal Investigation into the Shooting Death of Michael Brown

Darren Wilson during a struggle. Wilson defended himself and used deadly force to stop the threat.

The resulting news coverage was so negative and one-sided that a false narrative quickly developed. Millions of people believed – falsely[**], according to the U.S. Justice Department findings – that Brown had been shot with his hands up. "Hands Up, Don't Shoot" became a rallying cry for those who claim police are more likely to shoot Black suspects. After reviewing the crisis communications following the months-long controversy, it's hard not to conclude that the media strategy was ineffective.

There are many other police incidents that might require quick and strategic communications. Here are just a few.

- Anytime a police officer is charged with breaking the law, the apparent hypocrisy is enough to merit news coverage that would be more prominent than if, for example, the person charged were a plumber or a dentist.
- When an officer is alleged to have misused public funds or acted inappropriately while on duty, the news media may decide to cover the story.
- Police use of social media (even on personal time) can draw coverage if the sentiments the officer posts are well out of step with public opinion or appear to show some sort of prejudice.
- Lawsuits against law enforcement agencies have become commonplace and, despite their ubiquity, will almost certainly be featured in local news.
- The firing of a high-ranking police official will be newsworthy, particularly if the reasons for the firing suggest impropriety.

[**] Page 8, U.S. Department of Justice Report Regarding the Criminal Investigation into the Shooting Death of Michael Brown

- The arrest of young children or police injuring or killing a pet will draw negative attention and coverage.
- Credible allegations of bias – particularly racial bias – are a magnet for press attention. These stories rely on a well-worn narrative surrounding policework that, according to some research[*], is largely incorrect.

Finally, police leaders should remember that anytime there is video footage of officer misconduct or a controversial police encounter, the video is likely to be quickly shared on social media, which is a natural conduit to reporters. Video is more vivid and memorable than a written account or even an audio recording. As a result, the public impact of a controversial police video will be much longer lasting. Video makes a story stronger and gets TV news involved when they otherwise might have opted against coverage.

Building the Team

Every law enforcement agency needs to have a crisis communications team identified, trained, and prepared. In a typical local police department, the members may include the chief, deputy chief, PIO, and the attorney who advises the department. In larger agencies, there may need to be a crisis communications team in each division or sector. Ideally, the watch commander of each shift will be a member of the team or will have received the same training as the team. One key mistake is to limit crisis communications to first shift (day watch) employees. Because – like crime -- the potential for a media calamity exists at all hours of the day, police agencies must have the right people in position at all times.

Crisis communications teams typically need a subject matter expert but, given that there are so many different types of law enforcement crises, this decision may be deferred until the problem arises. If, for

[*] Heather MacDonald, *The War on Cops: How the New Attack on Law and Order Makes Everyone Less Safe,* Encounter Books (2016)

example, the crisis arises from a hostage situation, the on-scene SWAT commander will be added to the crisis communications team, since he or she will know the most about what is happening or what did happen on the ground. Conversely, if the news media interest is focused on allegations of on-duty impropriety by an officer, the internal affairs investigator assigned to the case may join the team as the subject matter expert. This seat at the crisis decision table will rotate based on the needs of the situation.

Training for Success

Public safety officers take a lot of training. Nearly every month, officers are updating skills in accident investigation, speed detection, leadership, and a wide variety of other topics. The designated team should be involved in at least two full days a year of crisis communications training. These should be a mix of lecture, discussion, and practical scenarios. Ideally, every member of the team will give several mock interviews in the varying styles for print, radio, TV, and news conference.

The Art of the Sound Bite

When I conduct this training, one of the more interesting exercises we do is sound bite training. People in my classes are often surprised that most TV and radio sound bites are less than 10 seconds. One of the most common complaints I hear from police professionals is that the TV interviews they give result in a final edited product that appears to take their statements out of context. I remind these students that it's likely they gave 45-60 second answers to each question while the reporter was only budgeting room for a ten second bite. Cutting 40 seconds out of a perfectly good answer to the question will indeed make the answer seem out of context.

Here's a good example of how that works. Let's say that raw interview footage for one particular question looks like this:

REPORTER: "Why did the responding officer have to shoot the suspect?"

POLICE OFFICIAL: "This was a very dangerous encounter. Our officer was warned that the suspect had just committed an armed robbery at a local gas station and that he shot at the store clerk. We also knew there was a felony warrant for the suspect. Our officer sensed danger, so he drew his service weapon and told the suspect to keep his hands visible. The man wouldn't listen to commands. His hands remained close to his waistband, and that's often a sign of a hidden weapon. When he put his hands under his shirt, it looked like he was reaching for a gun. Our officer had no choice but to fire."

This is about a 30-40 second answer. It's way too long. Unless the interview is being carried live, the reporter will take the video back to the station and edit it. The entire story – reporters call this the "package" – will usually be about 60-90 seconds. That will include the setup (or introduction) by the reporter, interview bites from a few different people, and the wrap up. Then comes the "toss" back to the anchor, who will transition to the next story. Among the interview bites is a slot for your comment and the available gap will be about 10 seconds.

In the above example, a fair reporter would probably take the sentence "When he put his hands under his shirt, it looked like he was reaching for a gun. Our officer had no choice but to fire." But the officer or PIO interviewed will be disappointed that the other information about the danger was excluded.

To be clear, because of the many thoughts put forward in the answer, a lazy or reckless reporter will grab any sentence, whether or not it fairly summarizes your position. Imagine watching the newscast and seeing the exchange this way:

REPORTER: "Why did the responding officer have to shoot the suspect?"

POLICE OFFICIAL: "The man wouldn't listen to commands."

Ouch. If that's all that's said from your side, some viewers might believe police shoot people who don't follow commands. Given how often that happens in law enforcement encounters, it would result in an underlying loss of respect for your work.

Ideally, your spokesperson would anticipate the nature of shorter TV sound bites, and the back and forth would look more like this:

REPORTER: "Why did the responding officer have to shoot the suspect?"

POLICE OFFICIAL: "This armed robbery suspect was dangerous and refused to listen to the officer's commands. When he looked like he was reaching for a gun, our officer had no choice but to fire."

This sound bite will fit easily into any news package and it essentially forces the reporter to use our message the way we intended it. To be sure, the reporter might ask other questions, but our spokesperson can and should pivot back to a similar sentiment, using different words.

You Don't Have to Answer the Question, but You Do Have to Provide a Response

Many police leaders are diligent and inveterate rule followers. This is a virtue. Yet this mindset can create for chaotic news interviews. Many of the questions that reporters ask law enforcement are straightforward. These can and should be answered directly. Here's an example:

REPORTER: "How many officers were on the scene when the suspect was arrested?"

WATCH COMMANDER: "Three officers were on the scene at that time."

But not every question asked by a reporter is objective or fair. Or, more commonly, the answer sought many contain information that cannot or should not be released. Yet the old "no comment" approach is one of the most destructive and ineffective responses possible. In these cases, providing a response is a better tactic than providing an answer. This hypothetical exchange illustrates the point. Imagine an internal affairs investigation into a lieutenant who is alleged to be having sex with a confidential informant. Investigators have strong initial evidence that the claim is true, but they have several more leads to chase. A reporter learns about the issue and approaches the chief at a public meeting.

REPORTER: "Chief, I have two sources who tell me that Lt. XX is having sex with an informant. Is there any truth to this?"

CHIEF: "Police departments often hear allegations about officers and we have a thorough process to see if the claims are true. We take every accusation seriously because we expect our employees to act professionally. When we have enough proof to move forward, we announce it publicly. That's all I can really say in response to questions about any particular officer."

Some naysayers will lament that sounds evasive or even squirrely. Yet your attorney – for good reason – will not want you to confirm any details in this case until charges are imminent. Rather than "no comment," the above response or something similar is a much better approach.

FREQUENCY OF TRAINING

Law enforcement agencies, more than most other organizations, understand the need to train. Crisis communications must be added to the training calendar and be conducted at least annually. One way to keep skills sharp is for the department PIO (or outside crisis communications professional) to stop by command staff meetings once a month and lead a 15-minute discussion on a hypothetical crisis. Departments that want to be especially prudent will extend these sessions to monthly roll call discussions.

When new officers join the force, they should be given a primer on basic press communications skills and the department's policy about dealing with reporters. At a minimum, they must be instructed to never say "no comment" when approached by a reporter. It would also be helpful – don't laugh here – to remind officers that intrusive reporters should not be arrested without approval from a commanding officer. You might be surprised how common a reaction that is when an over-caffeinated reporter perseveres in questioning a new officer.

Every few years, departments should structure a full day tabletop exercise and have command staff play their respective parts in responding to a hypothetical crisis with a detailed set of facts. When I conduct these sessions, I will interrupt the group a few times throughout the day with mock radio bulletins about the scenario. The facts shift, new allegations are made, and rumors are advanced as fact. Lest you think this sounds unrealistic, those who've been through actual controversies can attest that those conditions are extremely true-to-life.

MESSAGE

Perhaps more than any other government agency, citizens expect police to be truthful and forthright in their public remarks. This means the touchstone of all your responses must be accuracy. Don't release anything you don't know to be true. Bad guys lie and good guys tell the truth. Be the good guy.

Telling the truth does not mean revealing every bit of information you know. We've all had a friend ask us for honest feedback on a bad haircut. While the truth might be "that's an ugly haircut – go get your money back," most of us will find a more diplomatic way to respond. That might be "I've seen better haircuts, but no one really worries about stuff like that" or "it's just a haircut – you get a redo before too long!"

Beyond telling the truth, your responses should be infused with a clear sense of professionalism. Officers are trained to evince this trait on the witness stand in court; they must extend it to media encounters, as well. This includes avoiding practices such as use of most slang, unnecessarily demeaning others, and personalizing issues.

Your message should include the information likely to be of most interest to the public. If there's an immediate threat, what can people do to be safe? If a crime occurred, what happened and who is being charged? If police procedures are changing, what are they, what's the reason for the change and why is the new way a better way? Your PIO should have a good sense for the information that needs to be included.

When you can't release the details of a matter, consider using one of these four types of non-committal (but truthful) responses. Note that none of these responses needs to make reference to the details of the matter that's not ripe for public discussion.

Aspirational. This is a statement about your agency's mission, goals, or reasons for existing. Say why you do what you do and what you expect from your people. Explain why you care and assure people that you are diligent and working on the matter. Example: "We work hard to keep this community safe. Our officers make difficult, split-second decisions and they do their very best to enforce the law and protect others. We expect our people to follow policy and use good judgment."

Procedural. This is a description of the processes your department uses to deal with the issue or problem at hand. While it's true that this information is likely available in handbooks, policy manuals, or other public records, sharing them with the news media may allow you to survive the first few medias cycles until more information can be prepared for release. Example: "Before an officer is hired, we conduct background investigations and verify references. Those records are reviewed by our human resources office and command staff."

More to Come. This is a way to show you care about the public's desire to know more and that you're working diligently to provide it. It also allows you to demonstrate your commitment to taking the time to get the issue right. Example: "We understand people want to know why this officer took 15 minutes respond to the call. That's why we're working hard to gather all the facts, so we can report the verifiable facts about what happened. We want to be sure that the information we release is correct, and we'll release as much as we can as soon as we can."

Gag Order. This is the legal term for when a judge requires parties to a court case to avoid talking to the news media but in this context, it includes information that policies or prudence prohibit you from releasing. Too many attorneys believe that answers to questions in this vein require a "no comment" response, but they're under-informed. It's possible to avoid commenting without using those ill-fated words. Often, a simple explanation of the reason for your inability to speak will be your best gag order response. Example: "We have a policy that prohibits us from releasing the name of an uncharged suspect and we think it's the right thing to do to follow that policy."

MESSENGERS

Typically, the head of a law enforcement agency is the best person to convey the media message. There are others, however, who can be equally effective. Any command staff member can be a credible spokesperson, as can the department PIO. Occasionally, a department attorney can be a serviceable spokesperson.

No matter who you select to be interviewed, make sure that the designee has credibility, competence, and compassion. Credibility means being able to answer questions in detail. Competence means holding a position that citizens expect to be accountable. And compassion is a human emotion that is hard to define but easy to spot.

On occasion, when a case or matter has racial overtones, some departments seek out an African American spokesperson. If the chief is black, then there's no possibility for accusations of tokenism. But choosing a spokesperson based on optics should only occur after credibility, competence, and compassion have been considered.

OTHER KEY POINTS

Avoiding Jargon. Too many police officers talk like automated digital assistants like Alexa or Siri. Or they use words that make them sound far removed from the human race. Consider: "I exited my vehicle and approached the suspect" vs. "I got out of my car and walked over to the man I saw." I know that many police academies still train recruits to talk this way but it's time to change the habit. Beyond that, police work is rife with technical terms that most folks don't understand. Instead of saying "MDT" say "the computer in my cruiser. Replace "NCIC" with "the national computer system we use to check criminal records."

Releasing statements. Many agencies still cling to their news release the way a two-year-old grips his pacifier. There will be a lot of drama and whining before it's relinquished. News releases were once the easiest and best way to get out the news. I've written thousands of them and, on occasion, still use them. Yet the practice of using social media to release a short statement is quickly supplanting the old school news release. Similarly, short video statements released on social media (either embedded on YouTube or Facebook) or emailed or tweeted out with a link to a cloud download can be effective as well. Your PIO will know the local media outlets' respective needs and be able to advise you as to the best way to get your news to your community.

Maintain Perspective. Police deal with the saddest and darkest parts of society. This is the wellspring of cop humor. I firmly believe that the dark jokes and sarcasm that float around the squad room are a coping mechanism to deal with the sadness, pain, and misery found on every shift. Too many cops take that grim approach to talking to the press and it results in an unnecessarily antagonistic relationship. Remember that members of the media are your neighbors who are just doing an important job the best way they know how. They make mistakes, have doubts, and want to help people – the same way police officers do. Keep a bit of a sense of humor and don't take yourself too seriously. These attributes will help you weather your next media crisis.

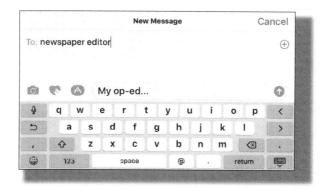

Op-eds

How to craft your own persuasive piece
for your local newspaper or website — with a
collection of my favorite offerings.

CHAPTER 4

Writing an op-ed that changes hearts and minds

Y ou're mad. Angry. Peeved. Or you're bursting with perspective. In a good way, or course. At parties, inquisitive people gather around you and pelt you with questions about your point of view.

Does this sound like you? Maybe it's time to share your opinion in written form, with a much larger audience. Perhaps an op-ed is the perfect place for you to express your expositions. It could be a thoroughfare for your thoughts. A window into your wit.

Allow me to alleviate the alliteration and put it the way it's expressed on a small leather desk placard in my office: It CAN be done. An op-ed is an excellent and time-honored way to express yourself.

Traditionally, newspapers offer the opinions of the publisher and editors in a column called an editorial. Perspectives of other people are often placed opposite the page that contains that editorial, hence the term op-ed.

Good newspapers seek out strong and smart writing to balance out their own editorials. Most prominent of this journalistic species is the work of syndicated columnists. Mixed in for interest are the opinions of local idea leaders who have something thought-provoking to offer. In large measure, this is where I've worked my way as a wordsmith.

Whether you're a business owner, government official, or just someone with a compelling perspective, an op-ed is a logical place to make your case. Your local weekly paper may be quite interested to print your submission. After all, they often have space to fill and a dearth of willing writers. A big-city daily newspaper is much different. It gets dozens of submissions every day and competition is steep. Knowing when, how, and why to write an op-ed can make the difference between an idea that gets read by millions of people and one that dies a digital death in the deep recesses of your cloud drive.

I've been fortunate enough to be published by several big-city daily newspapers, but it's always an arduous endeavor. When a news event sparks an idea in your mind, it's likely that a few thousand other people might have a similar notion. If only a fraction of them decide to put their perspective into writing and submit it for publication, you may be too late.

This cold reality has frequently resulted in me writing furiously into the threshold of dawn, just so my op-ed submission might be the first and most original in an editor's inbox. Perhaps there exist a few virtuosos of volubility who can be incisive and witty at 3 a.m., as the pangs of sleep starvation romp around the mind. Assuredly, I am not one of them. So, I try to limit my third-shift writing to those times when a news story is moving fast and could be out of the public consciousness in a few days.

Timeliness

As you can see, writing an effective op-ed requires a careful attention to circumstances in the news. If your idea for your opinion column is not relevant to what people are thinking and talking about, you might need a different notion.

The best approach is to take an issue currently in the news and address it with a compelling essay. I get my best ideas for op-eds when I'm driving or when I'm out for a walk or otherwise doing something mindless. Reading about a news story and then ruminating on it helps me think of the larger perspective, the historical perspective, or maybe the altogether-different perspective.

A Different Viewpoint

Op-eds advancing the conventional wisdom don't offer anything interesting to the readers of newspapers or other op-ed forums. We all agree motherhood is a good thing. Everyone wants to thank our troops for their service. The duck-billed platypus is sadly misunderstood. Thus, op-eds about those topics are less likely to be published.

When the stock price of Acme Widget Company goes down because of a widget recall, the conventional wisdom says this is bad for the company and stockholders will suffer. There's not much of an op-ed topic there. But try making the case that an Acme with less capital may force it to innovate more and, in the long run, be a much more profitable investment. That contrary perspective would make a fine op-ed in a business newspaper or personal finance blog.

When a politician breaks a campaign promise, the trite sentiment is that we should lose faith in that person and perhaps vote against him in the next election. That might be how you feel, but it won't catch the eye of an editorial page editor. Take a stab at composing a thoughtful piece about the fact that all of us have broken promises and hoped for forgiveness and that even appropriately contrite elected officials deserve some grace. That's enough of a novel viewpoint that it might be published or featured if submitted at the right time.

Length

Writing an op-ed is more art than science. But there are some certain scientific points that should be followed when you compose your essay. Here's what I mean: Most newspapers will have a limit on the length of your op-ed, both a minimum and a maximum. If you write less than 300 words, you might get consideration as a letter to the editor, but it won't be published as an op-ed.

On the other end of that, unless you're writing for a journal or online outlet that welcomes long submissions, if you submit more than 1,200 words, you're not likely to see your thoughts in print. For most American daily newspapers, an op-ed column between 600 and 900 words will meet the standards and be considered for publication. You shouldn't have to count the words by hand. When you use a word processing app and call up the spell check feature, it will tell you how many words you've written. In fact, if you have your program set up right, you'll see the number of words at the bottom of your screen even as you write.

Column length is important, but don't start out shooting for a certain number of words. It reminds me of some of my students, both in law school and grad school, who are keenly interested in precisely how many pages I want their writing projects to be. I often see some of them adjusting margins or font size to reach a certain page length. That's form over substance.

A good essay is, according to the old joke, like an attractive bathing suit: long enough to cover the subject, but short enough to be interesting. Don't start by thinking how long your essay is going to be. Start by thinking about the big point you want people to take away from your work. Sometimes you'll start your op-ed with that takeaway point; other times you'll end with it. But no matter which formula you employ, the reader should come away understanding your main point, because you either made it well, you made it repeatedly, or you made it in a creative and memorable fashion.

Grab the Reader's Attention

The first paragraph of your op-ed is your most important set of words. Here's why: No matter what headline you might choose to write for your piece, it's unlikely that the newspaper or another outlet will use the headline you suggest. I do put a headline on every one of my op-ed submissions because I'm trying to grab the opinion page editor's interest and broadcast exactly what my main point is. But only a few times have I seen the precise headline I suggested end up as the headline for the piece. This is most true, of course, in daily newspaper and magazine journalism, where reporters write the articles and editors write the headlines.

So, your first few sentences — journalists call this the "lede" — of your op-ed is the most important thing within your control. Casual readers will look at the headline, which, as I mentioned, is not of your choosing, but then they might scan the first few sentences to see whether the topic draws them in. And that's where creativity really matters.

Getting Started

Everyone has a different writing style, but my op-ed drafting style often goes like this: I begin writing my thoughts and purposely avoid composing the first few words or the first few sentences until I'm completely done. It sounds strange, but I'll often start writing in the middle of the piece and only later add the beginning and the end. That's because the middle is the main point and the proof factors for that point.

Let's say I'm trying to make the case — as I did in one op-ed included in this book — that the shark attacks of 1916 off the New Jersey coast are an interesting reminder of how experts can be wrong. I know I'm going to need to explain those shark attacks and how the experts of that era thought a giant snapping turtle, or tuna, or killer whale was responsible for the incidents. When I wrote that op-ed, I spent a few paragraphs explaining the history of the attacks and these mistaken opinions. Only after I had written that part did I realize that there's a relevant corollary between the mistakes of early 20th century experts and similar errors by modern experts.

Speaking of that op-ed, I got it published largely because I purposely waited to write and submit it until the 100th anniversary of the attacks. That's a great example of a historical news "hook" being used to draw lessons for contemporary readers. Simply looking through dates of history and matching them to a current event would provide anyone with a ready-made way to offer an opinion in an op-ed.

Almost as important as the lede is the "walk-off" — the last sentence or two of your piece. It should be punchy and hard-hitting. The reader should not only realize that you're done, but also what you've done. A good op-ed walk-off will generate a barely audible "huh" in the head of the reader. In my op-ed about the 1916 shark attacks, here was my walk-off:

"Nonetheless, press conferences were held, promises were made, and political reputations were bolstered. The sharks did what they sometimes do and the politicians did what they always do. A century later, nothing's changed."

You can see what I did there.

I try to write the walk-off last because that's when I understand the full sweep of what I've been trying to say.

Power Words

As you write, take a moment and think about word choice. You don't need to fuss and fight over every single word. After all, Paul McCartney reminds us there's no time for that, my friend.

But for certain words — like those in your main premise — you ought to dote and debate which word works best. Some word choices will evoke more passion and understanding in your reader.

When you got the bad news, can we say you cried or wept?

When you realized that someone you know got some great news, did you explode with envy or were you jealous?

If a politician does something without thinking, is he a dunce or a dimwit? A dummy or a dipstick? Maybe he's just daft. I'm not favoring one over the other; I just want you to pick one thoughtfully.

If there's an oil slick glossing over your favorite inlet and there's an oil company to blame, was it a leak or a spill? Is the beach soiled, sullied, or squalid? You pick it. Make your words count.

Is the AR-15 rifle an assault weapon or a defensive weapon? Is the culture debating gay marriage or marriage equality? On a more important note, are tater tots delicious or delectable?

The best words are those that bring about a distinct image in the reader's mind. I'll l give you a word and let me see if I can guess what image pops into your head.

Here we go: Plummet.

You probably thought of a person falling from a tall building or cliff. Or maybe an anvil. An Acme brand anvil. Plummet can mean to decrease quickly the way a stock price drops when bad things happen to a company. But the word itself creates mental images that should be considered by the prudent wordsmith.

Here's another: Terrorist.

If you're like many Americans, you probably thought of a young man in a far-off desert with his face covered. He may have a rifle and he and his other terrorists may have just finished doing the hand-over-hand horizontal ladder on the infamous terrorist monkey bars. That image comes from some stock footage of an Al-Qaeda training camp that has been run repeatedly on television since the terror attacks of September 11, 2001. Some people will pick a fight with me and say that terrorists can be male or female, desert-loving or local. But I'm not addressing politics here; this book is about writing. Just think through what mental images appear for different words before you select.

One more: Pitiful.

My guess is that you imagined a person crying. We often take pity on someone crying, so it's natural to associate pitiful with it. And if that's the image you want, then this is the word to use.

I do an exercise in my speech-writing classes. I show students a drawing of the scene where the humble shepherd boy David is preparing to use his slingshot on the mighty giant Goliath. Then I ask them to break into pairs and dream up a few power verbs, power adjectives, and power nouns that would help them tell that famous biblical tale. The results are often fascinating. It's a great way to think about power words.

When I need just the right word, there's a web page I use to help me brainstorm. It's a flexible word finder that can help you remember a word or point you toward one that you wouldn't have thought about on your own. Go to *http://tinyurl.com/TheRightWord* and try it out.

Editing and Proofing

Once you've assembled your strong opening, supporting points, and a punchy walk-off, replete with power words, you might think you're all set. Not true. You need an editor. Yes, you. I mean tater tot-loving *you*.

Everyone needs an editor. No one can edit himself. Your eyes will skip right past the mistakes, believing (as the rest of you does) that what you wrote was perfect and flawless in every way.

It's true that if you read a page backward, you can often spot misspellings. But with spellcheck, misspellings aren't the main concern anymore. A friend or family member who reads over what you wrote will spot things you've overlooked. In editing, we call that a fresh set of eyes. Those eyes can help you refine and improve your work.

Style

You or your editor should be aware of the different stylebooks that govern different kinds of writing. For most op-eds, you'll want to use the preferred style of the Associated Press — AP Style. The AP is the accepted source for journalists on when to capitalize, when to hyphenate, and when to hydrate. Maybe not that last one.

If you plan on doing a lot of writing for print, public relations, or op-ed submissions, you'll want to get your own copy of the venerable *AP Stylebook*. It's available both in hard copy and online. Learn more at *APstylebook.com*.

By writing and editing with AP style, you'll be saving your target newspaper from doing it for you. It's also a subtle clue that you're a pro. Amateurs get printed among the letters to the editor, if it all. Professional writers get consideration for op-eds.

Submission

Once the piece is ready to be submitted, you'll want to think through the pros and cons of where to send it and under what conditions. You can send one essay to several newspapers but, without a local hook, most will find it of little use. Your own local paper may be more likely to publish it since you live in the coverage area.

If you're submitting the op-ed exclusively to just one newspaper, mention that in your pitch email. It could increase your chance of getting the work in print. Whether you send it to one place or dozens, be aware that once it's printed in one outlet, other papers will likely refrain from publishing it. Most newspapers want their printed op-eds to be exclusive. In fact, some will insist on exclusivity as a condition of publishing it.

I recommend submitting your op-ed via email directly to the person at the media outlet who considers these submissions. Calling or emailing the newsroom and asking for this person's contact information will set you on the right path. Sometimes the contact information is listed on the website.

Don't send the op-ed as an attachment. Emails with attachments often get stuck in the newspaper's internal spam filters and may never be seen. Mention in the subject line that it's an op-ed submission and briefly state the topic. Some busy editors at bigger news outlets only skim the subject lines and don't even open many emails.

In the body of the email, offer up a short paragraph of your premise in the piece. Then list your pertinent contact information. After that, paste the words of the essay at the bottom of the email, as text.

At the end of your op-ed text, include a sentence or two of biographical information that's relevant to your subject. For example, when I submit an op-ed on legal topics, I'll often include a bio that points to my work as the Deputy Attorney General of Ohio or as a Spokesman for the United States Department of Justice. When I send op-eds to Pennsylvania newspapers, I will include in my bio description that I went to college there or grew up nearby. These descriptions can give you credibility — both to the editor and, eventually, to the readers.

Alternative Placements

If you can't get any news outlet to print your op-ed, don't give up. There's another way to reach people, in largely the same format.

The blog site *Medium.com* is well-suited to self-published op-eds. Create an account and post your op-ed there. It will appear among a mix of blog posts, opinion pieces, and op-eds from writers ranging from prominent to obscure. The search and linking features on Medium make it likely that people browsing may bump into your piece and then share it with others. Medium is more than a blog and it's useful for this precise purpose.

Another choice is to go to *Facebook.com/notes*. This is a powerful blogging platform that allows you to post updates, including op-eds. You can add photos and captions to make it even more readable. While it's not as print-focused as Medium, it's still a strong choice for reaching people on the world's most popular social media site.

Sharing on SM and Email

Whether you're published in the newspaper (and its online presence), on Medium, or on Facebook Notes, you should increase your reach by grabbing the link to your piece and sharing it digitally. If you have a Twitter, LinkedIn, or Facebook account, that's the first place to start. Send the link to friends and ask them to share it with their friends. You can do the same on other social media platforms.

You can also include a link and text in a mass email to the people on your contact list who might find it interesting. Don't overdo it and *don't* put all the email addresses in the "CC" part of your email. To learn why this is a problem, head on over to *PleaseBCC.me* and you'll see what I mean. Use a reputable email blast service like Mail Chimp or Constant Contact if you have a large list or plan on sharing a lot of mass emails.

A Final Thought

The op-eds in the first part of this book are just a handful of those I've written over the years. Some weeks I write multiple op-eds. In each case, I find it an intellectually stimulating endeavor. At the outset, it can feel like a cognitive burden, much like perusing all the puzzle pieces strewn across the kitchen table after you've opened and emptied a new jigsaw puzzle box. But, just like pushing in that last puzzle piece and stepping back to survey what you've done, the pleasure of completion is immense.

For the most part, the only op-ed you'll regret is the one you never write. Now get to it!

What follows are some of my best op-eds, with a description of the strategy and thinking behind each.

CHAPTER 5

Question Persists: Will Judge Act Like a Legislator or a Judge?

Giving your opinion to a friend over coffee is one thing. Having that same opinion read by tens of thousands of people while they drink their morning coffee is quite another. If that latter notion is alluring, crafting a strong op-ed submission to a newspaper or online news outlet should be your goal.

The column below was published by USA Today, which reaches three million readers daily. To date, it's one of the broadest reaches of my published commentary. Ironically, that outlet was not my original target. Only after sending it to a few large city dailies and the Wall Street Journal did I, on a whim, submit it to USA Today.

The idea for this column started months earlier, while I was reading a biography of Ulysses S. Grant. I noticed that the 14th Amendment was ratified in 1868 and did some quick math – the 150th anniversary would occur soon. I made a note on my calendar to use this timeliness hook to pitch an op-ed on the topic. I know a lot about this amendment, largely because of a grad school class that focused entirely on it. I'd always had strong views on the amendment, but those views aren't really germane without a relevant context. The 150th anniversary provided that context. As the date approached, President Trump was about to make his nomination to the Supreme Court and I realized that, if I included this hook in the piece, it would make the op-ed more interesting and timely. I was right.

As you examine the writing, note that I try to weave in a few pop culture references to make what could be a dry discussion more interesting and relatable. In the end, USA Today used a shorter version and the Cincinnati Enquirer used the full column.

Most op-eds I write take four or five hours to craft. This one took me fifteen hours or more. I started with far too much detail and spent most of the remaining time removing the least necessary portions. A sculptor once said that his task was to simply "take a big block of marble and just chip off all that isn't necessary for the figure." That was definitely my approach with this op-ed.

PUBLISHED: *USA Today* — July 5. 2018

Although Brett Kavanaugh was nominated to be a Supreme Court justice, he'll actually have his choice of two different jobs – a judge who resolves legal disputes or a legislator who makes policy. The approach he selects will be driven by his view of the Fourteenth Amendment, which was added to the Constitution 150 years ago this week.

Ratified amid the gusts of national changes following the Civil War, the portion of the amendment known as the equal protection clause was essentially intended to guarantee equal rights to newly freed slaves. There are academic tussles about this idea, but nearly everyone agrees federal judges have gone much further than that.

Some jurists who prefer a different policy outcome, shall we say, liberally use the amendment to strike down laws passed by state legislatures. In fact, federal judges invoke it as often as dads employ bad jokes. But while dad humor can be amusing, there's nothing funny about how misuse of the equal protection clause has shifted power from the people to the unelected federal judiciary.

Since the high court is largely split over how to apply the Fourteenth Amendment, this debate is timely. As the court's last term ended, some claimed that the justices have somehow "weaponized" the First Amendment. I disagree. A stronger case can be made that it's the

Fourteenth Amendment that's been used that way. In a constitutional framework of checks and balances, this particular provision is a check – a blank check.

Judge Kavanaugh certainly understands that the Constitution was drafted to strike a careful balance between state and federal power -- the relationship better known as federalism. The term relationship is apt. On minor issues, federal and state leaders quarrel like siblings, and, on major ones, they fight like ex-lovers. If it's misused by a Justice Kavanaugh, the equal protection clause will exacerbate those disputes and weaken our republic.

To a cloistered judge, it's no doubt intoxicating to have this or that social movement praise you as their savior. Just ask Justice Anthony Kennedy, whose retirement tributes include fulsome thanks for giving constitutional support to same sex marriage, after wielding – you guessed it – the equal protection clause. We saw similar farewell toasts to Justice Harry Blackmun, who, as the author of Roe v. Wade, unpacked the clause and discovered a pair of forgotten socks, some loose change, and a constitutional right to an abortion.

My argument is not that those two results are necessarily bad policy. Rather, in a representative democracy, thorny issues like gay marriage and whether women can legally abort their unborn children are best left to the elected, accountable representatives of the people – not to judges. Policies passed with such democratic accountability are more likely to be accepted by the nation than policy conjured by judges using the Fourteenth Amendment as a magic wand.

This became clear to me in grad school where I spent an entire semester discussing the meaning, application, and history of the Fourteenth Amendment. This class convinced me that local governance by state lawmakers is better governance than that offered by black-robed intervenors in Washington. This notion is more than just common sense – it's a floor joist of American government, firmly parallel to other foundational concepts like separation of powers and rule of law.

In 1835, French author Alexis de Tocqueville toured our nascent nation. He showed aptitude for both observation and prophecy when he remarked that, in America, every political issue ultimately becomes an issue for the courts. He pronounced this 33 years before the Fourteenth Amendment would make his reflection truer and the proof of it more commonplace.

Political questions belong in state legislatures, where, as a voter, you can toss out the rascals who pass laws you oppose. When policy issues come before unelected, life-tenured federal judges, the delicate balance of American law and government tilts against accountability.

In his confirmation hearing for the Court of Appeals, Judge Kavanaugh endorsed using the equal protection clause to get the right result yet, he has not employed judicial fiat to substitute his own policy choices for those of state legislators. These mixed views are worthy of inquiry by the Senate.

The president made his choice. Judge Kavanaugh now has a choice: will his role on the Supreme Court be the toadying showmanship of a lawmaker or the quiet reflections of a judge? An expansive reading of the amendment we remember this week could make Kavanaugh a giver of laws while an interpretation more in line with separation of powers and federalism will make him a guarantor of justice.

CHAPTER 6

Megan Barry's tenure didn't have to end like a sad country song

I work with a lot of clients in crisis. Many of them are high ranking government leaders. Lately, it seems like crisis and reputational risk surround politicians like cheap cologne on the boys' side of the dance floor at the freshman mixer.

Most work weeks find me trying to untangle a spun-up government or university public relations mess. While it's several yards short of a science, there are best practices that can be employed to help leaders protect, or even increase, their credibility during a crisis.

When bad news is bubbling up from the depths of stupidity in your organization, resist the urge to hold the bubbles under water. You already know they are going to eventually surface. Smart crisis communicators work to break their own bad news and explain to the public what happened – before critics take on the task.

I often travel to Nashville to give speeches and presentations. It's a vibrant and livable area and I have developed an affinity for it. Like the country music jangling and toinking from every loudspeaker in town, Nashville features a pleasing mix of fun, energy, and American spirit.

When I read about the once-popular mayor's scandal, I winced at how poorly she'd handled it. I could tell that someone in her circle has some crisis communications chops and could play some serious news media guitar but a few of the strings were out of tune and the melody they were playing fell flat.

*Working quickly -- before the mayor's resignation became old news –
I tapped out my initial thoughts on how she might have been able to
keep her job. Given the prominence of country music in this proud
town, I borrowed some imagery and allusions from that genre and
used them to frame the piece. I also made sure to use language and
local references that made the piece unique to that city.*

*Newspaper op-ed editors prefer to print local authors and, since I
don't live in Tennessee, I had to flash my country music bona fides
the way the banjo player auditioning for the bluegrass band warms up
with "Foggy Mountain Breakdown."*

*The editor must have been tapping his toe to the country drumbeat I
was playing, because he agreed to run the piece.*

*This is an example of how quick writing, knowledge of a subject, and
credibility in the locale can be a successful formula for a surefire op-
ed hit.*

PUBLISHED: *The Tennessean* — March 14, 2018

There are countless country music songs that include the phrase "I'm sorry."

The most famous is Brenda Lee's, where she laments her actions and asks, "Please accept my apology ... love was blind and I was too blind to see."

As if in reply, Blake Shelton sings a different tune, in the power ballad, "I'm Sorry," crooning: "Oh, you're sorry, you want it back the way it was ... but sometimes sorry just ain't good enough."

The Brenda Lee request from Megan Barry, the fallen mayor of country music's own hometown, was a hopeful plea for another chance. But the public's Blake Shelton response brought a discordant coda to her public life.

In the end, it was just another mournful refrain that resounded across town, from the tourist-pleasing cover joints on Broadway to the foam-padded studios along Music Row and far beyond the city limits.

As a frequent visitor to Nashville, I often speak to conferences here about crisis communications and how public officials can manage the fallout from a big mistake. You won't be surprised to hear that Megan Barry never took one of my classes.

Those of us who advise government leaders on how to respond to scandal watched the Barry episode with the same kind of grim foreboding of an air traffic controller eyeballing a damaged plane in sharp descent. We know how this flight ends.

The former mayor tried valiantly to rebound from her serious errors in judgment. In fact, many of her tactics evinced some competent counsel in her corner. Yet she nonetheless resigned, in shame, pleading guilty to a felony.

More people than Carrie Underwood are wondering what "Could've Been." Could the mayor have done something different to survive this shameful experience?

CHAPTER 7

Both sides misunderstand the role of the president

The ideas in this op-ed have been skittering around my mind for years. I've spoken about them in many of my public presentations and speeches but I've never condensed them down into a cogent argument. The opportunity arose in 2018, as I grew weary of the volcano of hyperbolic news coverage of President Donald Trump. In this endeavor, I sought to neither defend nor attack the president. My goal was more divertive -- to re-orient the reader's thinking about the role of the presidency itself.

Along the road to that obscure destination, I reached into my glove box and hauled out my metaphor toolkit. It's a well-worn binder and I keep it close at hand for jobs just like this. Hopefully, you just appreciated my use of a metaphor to describe how I select metaphors. If not, keep reading.

The word "metaphor" derives from the Greek for "to transfer" or to "carry over." It's an inventive way to explain one concept that a reader or listener may not know well by pointing to another concept and making a connection with that concept. Done right, metaphors can not only help someone understand your argument better but they can also add a lilt of inspiration and fancy that might otherwise be illusive.

In this piece, I employ several metaphors, the central one being the notion that government authority is like a cube of energy. Describing it that way advances and illustrates my underlying point that American representative democracy carves up that power and distributes it to different people, only one of whom is the president.

Other metaphors on display in this piece: "a bumper crop of challenges," "the snare of a jealous king," and the founding documents as "the owner's manuals for our republic."

I wielded parallel metaphors to describe the little-known psychological principle of cognitive dissonance. Given the relative complexity of the subject, I sought a memorable and palpable selection – soothing music (Pachelbel's Canon in D) vs. grating music (a toddler's piano punching of "Chopsticks.").

Metaphors, particularly striking and vivid ones, can be a strong way for you to persuade your reader.

PUBLISHED: *Cincinnati Enquirer* — January 26, 2018

A year ago, roughly half the country was celebrating the inauguration of a new president and the other half was lamenting the years to come. And nine years ago, those respective sides were in near turnabout. Barack Obama took the oath of office cheered by supporters giddy with victory, while the opposition grumbled with despair.

This discord isn't new, but it's growing deeper. And it yields a bumper crop of challenges. The problem is complex, yet many proposed responses are equal parts reflexive and reductive.

Much of this American anger focuses on who resides in the White House. Too often, when the candidate we opposed wins the presidency, we become gloomy about the fate of the nation.

This melancholy of the vanquished can be traced to at least one core misconception – the illusion that most of the government's power resides in the president. Those who view the president as the daddy of the country or the person "running the country" need remedial study in American government.

Power in the United States is peacefully given through the consent of the governed and then divided and separated among many leaders. The president is simply one of many holding that power.

Imagine all the power to run a nation condensed into a cube of energy. Throughout the sweep of time, monarchs, chieftains, and despots have jealously monopolized that powerful cube. The fates and fortunes of those governed rose or fell based on the whim of the cube-holder. Corrupt leaders grasping the full complement of power could rob their countrymen of everything, including their lives.

Our founding fathers were avid students of history and, having just escaped the snare of a jealous king, were keen to frame a system of governance that would confound the ability of any one person to bring down a nation.

Common bedside reading for the likes of James Madison and Alexander Hamilton was the work of French philosopher Baron de Montesquieu. Building on the division of powers in ancient Rome, Montesquieu noted that spreading power over many people limited the likelihood of wide-spread corruption or incompetence.

Thus, the Constitution, through the principles of separation of powers and federalism, takes that cube of energy and divides it at least nine different ways. The first three cuts occur left to right – the branches of government. These executive, legislative, and judicial slices split authority that, in most nations, had been housed in a single ruler.

The next division is top to bottom, three more slices of Neapolitan ice cream-inspired division. These federal, state and local layers distribute government power among officeholders in Washington, state capitols, and city halls.

After the slicing and dicing, power is divided among literally thousands of different people. No single person in that array – not even the president – can widely affect the power held by others.

Because executive branch leaders hold sway individually, presidents, governors, and mayors are more noticeable than legislators and judges. That's why people tend to focus more on them and it leads many to conclude that the character, competence, or credibility of a president matters more than for other leaders. It doesn't.

If you hated the last president and blame most of our nation's problems on him, you're wrong. And if you detest the current president and attribute most of our difficulties to him, you're equally wrong.

I know this perspective will clash in the minds of many. Our brain is much like our musical ear, which prefers Pachelbel's "Canon in D" to an overtired toddler's piano rendition of "Chopsticks." When we hold a strong belief, information from those who challenge that belief seems incorrect. Which is why cognitive dissonance is more than just choice "B" on your psych mid-term.

So don't take my word for this. Read the Declaration of Independence, the Constitution, and the Federalist Papers. These are the owner's manuals for our republic.

The occupant of the White House might lead the news every night and be the easiest person to argue about, but that doesn't make him the center of government power. Many presidents expected to run things only to discover that other officeholders also had their hands on the tiller of our ship of state.

President Truman groused, "I sit here all day trying to persuade people to do the things they ought to have sense enough to do without my persuading them. That's all the powers of the President amount to."

From township trustee to the commander in chief – every government role is consequential. By design, the power to govern America is less like a single guide star and more like the bright constellations glowing in a clear night sky. And understanding that will help you fully appreciate our galaxy of government.

CHAPTER 8

Accusations are easy, proof is hard part

As America roiled over the accusations of multiple women against certain men in power in business, government, and entertainment, I noticed that a key element was often missing from the discussion – the need for proof. It's more than a minor omission. It's the central factor in determining credibility.

I realized that, if I wrote about that, some might think I was defending the alleged behavior of the men caught up in what became known as the #MeToo movement. You'll see in this piece how I begin with my bona fides in the area of doing justice in cases of sexual assault before making my larger point. This can be an effective way to disarm a potential opponent to your planned argument. By removing the obvious knock on your own credibility before you begin to frame the debate, you've protected yourself from an easy attack.

Also note the liberty I took with the English language in order to increase reader interest when I wrote "Bloodletting in battle led to inkletting in statesmanship…" Although there's no word "inkletting," I thought it would create an interesting parallel construction with the prior use of bloodletting.

When writing for effect, it's less important to be square with your eighth-grade grammar teacher than it is to be persuasive. Used sparingly, the tactic of inventing a word that makes an argument sharper is worth your consideration.

Also note my use of alliteration in an attempt to create a memorable phrase – "rehab for reprobates." The latter word is a bit out of reach for the average reader (it means someone who does bad things) but I liked the ring of it.

As a rule, I try to write at the 8th or 9th grade level, similar to stories and opinion pieces you might read in USA Today. Given that most Americans don't have a college degree, this style will make your work more approachable. If you're unsure of what grade level you write at, use the Flesch Kincaid readability feature of your Microsoft Word program or paste your work into the analyzer at ScienceAndPublic.com. For example, this section you just read (according to that web site) has a 94% suitability rate for the general reading public.

PUBLISHED: *Cincinnati Enquirer—* Nov. 13, 2017

I was traveling with my wife and daughter last week when I told them I was contemplating writing a column entitled "In defense of Harvey Weinstein." They simultaneously grimaced.

I was quick to remind them that, given my experience prosecuting sex offenders and child rapists, no one is more repulsed by the poster boy of Hollywood excess and immorality than me. Ditto for U.S. Senator wannabe Roy Moore. But I also told them that while I despise the amoral attitudes those who prey on others, I cherish due process even more.

America was founded after royal subjects living in British North America became vexed at governmental abuses of power. The founding fathers and their ancestors had seen royal authority misused through search warrants that allowed soldiers to search any house at any time, government confiscation of property without compensation, and imprisonment and execution without anything resembling a fair trial. Indeed, the Declaration of Independence itself alleges that King George was "deaf to the voice of justice."

Bloodletting in battle led to ink-letting in statesmanship and the British gaps identified by the Declaration were filled by the American

Constitution. And the golden thread that holds together that Constitution's Bill of Rights is the notion of due process under the law.

As the heirs to those brave patriots who fought the American Revolution, we must not retreat from the ramparts they built. Due process was costly to achieve in battle and ought not to be conveniently ignored. When someone raises an allegation that the law has been violated, we must presume that the claim lacks merit until evidence is tested in a court of law and a judge or jury makes a ruling.

Mitt Romney recently announced that "innocent until proven guilty is for criminal convictions, not elections." Others have claimed that a news report is enough to determine someone's guilt.

But if we're truly committed to due process, in our heart we'll presume innocence even when we hear multiple sickening reports about the purported misdeeds of Harvey Weinstein, Kevin Spacey, and Roy Moore. It's hard to do. I struggle with it. But it's the right thing.

As a prosecutor, when I hear a criminal defense lawyer remind a jury that the person whom I genuinely believe is guilty must be presumed innocent, I bite my lip and shift uncomfortably in my chair. That's because I've reviewed the evidence and consoled the victim and I believe deep in my soul that the man I put on trial is guilty. But I allow the trial to take its course because I know requiring sworn testimony and evidence tested by cross-examination is the best way to discern the truth. And sticking to this standard is what keeps you and me from becoming accused and adjudged without credible evidence.

Some of the famous men who've been accused of sexual misdeeds have headed off to what news reports identify as sex addiction counseling. But such rehab for reprobates won't get at the root of the problem – a lack of moral character. Unless each of us acknowledges that there's a true north of what's right and what's wrong, no amount of counseling or psychobabble will stop us from doing what we want, when we want.

Men who abuse women share something with street thugs who rob, attack, and steal – they think they can avoid the natural result of violating basic tenets of right and wrong. Even beyond statutes passed by legislatures, there's an immutable moral law much like the law of gravity.

Far too much of Hollywood's product showcases characters who violate that moral law and avoid consequences. The entertainment industry's fetish for violence, sex, and nihilism leads many young people astray. And the people who write, act, and produce this garbage marinate in it themselves, affecting their own behavior and skewing their core values. We see this in other settings, as well.

Which brings me back to the uber-repulsive Harvey Weinstein. I describe him that way because, even if the accusations against him are untrue, the actions he admits to — adultery, cheating, bullying, make him a person that no person of good character will defend. But, as to whether he violated the law, we ought to wait on a court ruling. Due process requires it.

So, Harvey, if you're reading this, here's the good news: we should all withhold judgment about the sexual assault allegations until you get a fair trial. And, here's the bad news. If you're convicted, you should go to prison for the rest of your grubby little life.

CHAPTER 9

If you want new immigration policy, stop looking to the White House

In the first year of his presidency, Donald Trump was building a big, beautiful wall between Red America and Blue America. Nearly every action he took that year brought controversy. When he decided that President Obama's executive action to allow children of illegal immigrants to remain in America was improper, the usual paratroopers of polemics took to their respective battle stations and began to wage war.

As the din of the fight clanged on, I began to be frustrated that few people were focusing on what I thought was a much more big-picture concern – the discussion surrounding who gets to decide our nation's policy. So, without taking a stand on the substantive question of whether the people the media labeled "Dreamers" should be allowed to stay, I set out to remind those engaged in the battle that praising or pillorying President Trump fast forwards past the more appropriate point – Congress makes all of our policy.

As I often do, I began the piece by starting with an analogy most people can understand and asserting a premise few would dispute. This serves a dual purpose. It draws the reader into the column and begins to get that person agreeing with me. Once people agree with an early assertion, they are more likely to agree later in the argument.

If you've heard me give a public presentation, you'll recognize my voice in this piece. Founding fathers "parachuting out" of Great Britain and snarky references to popular culture, like the Broadway show, "Hamilton" are standard fare for me. This casual, informal language is how people talk to each other. It avoids the feel of a bad high school essay. It's genuine.

Finally, you'll see I used the "bookending" style here, which means I started and ended with the same illustration to give the reader a sense of completion and to hammer home my overarching point.

This is the only op-ed I've written that was published by two different newspapers on the same day. I had submitted it to both the Columbus Dispatch and the Cincinnati Enquirer in the hope that one would run it. They both chose to run it, the same day.

PUBLISHED: *The Columbus Dispatch and Cincinnati Enquirer* — September 8, 2017

We teach our children that cheating in school is dishonest. We tell them it's wrong and self-defeating to seek the outcome – a better grade – without achieving the very purpose of the enterprise: learning.

I thought about that concept this week as the left and the right engaged in social media slap fights over President Trump's decision to end what President Obama called a "temporary, stop-gap measure" of allowing certain children of illegal immigrants to remain in America. My own opinion about the fate of so-called DACA "dreamers" takes a back seat to my larger concern – who determines the policy?

Our founding fathers thought deeply about the kind of nation they wanted to build, given that they'd just parachuted out of what many believed was the greatest nation on earth. They knew future generations would scuffle and scrap about how government should operate, so they gave us the Constitution. That document acts as the guardrails along the path of managing the worst impulses of tyrants and tyrants in training.

A president might want to make treaties without interference, but the Constitution requires Senate ratification. Congress could try to make budget decisions alone, but the Constitution gives the president veto power. And federal judges may wish to gavel their whims into law but the Constitution allows Congress to impeach them if they fall short of "good behavior."

Article I of the Constitution gives "all legislative powers" to Congress. Unlike so many constitutional questions, that are as clear as the vista from a midnight sandstorm, who gets to decide federal policy is straightforward: 435 representatives and 100 senators.

That's why the policy question of whether bank robbery should be a federal crime belongs to Congress. What should the federal tax rate be? Ask Congress. And, most pertinently now, whether citizens of other countries can come to America and permanently live here is a question unequivocally left to Congress.

These are policy choices, and the founders wanted them to be made by just one part of government – the legislative branch. It makes sense. That's the branch most immediately accountable to voters with elections for all of the House and one-third of the Senate every two years.

Alexander Hamilton was a prolific booster of this approach. In fact, if you loved him on Broadway, you'll love him even more in the Federalist Papers, the pro-Constitution tracts he co-authored in 1788. Hamilton said (sorry, this was before he learned to rap): "It is essential to liberty that the government in general should have a common interest ... and an intimate sympathy with, the people. Frequent elections are unquestionably the only policy by which this dependence and sympathy can be effectually secured."

Federal law currently makes it illegal for a foreign national to remain here without permission. Indeed, the law that every elected official swore to uphold says that people here illegally "shall upon the order of the Attorney General be removed." That's the law currently in force, enacted by a Congress who, we must presume, acted with the legitimate mandate of those who elected them.

There's only one valid way to undo that law – pressure Congress to pass a different law. If this sounds a bit like eighth grade civics, that's because it is. But far too many of those shouting and shrieking over desired policy outcomes are ignoring these civic truths. They want what they want and to heck with the process. Yet even when Congress fails to enact the laws we want, our sole legal remedy is to change the Congress.

Which brings us back to the student who wants the good grade but doesn't want to get it the way the system was designed to give it – by studying and learning. The substantive process matters – often as much as the result.

There may be good policy reasons to allow "dreamers" to stay here. If that's your viewpoint, go instruct your member of Congress. If Congress doesn't fulfill your request, go elect a congressional majority that will.

Good ideas that have broad support tend to get passed into law, if only because legislators want to avoid the ire of angry constituents demanding action. When Congress doesn't act, it's fair to assume that not enough people back home have pressured them to do so.

President Obama's executive order was an end-around run of the policy-making structure given to us by Hamilton and his supporting cast. Bypassing that system by seeking a desired policy result from someone other than the designated policy maker is antidemocratic, unconstitutional, and – it's cheating.

CHAPTER 10

Don't derail the system by ignoring separation of powers

In 2015, people around the nation were horrified to learn of a high-speed AMTRAK train crash in Philadelphia where eight people died and many more were seriously injured. Investigators began to focus on the conduct of the train's engineer. Two years later, in 2017, a controversy arose when the elected prosecutor decided not to bring charges against the engineer, despite the fact he was operating the train at higher speeds than conditions warranted.

As a prosecutor, I understand the desire to seek justice in a case where someone's actions caused so many deaths. But the Philadelphia District Attorney, who was amidst his own corruption scandal and may have wanted a distraction from it via a high-profile trial, reviewed the evidence and saw no criminal case. One of the private attorneys suing AMTRAK decided to seek a different route to initiate an prosecution. He asked a judge to initiate the criminal case. Although I no longer live in the Philadelphia area, I still keep abreast with much of the news from the region and the story caught my eye.

I quickly determined that ignoring the local prosecutor by having a judge do the district attorney's job was a prominent example of seeking a certain result without caring about the process. In the previous chapter, you read how I raised a similar concern about such a system-bending tactic as it relates to children of illegal immigrants.

I knew that the Philadelphia newspaper – the Inquirer – would take note of any op-ed I submitted on the topic for three reasons. First, as a native of the region, my opinion was more relevant than someone with no local ties. The opening of the piece had a dual purpose: by citing my history in the area, I was establishing my bona fides and by envisioning a children's soccer game, I was setting up a key metaphor for my thesis. Also, when I introduced the concept of the constitution and the founding fathers, I made a local street reference and a nod to the local university, that was not only historically accurate but would resonate with area residents.

Secondly (and probably more importantly), I was taking a contrary, even unpopular stand. People were outraged and wanted action in the form of criminal charges. My argument about process was a cold splash of H20 on the burning desire to send the engineer to prison as recompense for lives lost.

Finally, I did some quick checking to see what was happening in olden Philadelphia around the same date of the judge's decision and (admittedly) stumbled into a coincidence of calendar that made the piece even more timely.

As usual, I wrote quickly, tapping out the piece the same day the news broke about the judge-borne charges. The Inquirer has published my work before, which helped them make their prompt decision to publish this somewhat-controversial piece.

I'll admit that my first take had several railroad similes. As I began to edit and advance the subsequent drafts, I realized that too much of such wordplay could be perceived as glib or insensitive to the families of those tragically killed. This is always a danger when opining about calamity and misfortune. It helps to have another person review your work, to determine if your fancy flourishes and punchy prose don't hurt more than it helps. But, you'll note, I could not resist including the "train" reference from the Declaration of Independence.

PUBLISHED: *The Philadelphia Inquirer* — May 19, 2017

P laying childhood soccer in the fields of Southeastern Pennsylvania, one thing quickly became clear to me: the younger the players, the more likely they are to follow the ball around in an eager clump of arms, legs, and colorful jerseys. Children all want to kick the ball, so the notion of patiently staying in their assigned positions is often elusive. In time, they learn that the goals of the game are better achieved when players stay in their lane to wait for the ball or defend against the other team.

If Municipal Court Judge Marsha Neifield better understood this concept, she wouldn't have resurrected the criminal case against Amtrak engineer Brandon Bostian, the key figure in the May 2015 derailment that left eight passengers dead and hundreds more injured.

The public is justly outraged at Bostian's apparent negligence, given that the train accelerated to 106 mph on a 50-mph curve. Many no doubt applauded the judge's decision. But, like a jumble of youthful soccer players, the judge was playing outside her designated position. She substituted her own judgment for the prosecutorial discretion of the elected district attorney, who had determined that there wasn't enough evidence to prove Bostian acted with the "conscious disregard" the law requires for a prosecution.

While a judge overruling a prosecutor -- particularly one under indictment like District Attorney Seth Williams – might seem like justice to some, it creates troubling issues with the separation of powers inherent in our government.

Our founding fathers spent quite a bit of time in Philadelphia discussing how to protect their new nation from the abuses of power by the British monarchy. Indeed, 230 years ago this week, delegates began to arrive here to start deliberations that would result in the approval of the Constitution.

It's not hard to imagine Virginia's James Madison and Philadelphia's own James Wilson strolling down Market Street, discussing the ideas of Aristotle, John Calvin, and John Locke -- all proponents of separating governmental power.

Wilson, who later served as a U.S. Supreme Court justice and was the first professor of law at what would become the University of Pennsylvania, saw a king who brandished the powers available to him in a way that created (in the words of the Declaration of Independence) "a long train of abuses and usurpations." Madison, Wilson, and their fellow delegates to the constitutional convention resolved to avoid the corruption that comes when too much power rests in any one office.

Their solution was as easy as the timeless childhood frolic of rock, paper, scissors. Everyone who plays this game quickly realizes that none of the symbols is all-powerful on its own. The same basic principle is the underlying reason why American checks and balances are fair. No branch has more power than the other.

Some judges don't like this notion much. They think the judicial branch gets the last word. They're mistaken.

Unlike judges, prosecutors are bound by rules of ethics that require them to only bring charges when they have good reason to believe they can prove each element of a crime. When that evidence is insufficient, they are ethically bound to decline prosecution. Indeed, Pennsylvania ethics rules give district attorneys a special role in the commonwealth's judicial system. They must not seek to simply prosecute and convict. They must, rather, be a "minister of justice." Sometimes, that means not bringing charges despite public demands.

In the criminal court system, district attorneys propose and judges and juries dispose. A judge has enough to worry about without taking on the responsibility of another player.

To the delight of the plaintiff's attorneys seeking millions of dollars for their clients, the victims of this horrific crash, Pennsylvania Attorney General Josh Shapiro has played along and agreed to prosecute. Keystone state residents ought to wonder whether that decision was more about achieving justice in the court of law or, more worrisome, achieving headlines in the court of public opinion.

When an Amtrak engineer derails a train, it can cause a lot of damage. But when a judge derails the separation of powers that keeps corruption and tyranny at bay, other types of damage ensue. We'd be wise to be concerned about both.

CHAPTER 11

Women and politics: What you think may be wrong

I lived in Washington, D.C., for years before moving to Ohio. Visiting there in January 2017, I was an eyewitness to the crowds and craziness surrounding the right-leaning Trump inauguration and the left-leaning "Women's March on Washington," which took place just a day apart from each other.

As I walked among the gathered partisans of both camps, it was clear to me that women were ubiquitous there. Mingling among the mall and monuments, some wore red baseball caps lauding President Trump, others had pink knit hats with cat ears meant to deride him. Each side glibly suggested it somehow represented the majority of American women. Some in the news media weighed in on this notion, as well.

Both sides of that assertion — and the media outlets that indulged them — were wrong.

Over the years working with many different women leaders, I've grown weary rebuffing the lazy and false narrative that women largely share the same political views. So, returning from a brisk walk among the competing voices (accompanied by my wife, Lori, and our daughter, Jamieson), I metaphorically brushed the remnant specks of angry partisan brickbats off my coat and sat down at my laptop to set the record straight.

Within 36 hours, one of the largest newspapers in Ohio agreed to run my op-ed, without suggesting a single change or edit. I woke up the morning of its publication to a series of texts and email messages from friends and colleagues who had enjoyed the piece.

Later in the week, I stumbled across this op-ed posted on a wide variety of social media sites. Predictably, the two sides claiming to represent American women were duking it out in the comment sections.

There are a few lessons aspiring writers can take from this piece. Although I have my own strong opinions on many issues currently being discussed, I used this column to advance what is sometimes called "triangulation." It simply means identifying the space between two competing viewpoints as a place of common sense and common ground.

At its worst, this concept can be cynically employed to pit political factions against each other. I prefer to use it to calm roiling waters and bring people together. In a nation as divided as America, cooler arguments may quench the burning need for resolution and harmony. Here I chose to use the written word to rebuff attacks, reduce the clanging dissonance of emotional arguments, and remind all involved that we are bound by an American credo.

Let us never forget that ours is a credo of self-governance that stemmed from a "firm reliance on the protection of divine providence" as described by Maestro Jefferson's coda in the verbal symphony that is the Declaration of Independence. Together, we can and we must renew the bonds that, to borrow and amend a phrase from a red ball cap, Made America Great in the first place.

PUBLISHED: *The Columbus Dispatch* — January 24, 2017

T his week, millions of women rejoiced at the inauguration of Donald Trump, many of them trekking to Washington to be heard. Other women, also in the millions, decried President Trump's ascension to power, some also heading to the nation's capital or nearby venues to protest. What do these women — or women in general — have in common? Almost nothing. And, when it comes to politics, that's a good thing.

For example, nearly every poll tells us that women are about equally split on whether they identify as pro-life or pro-choice on abortion. There's no "women's position" on that issue, or, for that matter, any issue. Every issue is a woman's issue — and a man's issue. And, while there's a "gender gap" in some election results, factors like race, locale, and age are much stronger predictors of partisan leanings than a voter's sex.

Even if a stray issue here or there does show a marginal difference between attitudes of men and women, there's no intellectually honest claim that women's views are monolithic. Yet news media coverage often suggests otherwise.

As my byline suggests, I'm not a woman. But the notion that only women can accurately analyze the views of women and politics is as wrongheaded and over-simplistic as the assumption that women are some odd species whose attitudes are fully in sync with one another. Nowhere is that common fallacy more destructive than politics and policymaking.

When people who make our laws believe women naturally think one way and men another, the result can be regulations that perpetuate a troubling Balkanization of the sexes. In a nation where our motto is *from many, one*, we must strive to divert from this direction lest we all become denizens of division. Indeed, pernicious identity politics should have no place in a country where the only relevant identity is being American.

Several times a year, I speak at women's leadership conferences. I often help develop opportunities for young women to be more involved in public affairs and government. Indeed, I was proud to see my wife and daughter become active in these programs and glad to see others benefit from them as well. I support these efforts not because women have a unique voice that must be heard. Female perspectives are multiple and varied, not uniform. To claim otherwise is to diminish women's role as equal partners in politics.

So, women ought to be involved in the process of self-governance not because there's a "woman's viewpoint," but because when we're all in it together, our decisions are usually better. When women — conservative, moderate, and liberal — are less involved in a government of, by, and for the people, the resolutions of our republic may be rejected. Indeed, it was Founding Mother Abigail Adams who reminded her husband John that women *"will not hold ourselves bound by any laws in which we have no voice or representation."*

Years ago, I moved to Ohio to work as the deputy attorney general for Betty Montgomery — the first woman elected as our state attorney general. Yet her place in history was secured by her character, vision, and dedication to this state. Her gender was more footnote than foundation.

Electing a woman simply because she's a woman is as ill-considered and small-minded as voting against a woman for the same reason. And as we begin the administration of President Trump, one-dimensional views of whether women support or oppose his policies have the ironic effect of advancing that which so many feminists reject: the notion that women should be of one mind on anything. Politically speaking, men are complicated. It's not breaking news that women are, as well.

Women, whether in the era of Obama or Trump, should march on Washington to counter leaders and legislation they oppose. But that burden of representative democracy also falls to men. Americans are the shareholders of this nation and we ought not be silent partners in it. And this mandate applies without regard to gender, since the chromosomes of our body matter infinitely less than the DNA of our democracy.

CHAPTER 12

How to avoid political heartburn at a family dinner

In the wake of the presidential election of 2016, America was largely divided between those who were glad Donald Trump won and those who were not. While that's not an unusual state of affairs after a contested election, something about the 2016 campaign seemed to bring out the worst in many people. Social media was aflame with people who ought to be friends acting downright unfriendly to those who had voted for the opposing candidate.

Knowing that Thanksgiving 2016 would bring family members of differing views together at the same dinner table, I penned this op-ed with the hope of reminding people of the importance of civil discourse and the need to see the larger picture. The arguments I make here are based on simple notions of civility and, in another setting, might well have been unnecessary.

I was glad when the major daily newspaper in Cincinnati, Ohio, agreed to run this in their Thanksgiving edition, which — hopefully — allowed my thoughts to be fresh in the minds of those gathering around the table.

You can see that I used familiar Thanksgiving references throughout the piece to act as the framework and give it more relevance. Maintaining consistency with such a theme can be helpful, as long as it's not over-cooked.

PUBLISHED: *The Cincinnati Enquirer* — November 23, 2016

T here may be more than turkey, gravy, and stuffing being passed around the table this Thanksgiving. There could also be family-sized servings of acrimony, anger, and antagonism. Usually, November begins with Election Day dissonance and ends with Thanksgiving harmony. This year may be different. Unless families have a game plan to address disparate political views, the post-dinner TV football won't be the only display of unnecessary roughness.

It's long been noted that we can pick our friends but not our family. It's not new that relatives often hold differing political views from one another. But the rancor of the 2016 election could set the table for a meal that leaves no one feeling very thankful. Yet calm and civil discourse is possible if all involved are willing to observe some basic guidelines.

First on the menu ought to be understanding different perspectives. With our country about evenly divided between those who hate Hillary Clinton and those who revile Donald Trump, remember that American politics is largely a two-sided coin. In 2008, the coin landed heads up for Democrats, and face down for Republicans. One side was elated and foresaw a bright future. The other was dejected and predicted national ruin. We now know that neither perspective was completely correct.

This year, Republicans won the toss. They're gleeful and certain of rosy days ahead. Democrats are sadder than a hungry vegetarian at the turkey carving station. They're sure America is on the skids. If history is any judge, neither party will be fully vindicated.

Appreciating that perspective really matters. It can help abate the arrogance of the winners and assuage the anger of the losers. Every kid who's ever sat on a playground teeter totter knows that the exhilarating view from the up position is tempered by the knowledge that the down spot will soon arrive with a jolt.

Next, if you do decide to engage in verbal arm-wrestling alongside the cranberry sauce, try to avoid the more egregious mistakes people make in political discussions. The worst of these is the *ad hominem* attack — personally criticizing someone instead of addressing his or her point.

Let's say your tipsy aunt wobbles by and remarks, "Millard Fillmore was the greatest president of the nineteenth century." You then reply, "only an idiot would think that." You've made an *ad hominem* attack and fallen short of how responsible adults should discuss personal beliefs. A better retort might involve pointing out that President Fillmore and Abraham Lincoln served in the same century and Lincoln was the one who preserved the nation during the Civil War.

Among the most over-used *ad hominem* attacks is calling someone a racist, sexist, or some other form of hater. These are uncivil personal slurs that lack a universally agreed-upon definition. Casually and frequently using such epithets suggests your position lacks substance. Criticize arguments, not people.

Another common underhanded discussion technique is the straw man argument. This occurs when your verbal adversary summarizes your own view for you, conveniently stripping out the nuance and logic of your stance.

Imagine that your annoying cousin tells the family members huddled around the after-dinner mints that you support giving handguns to toddlers. You wonder how your support for the Second Amendment could be construed that way, but wonder no more. Your cousin helpfully created a political straw man position for you, one that you can easily knock down. Simply smile and say, "if you don't mind, I can describe my own opinion, and here's what it is."

Finally, leave the offensive fouls to the football players. Saying "I'm offended" or "that's offensive" when you really mean "I disagree," is unnecessarily aggressive and doesn't advance your argument. Anyone can claim to be offended about anything. What if the person you're arguing with is offended that you're offended? You'll both be dizzy in a roundabout of offensiveness.

Unlike Facebook or Twitter, where relatives who vex you with their political views can be quieted with a click, bringing serenity to the

Thanksgiving table requires more effort. Quoting founding father Thomas Jefferson might help. Attempting to resolve a quarrel with a friend, Mr. Jefferson wrote: *"I never considered a difference of opinion in politics, in religion, in philosophy, as cause for withdrawing from a friend."* While that sentiment was meant to heal a friendship, it can help repair a rift in the family, as well.

If all else fails, remember this. Imagine, that, as the dishes are cleared away, your uncle announces to the family that he's recently been diagnosed with a terminal disease and has only a few months left to live. If this were to occur, you ought to set aside your objection to whichever candidate he supported and immediately embrace and comfort him. If you don't, you'll be acting as hateful as whichever candidate you abhor.

Thanksgiving is a time for reflection, appreciation, and graciousness. If you get lucky and pull the larger piece of the wishbone, make a wish that this special day will be a time when we all remember what — and who — is truly important in our lives.

CHAPTER 13

Students vulnerable to unpatriotic stunts in sports

In the autumn of 2016, Americans were debating whether a group calling itself Black Lives Matter was accurate in its claims that police officers have a racist attitude toward African-Americans. Most public opinion polls showed Americans siding with police and rejecting most of the Black Lives Matter agenda, yet the controversy persisted.

A flashpoint occurred when a professional football player named Colin Kaepernick announced that he would make his own form of protest against the police, by refusing to stand during the pre-game national anthem. A few high school football players began to imitate this disrespectful defiance, garnering news coverage. For years, I'd been pondering why many Americans are quick to publicly criticize their country (which has flaws like every other country) in a way that they wouldn't dare do about their (similarly flawed) family. Writing this column gave me a chance to expound on the idea.

PUBLISHED: *The Zanesville Times Recorder* and additional USA TODAY Network publications — September 27, 2016

The unpatriotic unwillingness of Colin Kaepernick to stand during the national anthem is now creeping into a handful of high school football games around the country, the way fungus blights a few leaves on every tree.

The dictionary defines patriotism as the act of vigorously support-ing or loving one's country. People who argue that doing the opposite of supporting or loving America is also patriotism either don't under-stand what the word means or are trying to redefine it. The former dis-plays ignorance and the latter shows malice.

Abraham Lincoln once observed that calling a dog's tail a leg "doesn't make it a leg." Describing criticism of America as patriotism is similarly inappropriate.

That's not to say that being unpatriotic is illegal. It's not, nor should it be. The First Amendment is alive and well and it applies here in full measure. The fact that, unlike authoritarian countries like North Korea, we allow abundant criticism of our government speaks to the greatness of America.

This can be an incendiary topic, as too many people conflate their own political opinion with the larger issue. That leads to uncritical thinking and an erroneous result. It may help to examine this subject through another lens.

There have been countless bad mothers through the course of American history. In the 20th century, Marie Noe murdered eight of her ten children. In the century before that, Mary Ann Cotton killed all 12 of her kids. The list of maternal evils, despite being a small and un-representative fraction of mothers, goes on.

Each of these mothers deserves sharp and energetic criticism. I wouldn't stand up to honor any of them. But motherhood — the idea of a lifetime of loving self-sacrifice for the benefit of another — is one of the worthiest notions of all time. It would be hard to find someone unwilling to stand up for the notion of motherhood. It's possible — even morally right — to criticize specific evil mothers while still honor-ing the ideal of motherhood.

Our country has seen individual people do bad things, leaders and regular citizens alike. While our system remains superior to any other country, we've still fallen short of the ideal. Conjure up your favorite example of American misstep or misdeed for a moment. While that instance may deserve our denunciation, the stated aspirations of America unquestionably do not.

Standing during the national anthem is a tradition we share as part of our American culture. After all, despite a few shrieks from the campus crowd and the for-profit diversity education community, we're not a multicultural country — we're multi-ethnic. We share one culture and that includes a reverence for the creed set out in the Declaration of Independence: All of us were created equal and endowed by God with certain basic rights.

If reading that assertion rankles, remember that it's neither a controversial statement nor a political ideology. It's the stated essence of what it means to be an American — as written, discussed, and ratified by the founders — who, as a group, risked more than anyone alive today to acquire that designation.

If your local city council passes a law you oppose, show up at a meeting and give them an earful. If government bureaucrats write a regulation that will deprive you of a job, carry a picket sign outside their office building. And if you believe a police officer has made a mistake, report it, denounce it, and tell the world about it.

But just as you wouldn't publicly criticize motherhood (or your own mother, for that matter) for the mistakes of individual mothers, nor should you disrespect the national anthem for the misdeeds of individual Americans.

If Colin Kaepernick or any other misguided athlete wants to sit on the bench while thousands of other people in the stadium stand and cheer the police who risk their lives for others, I would disagree with him. I would acknowledge that his protest was at least aimed at the specific occupation he's mad at most.

But failing to stand for the national anthem as a way of highlighting particular mistakes in our country is wrong. It's actually — allow me to briefly borrow a term overused by the armies of the aggrieved — offensive. Indeed, just as the Confederate flag is deeply offensive to millions of Americans, refusing to show honor to the national anthem of the United States is deeply offensive to many, many more.

And it's one thing for a wealthy, pampered professional athlete to do so and quite another for impressionable high school student athletes. Everything that happens at and through a school is meant to be a learning opportunity. Coaches and parent leaders who see a student following the unpatriotic example of Colin Kaepernick ought to have a direct dialogue with that teen.

In fact, taking a few minutes to discuss the difference between the constitutional right to protest and the American responsibility to embrace and support our national creed could be the best lesson ever. Especially in the land of the free and the home of the brave.

CHAPTER 14

Crowdsourcing justice can mean denying it

Americans are now enjoying and discussing new online entertainment programs that take real criminal cases and examine them in a weekly progression that draws people in the way episodic television dramas have for decades. As someone who has tried several cases in court and prosecuted violent felons in front of a jury, I have a general aversion for how Hollywood overdramatizes legal matters. But the podcast "Serial" and Netflix program "Making A Murderer" looked like they might be different. After friends and family asked for my opinion on these programs, I reviewed them and came away unimpressed and a bit concerned. This column was my way of explaining why.

PUBLISHED: *The Cincinnati Enquirer* and other USA TODAY Network publications — September 19, 2016

Courtroom dramas are becoming courtroom documentaries and Americans are hooked.

Millions discovered an audio podcast called *Serial*, which, during its first season, spent several hours scrutinizing the case of a Baltimore man convicted of the murder of his ex-girlfriend. Others have binge-watched the Netflix program *Making a Murderer*, a series surrounding the trials of a man and his nephew for the murder of a local woman. Now, *The Cincinnati Enquirer* has waded in with its compelling online series titled *Accused*.

In these programs, the multimedia content is delivered over the internet, where a culture exists that encourages anyone with a Wi-Fi connection to explore facts and theories, often sending tips to producers for broadcast use in future episodes. To many, it's good fun to use internet podcasts to cobble clues together to solve a heinous crime.

But good fun isn't good justice. Given the inherent limitations and over-dramatization of criminal cases offered for popular consumption, using the wisdom of the masses — often called "crowdsourcing" — to ascertain the truth can do more harm than good.

Crowdsourcing gourmet reviews makes some restaurant owners yip and Yelp with fear and using an app to summon a ride from passing cars is undoubtedly Uber convenient. Money is made and consumers are gratified. Yet using the internet to crowdsource justice may well be no justice at all.

As someone who's served as both a prosecutor and a magistrate, I'm concerned. Here's why: It may be interesting to see the perspective of these media producers, but their opinions of guilt or innocence don't really matter. Your opinion doesn't matter, either. Or mine.

What matters are the views of the jurors who spent weeks listening to evidence, observing and evaluating the demeanor of witnesses, and rendering a verdict. Juries have been doing that for centuries. Yet now these profit-making programs seek to second guess that work and even imply that the internet audience is somehow better suited to reach a just verdict.

While the First Amendment protects their right to do so and many find it compelling, it doesn't mean that the audiences have heard the truth or seen the complete view of the case. Without being present in the courtroom for the entire case, that's impossible.

Some may point to recent court actions where some of the defendants in these programs have been given new trials as proof that these offerings have brought forth previously-unseen perspectives. But many judges, including appeals court judges, are elected and, as a result, they may be more persuaded by the public opinion stirred by these media sensations than by new evidence or the relevant jurisprudence.

Nearly every criminal case is a tangle of conflicting accounts, varying degrees of persuasive evidence, and a fallible jury or judge. Almost any microscope applied retrospectively to this messy process will yield more questions as well as second, third, and fourth-guessing.

Near the end of the *Serial* podcast, the host ponders aloud "did we just spend a year applying excessive scrutiny to a perfectly ordinary case?"

Sorry, but yes. That's precisely what you did. And so did *Making A Murderer* and *Accused*.

Every day, courts across the nation wrestle with facts, evidence, and testimony that can be as confounding as a Rubik's cube with half of the color stickers torn off. Jurors and judges are tasked with using the same common sense they use in their most important life decisions to weed out the truth.

And — here's the crucial part — to convict someone, they must simply decide that the prosecution has proved its case "beyond a reasonable doubt." Not beyond a shadow of a doubt. Not beyond any doubt at all. The standard is lower than what many people think.

Jurors will often leave a trial where they convicted someone and still harbor a nagging doubt about whether they did the right thing. That's natural. Human endeavor brings with it the possibility of mistake. Even the exacting truth-determining process of a trial can result in error.

When it comes right down to it, our justice system isn't perfect. It can't be since imperfect humans are making the decisions. When a trial court makes a mistake, an appellate court can and should correct it. When new evidence is brought to light within court rules and legal standards, post-conviction hearings can and ought to consider it.

The sort of debate, discussion, and review of the conflicting evidence in these shows is much like what occurs in the private room where jurors deliberate the case. But, the procedure these programs employed was flawed from the very start, which is ironic because they undertook to correct what they saw as a flawed trial process. The problems abound.

First, the legal system has detailed rules about what sort of evidence is appropriate for jurors to hear. Hearsay — things people who aren't in court might have said — is typically not allowed to be considered.

Polygraph examinations are almost never admitted into evidence. Personal opinions of the lawyers involved are similarly barred.

In court, evidence is subject to rules of admissibility and then tested by cross-examination by legal professionals trained to pierce the fog of evasion and reveal what really happened. For centuries, observers have rightfully called this process the "greatest legal engine ever invented for the discovery of truth."

But that engine sputters and dies in these entertainment programs. Fans review perspectives that would never be allowed in court and, even if such evidence were, would be subject to aggressive questioning by both sides.

Suggesting that casual consumers of internet entertainment can provide the same quality of focus and review as a jury is to misunderstand and underestimate our legal system.

So, go ahead, binge watch another trial, put on a new podcast, and eagerly debate the competing theories with your friends. This trend may become a model of modern entertainment. It just won't be a model of justice.

CHAPTER 15

When the prosecutor is really a persecutor

This is the last of three columns I wrote in The Baltimore Sun addressing the criminal charges brought against police who arrested a young African American man suspected of dealing drugs. When the man died in police custody, riots and violent lawlessness gripped Baltimore in a way that focused the world's attention. Despite little or no evidence of wrongdoing by the police, the elected prosecutor in Baltimore brought felony charges against several officers.

I discussed her vitriolic and unprofessional news conference in the first column, while the second op-ed addressed a ruling by the judge attempting to limit the First Amendment rights of jurors to speak about the first trial. In the column below, I continued my notes of concern for how the local prosecutor abused her power to twist the justice system beyond what the Constitution and laws permit. It was meant to be the postscript of a shameful episode in American legal history.

I initially thought the penultimate line about Lady Justice should have been the walk-off for the piece, because I thought it was a strong ending. But eventually, I opted for a more conclusory walk-off. You can decide which one would have worked better.

PUBLISHED: *The Baltimore Sun* — July 28, 2016

People of good will can disagree on whether Freddie Gray should ever have been arrested by Baltimore Police. But there's no credible argument that the officers involved in his arrest should have been charged with crimes.

A recent editorial from *The Baltimore Sun* outlined what it sees as positive outcomes that came from the indictments and trials of the police officers involved. But the purpose of the criminal justice system is not to bring about general societal good. This system, built upon centuries of careful deliberation and adjustment, solely reviews cases when — and only when — probable cause exists to believe that someone committed a crime. Other uses of the justice system are illegal, improper, and — by definition — unjust.

While many people have used the death of Freddie Gray to advance their own agendas and refine their own reputations, one person alone bears the burden of responsibility in court: State's Attorney Marilyn Mosby. In our impatient yearning to speak our minds on inflamed issues like this, the rest of us are only constrained by the law and our conscience. Ms. Mosby is further constrained by Maryland's rules of legal ethics, and the penalty for abuse includes the possibility of losing her license to practice law.

A prosecutor who brings a criminal case for any reason other than probable cause violates her oath of office, the law, and ethics rules. While she denies it bitterly and with the political passion of a demagogue, the facts show that much of what Ms. Mosby has done in this case has been ethically dubious.

It started with her news conference announcing the indictments. The law school class I teach examines the rules surrounding what lawyers can say to the press ahead of and during litigation. Ever since the Duke lacrosse case, we've spent an entire class examining that North Carolina prosecutor's unethical media statements and actions. He went on to be disbarred and jailed. Going forward, my class will study the unethical media statements and actions of Marilyn Mosby.

By essentially telling local youth that their outcries of outrage were a primary reason for bringing charges, Ms. Mosby started a political persecution under the pretense of a prosecution. Along the way, she withheld evidence, defamed police, and brought such weak cases that the judge rivaled land speed records in issuing his acquittals.

Even in the more recent news conference, where she announced that she was dismissing the remaining cases, Ms. Mosby stumbled ethically. First, she said her original charges were meant to "seek justice" for Freddie Gray. She fundamentally misunderstands her role. It's the lawyers who represent Freddie Gray's family in civil actions against the police who are tasked with seeking justice for Freddie Gray. A prosecutor represents the entire state, not any one person. Her job is not to seek justice "for" a particular person. Her job is to simply seek justice.

This is more than a distinction without a difference. As a felony-level prosecutor, I've felt the pull of wanting to bring certain charges and take actions that crime victims and their families demand. But prosecutors are called to do what's right for everyone, not just those who've been victimized. It's a hard truth to accept, but no one becomes a prosecutor under duress.

I've seen this issue from both sides. When I worked at the United States Department of Justice in Washington, I worked side-by-side with prosecutors advancing cases against genuine and horrific police brutality. Later in my career, I've also helped speak out against those who evilly target police for violence and vitriol.

Our nation is at a dangerous crossroads where trust between those enforcing the laws and those protected by the law is eroding. Justice ought not need its own advocate, but when it does, those who swore the oath of a prosecutor must be in the vanguard of its defense. Yet Ms. Mosby pursues another path. She bristles with words of contempt for police and those who dare to criticize her actions. While passion and pride are laudable attributes in a public official, anger and agitation do not wear well.

In announcing the dismissal of all further charges (something any sentient observer could have predicted), Ms. Mosby shouted her points in a style reminiscent of a hyper-charged political rally. She spit words of affront in a pattern that belied her obligation to be even-handed and even-tempered.

An overheated statement by an officer of the court that encourages and prompts cries of approval from an impassioned crowd has no place in our justice system. If Lady Justice didn't already have her hands full with scales and a sword, she would have covered her ears.

What's worse, in announcing the dismissals, Ms. Mosby said she had to consider the "dismal likelihood of conviction" in dropping these charges. As this shameful episode of American jurisprudence begins to fade into history, we can all agree that justice would've been served had she made such a consideration before filing her charges.

CHAPTER 16

Ohio's grand jury system innocent of wrongdoing

Most Americans will never see the inside of a grand jury. Since its earliest use in Britain, it's given government power to citizens as a bulwark against government abuse. And grand jurors meet in secret.

Following some high-profile police shootings cases around the country, activists — largely critical of police — began demanding more openness in the grand jury process. Ohio officials began discussing changes to grand juries.

As a prosecutor, I've argued many cases to grand juries and I know their value as an investigative process. In this op-ed, perhaps more than the others, I address the concerns raised by reformers and use a sweeping review of civics to show why the suggested changes are unnecessary and likely to skew the delicate balance of our judicial system.

I often encourage writers to strengthen their work with the use of carefully chosen power words. Here you'll see me taking my own advice, with such words as raucous, agitating, clamor, and denigration. I also used the vernacular phrase of the defense lawyer "innocent of wrongdoing" to defend the grand jury, which is actually the province of the prosecutor. Call it poetic justice.

PUBLISHED: *Lima News* — July 11, 2016

When a police officer must use deadly force in confronting a potential suspect, a stadium full of Monday morning quarterbacks are quick to offer an opinion. Some people will reflexively side with the officer. Others will favor the suspect.

Who decides which side was right?

Our finely-tuned justice system, with a wide array of checks and balances, will make that decision. But now, based on a handful of cases, a tiny but raucous group of special interests are agitating to change the system. They are unabashed in their hope to change outcomes in cases to achieve results they have decided represent justice.

These groups point to the Tamir Rice case in Cleveland, where officers responding to a 911 call about a man with a gun, shot a young man wielding a realistic looking airsoft gun. The result was tragic but the notion that the grand jury system needs to be changed as a result is wrongheaded and rash. Justice is a process, not a result. And we ought to deny those who clamor for certain outcomes the ability to rig the justice system to align with their viewpoint.

Nonetheless, in response, the Ohio Supreme Court has created a task force to review whether grand jury laws ought to be changed. On behalf of the Ohio Fraternal Order of Police and the 25,000 police officers it represents, I've publicly asked that task force to leave the current system unchanged.

As a prosecutor, I've presented to numerous grand juries and I've also been on the prosecution team investigating allegations against police officers and other law enforcement officials. I've seen this issue up close.

The media narrative that somehow prosecutors and grand juries can't fairly handle and review cases involving law enforcement officers ignores more than two centuries of careful examination and proper handling of such cases.

In fact, those who drafted our state constitution wisely built a criminal justice system replete with multiple checks and balances to ensure fairness and guarantee individual liberties. As was done with the U.S. Constitution years before, the Ohio framers took power and divided it horizontally and vertically so it couldn't be abused by any one person or even small group of people.

For example, Ohio's prosecuting attorneys are elected by the people and thus must be responsive to their communities. Prosecuting attorneys also must be a member of the Ohio Supreme Court Bar and abide by the Ohio Rules of Professional Conduct, which are the ethics rules for all lawyers.

All county and municipal law enforcement officers work in an agency overseen by an elected officeholder such as a mayor or a sheriff. Collective bargaining laws provide a system for discipline and removal if there's misconduct.

In Ohio, grand jurors are bound by a solemn oath that includes a pledge that he or she *"will not leave unindicted any person through fear, favor, or affection, or for any reward or hope thereof."* Grand jurors — common citizens who live in the county where the incident under scrutiny took place — are able (indeed, they have a sworn duty) to indict those who break the law, including police. This is a significant responsibility.

Some suggest that a special prosecutor is better suited to make a prosecution decision about alleged police misconduct than an elected prosecuting attorney. Even if that's true, special prosecutors rarely, if ever, live in the county where they prosecute and are not accountable to the community.

All of these examples — and there are many more — meet the stated goals of the would-be reformers: to ensure justice and make needed change. No further systemic reforms are necessary. Indeed, the kind of reforms currently being discussed may well result in a wide variety of unintended consequences and may result in less justice and accountability.

Some people suggest that the grand jury process should only be changed in cases where police officers are under scrutiny. If that happens, it will have the effect of removing due process rights for the class of people most at risk of criminal violence. It will send a message to every officer and those considering law enforcement as a career that their lives and their rights are of less value than say, a child molester who would still have his grand jury proceedings kept private. The people of Ohio would not stand for this sort of discrimination and denigration of law enforcement officers.

Ohio's grand jury system has been unfairly accused. The system is innocent of wrongdoing.

CHAPTER 17

Taking a bite out of expert opinion

In my youth, I spent many summers body-surfing and otherwise ca-vorting in the waters off Ocean City, New Jersey. While I didn't see many sharks, I saw lots of people looking out for them. To many folks, there's toothy danger lurking in every swell. While there have been some scary shark encounters in U.S. waters over the years, sharks and humans usually leave each other alone.

One notable exception happened in New Jersey, during the summer of 1916. Knowing that the centennial of those shark attacks was ap-proaching, I set out to write this op-ed and remind readers of what was then the biggest news story in the country. Along the way, I de-cided that the piece would be as much about the danger of relying too heavily on proclaimed experts as the danger from man-eaters from the deep.

In this op-ed, I used historical resources (particularly a book I read called Close to Shore) to tell the story of not-so-funny terror of shark attacks and the somewhat funny response of politicians. Because the Discovery Channel's annual TV special "Shark Week" had just aired, I essentially had a double hook — the 100th anniversary of the at-tacks and the end of television Shark Week.

My walk-off in this piece came to me at the very end of my writing process and it's one of my all-time favorite ending to an op-ed.

PUBLISHED: *The Newark Advocate* — July 9, 2016

One hundred years ago this week, much of the eastern seaboard of America was terrified. Despite the blistering hot temperatures, most people near the ocean didn't dare go in the water. It was such a national calamity that the President of the United States ordered the Coast Guard to deal with the problem. Their assignment was clear: Kill the sea monster.

Over the first two weeks of July 1916, five people were attacked in the waters off New Jersey. All but one died. Their bodies were horribly mutilated. Local authorities were unsure what creature had caused the first attack on a Philadelphia salesman out for a leisurely swim. Whatever killed him in the three feet deep surf was powerful — his entire left leg was missing.

Reporters peppered local fisherman with questions, particularly, what could have caused this death? Some said a giant tuna must have done it. Others said that only a large sea turtle would have such biting strength.

The victim of the second attack, a bellboy at a beachside hotel, told his rescuers that it was a shark that bit his legs off. He later died of his wounds. But when authorities summoned one of the top shark experts in America to examine the body, the dying man's statements were shunted aside. The expert simply didn't believe sharks were likely to kill humans. He was certain it must have been a killer whale.

The mistaken killer whale theory persisted for days. Eventually, three more people would be attacked and, in the end, the culprit was determined to be a Great White shark. But the people who initially rebuffed the notion of a shark being responsible were not alone.

A few years earlier, a wealthy American adventurer, wanting to vindicate his own personal belief, had offered a $500 reward "for an authenticated case of a man having been attacked by a shark" in waters anywhere north of the Carolinas. No one claimed the money.

Some of the most esteemed experts boldly declared that a shark was unable to kill a human, believing that a shark's jaws simply lacked the biting power to sever a person's leg. The most renowned shark expert in America was the Director of the American Museum of Natural History. A few months before the attacks began, he told a reporter that *"it is beyond the power even of the largest [shark] to sever the leg of an adult man."*

Academics and even veteran fisherman also doubted a shark could swim in the fresh water of a river, even one that connects to the ocean. Yet two of the shark attack victims that July were in a river several miles upstream from the ocean. Nearly everyone was wrong.

As we think back to the horrific events of a century ago, what can we learn from this episode in history? The primary lesson is this: Many of the people we call experts are just guessing. That doesn't make them stupid or dishonest, just sometimes wrong. Countless things remain beyond the knowledge of science and it often takes an episode like the 1916 shark attacks to cause scientists to rethink their assumptions.

The second lesson is less obvious, but just as important. As those shark attacks were happening, many Americans were panicking. Some even took swimming lessons that featured ways to swim that supposedly would outwit sharks. People desperately in search of something to keep them safe often look to politicians for protection. Yet there's little or nothing government can do to solve certain problems.

In some newspapers, shark news received more coverage than the deaths of tens of thousands of British soldiers in the Battle of Somme, which was occurring in Europe at the same time. Such intense media coverage draws politicians to an issue like, well, sharks to blood.

And respond they did. New Jersey Gov. James Fielder suggested every coastal town should build some type of sea net. A congressman introduced a bill to give $5,000 to the federal Bureaus of Fisheries to exterminate "the man-eating sharks now infesting the Atlantic Ocean." Both ideas (which were ridiculous when subjected to any logical scrutiny) went nowhere.

But it was President Woodrow Wilson who showed the most political gall. Despite the fact that only Congress can declare war, many presidents like to metaphorically declare war. Presidents have declared war on poverty, drugs, and terror. But it was Woodrow Wilson who literally declared a "war on sharks." The president sent in the Coast Guard, who could, essentially, do nothing.

Nonetheless, press conferences were held, promises were made, and political reputations were bolstered. The sharks did what they sometimes do and the politicians did what they always do. A century later, nothing's changed.

.

CHAPTER 18

In retail: "Buyer beware." In politics: "Voter beware."

You're reading this now, knowing full well that Donald Trump was elected president in 2016. Yet, when I wrote the essay below, that notion was far-fetched to most people. While my column mentioned the candidates, it wasn't really about Donald Trump, Bernie Sanders, or Hillary Clinton.

Rather, I was then (and am now) deeply concerned that too many Americans are just barely paying attention to the process of electing government officials. That casual attitude leads some to believe simplistic promises from candidates and expect easy answers to complex problems. This is just not a responsible way to run the greatest nation in the history of the world.

Following the 2016 election, given some of the more irrational fears from those who were bemoaning the election of Donald Trump, I found myself trying to calm some of them by quoting from the final paragraph of this op-ed — specifically, I pointed to the genius of the framers of the Constitution who crafted a system of shared power that no single person can undermine.

I genuinely believe these words and this sentiment have been true for the first two centuries of America and will remain true for the American millennia to come.

PUBLISHED: *The Cincinnati Enquirer* — May 6, 2016

The presidential election of 2016 baffles and astounds. Nearly every day someone asks me some variation of "what the heck is going in American politics?" People want someone to help them make sense of it all.

The rise of Hillary Clinton is expected, given the Clinton family stranglehold on the establishment wing of the Democratic party. What's more remarkable is the amazing electoral successes and improbable popularity of avowed Socialist Bernie Sanders and political newcomer Donald Trump. This terra incognita can be traced to at least one primary source and one probable cause: Too many voters refuse to do their homework and too few look close enough to spot a charlatan. That's not to call any particular candidate a charlatan — each of these candidates made compelling cases for their cause. Rather, at all levels of politics, prevaricating politicians are all too common to the breed.

Many politicians and strategists believe American voters are stupid. I disagree. I think most voters are so fed up with government and politics that they've given up paying careful attention. And, with an ever-expanding information buffet of internet, cable TV, etc., voters would rather indulge in something — anything — other than politics.

Irresponsible candidates thrive in a political environment in which voters don't give much thought to policy. Their simplistic, almost cartoonish, issue positions are easy to remember and appealing at a surface level. But anyone who spends more than a moment thinking through the details will see through the charade and realize that Clinton, Sanders, and Trump have defined themselves with promises and pronouncements that, in many cases, can't withstand scrutiny.

Let's start with Trump. The notion that America should build a wall to keep out illegal aliens and stem the tide of deadly heroin is popular with most Americans and has merit to it. But Mr. Trump offers no details about how such an undertaking is possible. Promising to build a 2,000-mile wall and make Mexico pay for it is a memorable sound bite. But no one who truly understands policy and logistics thinks a physical wall can be easily built or that a foreign government can be made to pay for it. Yet candidate Trump trumpets the promise at every rally, enthralling the amped-up audience with their favorite "build the wall" one-liner.

Hillary Clinton's speeches are so replete with political palaver that they sound like they were spawned following an endless series of focus groups and more marketing meetings than a Mad Men binge-watching session. In her fantasy world, her critics are all wrong, her own motives are all pure, and her policy solutions are all perfect. Believing that suggests she's a few deleted emails short of a full hard drive.

Sanders' appeal is equally simplistic. As a Socialist, the cornerstone of his candidacy is to offer "free" goods and services, most notably free college to all. When quizzed on how he would cover the $750 billion price tag for just 10 years of such munificence, he says he'll tax "Wall Street speculation." That's code for taking money from everyone who has a pension, individual retirement account, or college savings plan. Retired teachers, nurses, and firefighters on fixed incomes would see their income reduced to pay for Sanders' plan. And experts say even that tax hike wouldn't be enough to cover the tab. But, just like some of the fantastical solutions offered by Trump and Clinton, the magic Bernie Sanders free college is an appealing notion that's easy to remember.

These fast-talkers aren't the first politicians to over-promise just to win votes. But, more than most, their promises defy basic notions of economics, logistics, and even separation of powers. These candidates fail to mention that their plans would require the acquiescence of the Congress, but none has the support among lawmakers to get much done. Reality intrudes into their rhetoric, but voters pay little notice.

The party-bots who cheer for Clinton despite her deep personal failings and the disaffected who defend Trump's simple solutions and sharp name-calling all owe it to themselves and their countrymen to give a bit more thought to the practicality and wisdom of these appeals. And the fevered college students marching, cheering, and snapchatting in support of Sander's promises of a government that has a bag of toys deeper than jolly old St. Nick's ought to realize that myths are fun to believe, but heartbreaking when exposed. At least with respect to this issue, believing in Santa will bring less disappointment than believing Sanders.

Our parents taught us that when something looks too good to be true, it probably is. Too many politicians — of both parties — are counting on us to forget that warning when we go into the voting booth. If we're taken in, we have only ourselves to blame.

America will survive no matter who wins the presidency. Our nation was built to withstand category 5 demagoguery and remain intact despite gale force blowhards. But the rise of Trump, Clinton, and Sanders will test our foundation. And the only way to reinforce the structure of our government is for voters to arm themselves with information and gird themselves with common sense.

CHAPTER 19

Stanford swimmer sex assault case shouldn't surprise

Sexual assaults on college campuses have been a problem for as long as men and women have met and mingled among the ivy walls and ivory towers. But recently, the issue of what constitutes consent to sex and whether university administrators ought to be the ones investigating assault allegations have become much more than an academic issue.

I began my legal career as a student lawyer in my undergraduate years. I represented students charged with violating college policies. Many of them faced suspension and expulsion. In my most controversial case, I successfully defended a student falsely accused of rape. After becoming an actual lawyer, I chose to work more as a prosecutor, helping to send sex offenders to prison.

This column was spurred by what I believed to be a newfound outrage at leniency in sentencing. The student involved certainly deserved a lengthy prison term but I was, and continue to be, worried that selective outrage at the controversial headline of the moment is a poor substitute for a consistent advocacy for helping police and prosecutors do their difficult work.

I use the time-proven technique of telling a compelling story in the opening of the piece to draw in the reader and set the stage for the more substantive points to come.

PUBLISHED: *The Cincinnati Enquirer* — June 20, 2016

I'll never forget the scene. I was prosecuting a child molester. He was an older man who had sexually assaulted his granddaughter multiple times. After his conviction, the time had come for the judge to decide the man's punishment. A crowd had gathered in the courtroom and there was tension in the air as I stood up to make my recommendation for a long prison sentence.

Citing the emotional trauma to the young girl and the fact that this defendant would likely continue his crimes if allowed to remain free, I urged the judge to send him to prison for a lengthy term. After I finished, the defense attorney called several witnesses — all of them family members — who begged the judge to allow this sex offender to go free on probation.

Despite being related to both the victim and the offender, each one of these family members chose to overlook the pain of the little girl and side with the man who had violated her. Other than me, no one spoke on behalf of the victim.

The judge sent the man to prison, and the mood among the family members was surly. As I walked out of the courtroom, I heard a terse voice behind me call out my name. I turned on my heel, expecting to be verbally assaulted for my efforts but, instead, I got quite a surprise.

One of the women in the gallery, who had not testified as a character witness, said to me: "I'm embarrassed by how my family acted in there. I just want to thank you for speaking up for that child when none of us did."

I thought of the pain of crime victims when I read about the recent case where a Stanford student was convicted of sexual assault. The man, a competitive university swimmer, met the woman at a college party. A jury convicted him of sexual assaulting her while they were both intoxicated.

Prior to sentencing, the victim offered a moving in-court statement about the defendant's impact on her life. Her eloquent words have reverberated across the internet and social media. Suddenly, millions of people are lamenting the plight of crime victims and calling for tougher sentences. There's even a growing effort to remove the judge for what many are calling a lenient sentence.

All I can say to those agitating and anguishing over this case is: welcome to the cause.

I applaud this brave young woman for speaking out, but I'm honestly surprised at the public reaction. Sadly, her case is not unique. In fact, violent crime, distraught victims, and light sentences are all too common. The FBI reports that more than five million violent crimes are committed every year. That's five million victims with traumatic tales to share.

Americans should realize that similar painful statements are read every day in courthouses across the land by courageous victims of violent crime. Tragically, the public galleries often stand empty. No one tweets or updates Facebook with calls to action about what was said. The tears on the crumpled tissues are barely dry before another criminal case tumbles into the courtroom.

If you're mad about all this, you might wonder what you can do to bring about change. You can start by ensuring that this case and this victim's agony will become more than just another viral moment. To help crime victims achieve justice and return to as normal a life as possible, we should rally behind them *before* judges impose lenient sentences.

We also must support police and prosecutors who work diligently to protect and defend victims of crime like this. Our concern about injustice and our caring for those who are hurt by it must be more than just a one and done proposition.

Activists and politicians who decry so-called "stop and frisk" policies neglect to mention that police officers are typically investigating a crime with a vulnerable victim seeking justice. When victims give a description of the person who hurt them, police go looking for people who match that description. It's not discrimination, it's common sense police work.

And Hollywood filmmakers who depict prosecutors as conspiratorial or dishonest do a disservice to the hard-working lawyers seeking to defend crime victims and enforce our laws every day. In fact, part of the Stanford victim's stirring statement involved thanking the police and prosecutors in her case. She recognizes, as we all should, that these professionals are a force for good in a world beset by evil.

So, let's not let this viral internet moment get swallowed up by the next interesting online meme. Let's remember the victim in this case and the granddaughter victimized at the hands of her grandfather in my case. And let's join with police and prosecutors who seek justice from the five million violent criminals who victimize people every year.

CHAPTER 20

President, Senate are equal partners in appointments

At the Department of Justice, my boss was Assistant Attorney General William Bradford Reynolds. When he retired, the department hosted a reception in the Attorney General's suite to honor him. I got there early and soon noticed a man standing alone, away from the others gathering. After a double take, I realized it was Supreme Court Justice Antonin Scalia, a friend of my boss. Not wanting to miss the chance to meet such an important figure in American history, I sidled over to him and introduced myself. I was pleased to find that he was warm and engaging. We had a lively conversation for a few moments. I never met Justice Scalia again but I later devoted my law school independent study project to his jurisprudence.

When he died in 2016, our nation lost a brilliant and principled jurist. The political fight to fill his empty seat on the high court quickly melded into the presidential contest. Republicans sought to hold off on appointing a new justice until a new president was elected. On the other side were Democrats, who wanted President Obama to make this nomination. While I had my own opinions about that dispute, I wrote this op-ed for a much different reason. I noticed that too many people arguing the issue misunderstood the basic process for federal judicial selection. As you'll read below, it's more nuanced than often thought.

Whatever your opinion about the Republican or Democrat arguments, I hope this op-ed will illuminate for you that the Constitution makes selecting judges and justice in the judicial branch a joint and co-equal responsibility of the executive and legislative branches — not a power of the president alone.

In my classes, I urge my students to use metaphors whenever possible. This literary device allows a writer or speaker to explain more complicated or unknown information by relating it to a better known, more easily understood notion. You'll see how I employed the example of rock, paper, scissors as a metaphor in this op-ed.

PUBLISHED: *The Cincinnati Enquirer* — March 17, 2016

There's an easy way to win a bet about American government. Ask someone what the U.S. Constitution says about how long a Supreme Court justice serves in office. The other person will claim that a justice is appointed for life. You'll win the bet when you tell your unsuspecting mark to whip out a phone and check Article Three, Section One, where the Constitution states that "Judges" of the Supreme Court may serve only "during good behavior." Judges can be impeached by the Congress and lose whatever life tenure they imagined they had.

This is just one example of how the text of the Constitution can differ markedly from what most Americans think. There's another much more practical example and it's squarely on display in the political skirmish surrounding President Obama's nomination of Merrick Garland to replace Supreme Court Justice Antonin Scalia.

Get ready to lose another bet if you agree with this assertion: The president appoints justices to the Supreme Court.

Again, reading the Constitution helps disprove this common claim. The president's authority in this area derives from Article Two, Section Two, which states he *"shall nominate, and by and with the Advice and Consent of the Senate, shall appoint ... Judges of the Supreme Court."*

The first verb — "nominate" — spells out what the president may do. The second verb — "appoint" — describes what the president and the Senate may do together. These different words instruct our leaders to take different, co-equal roles in this process.

All Americans, born here or naturalized, trace our national lineage to those brave souls who landed on the shores of this continent in search of freedom from religious and government oppression inflicted by the power players of Europe. These pioneers of democracy withstood British rule long enough to win independence and then find the right men who could build a new nation girded by the consent of the governed.

One of the most vexing issues confronting those men, the framers of our Constitution, was how to ensure that no official could employ government power as a spear against the people whom it was meant to shield. They knew, as do we, that unchecked leaders can use power for profit, plunder, and prejudice.

Their solution was as easy as the timeless childhood frolic of rock, paper, scissors. Everyone who plays this game quickly realizes that none of the symbols is all-powerful on its own. Rock might crush scissors, but paper covers rock. The basic principle of why rock, paper, scissors is competitive is the underlying reason why American checks and balances are fair. No one government branch has more power than the other.

Unfortunately, American public opinion on this topic has shifted. Far too many people think, incorrectly, that the president is somehow "in charge of" the country. But American government is designed to be an amalgam of federal, state and local officials who serve in three branches at each of those levels: executive, legislative and judicial. Spreading the power reduces the risk of corruption. Federalism advances this crucial principle even further by distributing power widely between federal officials and the thousands of state and local authorities around the nation.

So, who gets to fill a vacancy on the Supreme Court? If you think it's the president, you're right. And if you think it's the Senate, you're also right.

Alexander Hamilton did far more than inspire a popular Broadway musical. In *Federalist 76*, Hamilton discusses the important difference between nominating and appointing. He even pushes back against those who think the power of selecting justice should rest solely with the president. He describes the advice and consent clause as a "powerful" and "excellent check" against potential presidential misuse of power. And, in *Federalist 67*, Hamilton reminds us that, under the Constitution, *"the ordinary power of appointment is confined to the President and Senate jointly."* Jointly.

This means that Mr. Obama has every right to nominate someone without any legal quarrel or question. And, his equal partner in the appointment — the Senate — has every right to give their advice and consent. The Senate decision could be to approve or reject the nominee. And, yes, the Senate is well within its constitutional prerogative to determine that its members do not think the time is right to confirm someone. And, as with the president, it may do so without legal quarrel or question.

We're all entitled to our own opinion as to what the president or the Senate *ought to* do in the face of a high court vacancy. But the words of the Constitution spell out what they are each *permitted* to do.

And, in an election year like this, the safest bet is that Democrats and Republicans alike will cloak themselves in constitutional rhetoric while advancing a position that will benefit them politically.

CHAPTER 21

Let the Freddie Gray jurors speak

Throughout 2015, Americans debated whether Baltimore resident Freddie Gray died in a police transport van due to an accident or criminal actions by officers. The first officer's trial ended with a hung jury. The judge dismissed the jury, freeing them from that case forever. News reports indicated that the judge ordered jurors not to speak about the case, at least until the other five police defendants had their trials — which could take years.

I knew that the judge's order, however well-intentioned it was to protect the five defendant's fair trial rights, was likely a violation of the First Amendment rights of the jurors. The major daily newspaper in Baltimore agreed to print this op-ed column to provide my legal analysis perspective.

PUBLISHED: *The Baltimore Sun* — January 4, 2016

Marylanders now know that Baltimore Circuit Court Judge Barry Williams strongly suggested to jurors in the trial of William Porter, one of six city police officers charged in connection with the death of Freddie Gray, that they not speak publicly about the case after its conclusion. While the judge is admirably trying to balance the interests of a fair trial with free speech rights, he appears to have gone too far.

One juror was quoted by reporters as saying, "I would very much like to talk about my experience as a juror," but she feels obligated to follow the judge's suggestion to abstain. She need not feel so compelled.

As a magistrate in a local court in Ohio, I've presided over hundreds of criminal cases. I know the burden of trying to be fair to all sides while keeping an eye on the often-complicated rules of evidence and criminal procedure. It's a daunting challenge. And, given that there are more trials of Baltimore police officers coming, a responsible jurist must make rulings that will protect the ability of prosecutors and defense attorneys to impanel jurors who can review these cases fairly.

But, even with those factors in mind, there's little or no chance that allowing the Porter case jurors to speak publicly will bias future trials.

Given that jurors were barred from reading news coverage, many members of the public know more about what happened during the trial than the jury. Their commentary may provide insight into what happened in the jury room, but it can't offer new evidence that could taint future trials. These jurors only heard and considered evidence that was first reviewed and permitted by the judge.

If jurors were to share their thoughts of that admitted evidence, the revelation and insight might be interesting, but it still wouldn't affect the ability of future juries to bring an open mind to the remaining trials. Evidence the jury weighed has been thoroughly discussed in the press already.

Yet the merits of allowing jurors to speak publicly go far beyond the fact that it won't hinder the work of future juries. It's a matter of constitutional law.

Courts have often ruled that a judge may protect jurors from press harassment and limit or even bar reporters from contacting them after a trial. If that were the extent of Judge Williams' order, it would likely withstand constitutional review. The judge also probably can protect the jurors' identities from public release. And in a few states (not Maryland), jurors are legally barred from writing a book for at least 90 days after being dismissed from duty.

However, if jurors want to speak out, be interviewed or even blog about their experience, they have a First Amendment right to do so. To the extent the judge has chilled their ability to speak, he has exceeded his authority.

It's well-settled by the U.S. Supreme Court that most of the individual rights in the first 10 amendments to the Constitution are "fundamental," meaning they can only be abridged when government has a compelling interest to do so. And, when such a compelling government interest exists, the proposed government action must be narrowly tailored to advance that compelling interest.

How does this apply to the Porter case jurors? In the case of their fundamental right to freedom of speech, the law disfavors a judge from prohibiting speech that may occur in the future, such as a juror posting a Facebook update about the deliberation. These "prior restraints" of speech are almost never permitted. Indeed, given that it could potentially take months or even years to try and retry all the remaining defendants, it's unimaginable that an appeals court would allow even a permissible prior restraint to last that long.

What's the solution? Judge Williams should enter his instructions to the jury as part of a journal entry. This is the written public record of what a judge has done. He could balance the interests of this case with a short declaration making it clear that, while jurors may decline to speak publicly about the case, those who wish may indeed speak out publicly.

The result will permit future trials to be fair, while giving an already-skeptical public a fuller sense of transparency about this important case.

CHAPTER 22

College students should be treated as adults

Heated passions were fully on display at the University of Missouri and other American colleges in 2015 as some students protested and made demands to administrators. The trend has continued and many campuses are aflame with anger and vehement.

As I read through the various accounts, I realized the people who run these institutions of higher education may have lost sight of their ultimate responsibility: preparing students for the life ahead. I was appreciative when the major daily newspaper in Columbus allowed me to elaborate on my views in this op-ed column. Note the use of the words "Sherpa" and "training wheels" as metaphors.

PUBLISHED: *The Columbus Dispatch* — November 15, 2015

College students are dizzy in the whirlwind of change from the teenage drama years to the vastly different burdens and joys of adulthood.

Payers of tuition, parents, and students alike, expect university officials to be wise Sherpas, accompanying those students along that rocky climb. Yet recent incidents at the University of Missouri, Ithaca College, and Yale University have shown that those who lead many of our colleges and universities are failing in their responsibilities.

My perspective on this is manifold and sweeps over several decades. As a student-government leader at a large state university, I negotiated with administrators and trustees over student demands. In graduate school, I was the resident director in charge of two big freshman dormitories. Today, I teach at three major universities and my two children are college students.

Each aspect of university life is, and ought to be, a learning experience. Ideas of every type should be discussed, debated, and considered during these years that are made for acquiring the knowledge that will guide and govern the travails of life. But there's a dichotomy that sets the table for the trouble we're seeing today.

When it comes to issues such as alcohol use, sexual activity, and political participation, many college students desperately want to be treated like hardy adults. But those who demand "safe space" and college-enforced protection from offensive words or ideas incongruently are asking university officials to treat them like fragile children.

These paradoxes shouldn't surprise us. Research shows the human brain doesn't fully develop until age 25. For that reason, our call for redress should primarily be aimed at those who've been educated and trained to help young adults thrive and mature in a college setting. Yet it's precisely those administrators who too often seem to instill a culture of cowardliness when this crucial challenge calls for them to be people of principle.

The most glaring example of this is Timothy Wolfe, who stepped down as the president of the University of Missouri under pressure from a losing football team refusing to play, a fraction of the student body boycotting classes, and a solitary student declaring he would not eat until the president resigned. The entire offbeat episode evoked the unmistakable analogy of a spoiled toddler threatening to hold his breath until he gets his own way.

None of this is to say that some of the concerns raised by the students, such as issues of racial division or social unrest are unserious or unworthy of substantive debate. Rather, the notion that students with grievances —perceived or actual — claiming the forced resignation of a university president as a trophy should be as offensive to those of us who revere higher education as the recent poaching of Cecil the lion was to those who love animals.

And lost in the noisy swirl of chants, declarations of being offended, and accusations of so-called micro-aggressions is a larger, more durable concern. At least at public universities, which are unequivocally bound by the restraints of the U.S. Constitution, the willingness of the army of the aggrieved to deny the value and applicability of First Amendment free-speech protections is deeply troubling.

One student leader at the University of Missouri gave a national TV interview in which she declared that she was tired of those who cite to the First Amendment as a reason why she might have to allow others to speak. Funny thing about the Constitution: it's not optional.

Such a misshapen view of basic American tenets is a prime opportunity for college leaders to step in and advocate for civil dialogue from all sides. Yet, as resignations hung in the air, most were too intimidated to do so.

I've taught hundreds of students over the years. I've learned as much from them as they did from me. Our exchange of information took place in and out of the classroom on a wide variety of topics, some of which were nowhere in my syllabus.

Foremost in my mind in those interactions was the hope that these young people could get something from my class that would better prepare them for the vexing challenges that awaited them beyond the wide green expanses and metaphorical training wheels of campus life.

University leaders must not shrink from their duties to be the rock of principle in a rushing stream of anger, confusion, and unrest. Students won't always like it when they don't get all they ask for. But they will learn a great deal about the real world of family life and career, where angry demands are not always met and shouted grievances are usually rebuffed.

CHAPTER 23

Disgraced Attorney General undermines her office's work

Although I'm now an Ohioan, I was born, raised, and worked for years in Pennsylvania. I still have many clients and friends in Pennsylvania, so I keep up with the news there. When I saw the Pennsylvania Attorney General enmeshed in scandal and dragging down the morale and reputation of the professionals who work in her office, I felt the need to speak up.

Sitting alone in a Pennsylvania diner, I ate a long lunch and composed this op-ed on my laptop. I was appreciative when the major daily newspaper in the Lehigh Valley region of Pennsylvania agreed to publish it.

Coincidently, exactly one year to the date of this op-ed, the beleaguered Attorney General finally stepped down, as I had predicted she would. She also was convicted and ordered to prison.

I encourage writers and speakers who I mentor to use similes to help strengthen their persuasion effort. In this piece, I used the simile of a driver heading down a dead-end road to describe what was happening in a way that might resonate well with readers.

PUBLISHED: *The Allentown Morning Call* — August 17, 2015

It's no exaggeration to say that the professionals in the Pennsylvania attorney general's office save lives and protect the commonwealth's interests every day. But it's just as clear that Attorney General Kathleen Kane, who was elected to lead that office, is hindering that mission.

As a proud native Pennsylvanian who now lives next door in Ohio, I've watched with sadness as my home state is embarrassed by the immature and imprudent antics of a state attorney general who doesn't have enough sense to see the troubled road ahead for her or her fellow Pennsylvanians. And as someone who has worked for the U.S. Attorney General, in a state attorney general's office, and with several different attorneys general, I can see that her office is in turmoil, to the point of severe dysfunction. Other recent attorney general scandals can inform this discussion.

Indeed, one only need look to the respective tenures of disgraced ex-Ohio Attorney General Marc Dann (a Democrat) and dishonored ex-Pennsylvania Attorney General Ernie Preate Jr. (a Republican) to predict with confidence how the Kathleen Kane movie will end. Spoiler alert: She resigns.

Dann was forced to resign in 2008 amid evidence of criminal corruption, ethics violations, and a sex scandal. He was convicted and lost his law license. Preate resigned in 1995 after pleading guilty to hiding illegal campaign contributions and later served prison time. In each of those cases, there were obvious warning signs of a law enforcement office well off course.

Earlier this year, while speaking at a statewide conference of Pennsylvania district attorneys, I interacted with these prosecutors and it became clear that many of them are disconcerted by Kane's poor judgment. Just last week, while speaking at the Fraternal Order of Police conference in Pittsburgh, I observed the same concerns among rank-and-file police.

While I don't know the career employees of the Pennsylvania attorney general's office, I do know that their Ohio counterparts were humiliated and dispirited when their boss dragged out a game of political Twister, as he tried to deny his manifest misdeeds. Like a reckless driver speeding down the same dead-end road, Kane is now engaged in that same futile endeavor.

Just by reading the details of the Kane investigation, it's apparent that she's putting her staff under great stress as they do their already-difficult jobs. Here are just a few tip-offs.

While the traditional title of an attorney general is "General" as in "Gen. Kane" or "the General," most state attorneys general shun the designation. Even when I worked for former Pennsylvania Gov. Dick Thornburgh while he was U.S. Attorney General, he preferred to be called "governor," which is how I — and others — addressed him. At the national conferences attended by state attorneys general, senior staff and longtime officeholders roll their eyes when they hear the obsequious term "General" used and overused. Internal records show that Kane's politically appointed senior staff referred to her as "the General" frequently, often as a way of pulling rank on other employees. It's an unmistakable sign of hubris.

But there are other indicators of trouble afoot. Kane routinely travels with two law enforcement agents, essentially bodyguards. Many attorneys general do just fine with one. Some travel with none. Unless there's an active threat, a state attorney general is no more a target for violence than any other state officeholder, such as the auditor general. Most district attorneys, who actually come face to face with dangerous felons on a constant basis, rarely have security agents travel with them.

Kane exacerbated this problem when she was arraigned recently, adding two undercover narcotics agents to her detail to escort her the few yards from her car to the court entrance. That's a dubious use of undercover cops, and her obsession with security suggests an attitude of importance far beyond her role.

Finally, her own words show us that she's putting her political sensibilities ahead of the mission of her office. "This is war," she boldly declared to an adviser. She wasn't speaking of the fight against heroin or organized crime. No, this hyperbole was reserved for her political rivalry with a career prosecutor in the Philadelphia district attorney's office who had uncovered some of Kane's misdeeds. An imprudent squabble to be sure, but not a war.

Last week, in her odd news conference, she criticized those holding her to account for her actions and endeavored to order a judge to violate the grand jury secrecy law. And that performance was merely the capstone of two years of bizarre behavior that included mischaracterizing investigations, showing up to an editorial interview represented by a lawyer who refused to allow her to talk, and managing a press office with a revolving door of speechless spokespeople. The Kane chronicles will be long studied by students of Pennsylvania history and puzzled over by ethics experts and psychologists alike.

Kathleen Kane is not the first politician to believe her own press releases. Nor is she the only person in government to live in a self-induced state of paranoia. But the work of her office is too important to be sidetracked by such inanity.

On the criminal charges, she's entitled to her day in court. But she's undoubtedly guilty of feckless leadership, questionable judgment, and — worst of all — casting a shadow on a proud group of professionals who've devoted their careers to justice.

CHAPTER 24

Religious freedom squabble brings more heat than light

As a law student, one of my more interesting courses was a class where we spent an entire semester learning about just one phrase in the First Amendment: "Congress shall make no law respecting an establishment of religion." This is the "Establishment Clause," and its primary purpose was to ensure that America would not end up with a national religion run by government leaders, the way the Church of England once dominated Britain.

Yet decades of judicial rulings have so twisted and bent the Establishment Clause that it's as misshapen as a cowboy hat that's been stampeded by a herd of annoyed buffalo. The next phrase in the First Amendment — the "Free Exercise Clause" is similarly adrift from its original moorings. Worse yet, the Free Exercise Clause is sinking under the weight of the transmogrified Establishment Clause. Mixed metaphors intended, as such is the confusing fog of modern American constitutional law.

In 2015, after the U.S. Supreme Court essentially affirmed the legal status of gay marriage, the national debate moved to the issue of whether government can compel private citizens to violate their religious beliefs (protected by the Free Exercise Clause) and participate in a gay marriage ceremony.

After Indiana and Arkansas passed a law that underscored Free Exercise Clause protections, the cable news bobbleheads were chattering with passion over whether the new state laws would meet constitutional muster. I undertook this op-ed to offer some legal and historical insights to the issue. The debate was taking place during Holy Week, as Easter and Passover approached — a key news hook for this op-ed.

One of the techniques I used here is taking the rule proposed by the side I oppose and applying that same logic to a group that might be more sympathetic to my verbal adversary. It's a powerful and effective way to force opponents into acknowledging your point or backing away from their original premise.

PUBLISHED: *The Cincinnati Enquirer* — April 5, 2015

This past week, with Christian and Jewish celebrations underway, politicians and activists in Indiana and Arkansas weren't slicing Easter hams or Passover brisket but rather carving up the rights of religious people.

They were derailing state measures modeled after a popular federal law signed years ago by President Bill Clinton. These laws make no mention of sexual orientation, rather they seek to curb a type of discrimination that's rarely confronted: anti-religious bigotry or government action that seeks to force religious adherents to act contrary to their faith.

People of faith who fled European religious persecution settled America. With that in mind, our founding fathers built a republic that, first and foremost, requires government to refrain from "prohibiting the free exercise" of religion.

Most people support this. Polling shows 81 percent of Americans believe government ought to "leave people free to follow their belief about marriage as they live their daily lives at work and in the way they run their businesses." Notably, in these polarized times, 81 percent of Americans rarely agree on anything. But religious freedom underscores our American creed.

Hatred toward gays and lesbians is morally wrong. But so is hatred toward those Christians, Jews, and Muslims who respect scriptural teachings about homosexuality. That mean government laws and enforcement efforts to compel a religious person (such as a professional photographer) to attend and participate in a gay marriage ceremony are bigoted and intolerant.

Balancing these competing interests requires thoughtful dialogue. But, sadly, some rhetoric is inflamed and well out of proportion. Apple CEO Tim Cook called Indiana "dangerous" for protecting religious freedom. Yet Apple recently expanded operations into Saudi Arabia, where it's legal to stone gay people to death. Now *that's* a dangerous place.

A Stanford law professor, who also served as an appellate court judge, pointed out this week that, in the decades since states and the federal government have passed religious freedom statutes similar to the Indiana law, no business has been given the right to discriminate against gay customers or anyone else. But such reasoned argument doesn't make great news copy or cable TV segments.

Here's the common-sense consensus: Store owners have a legal and moral obligation to sell products to anyone who possesses the money to pay. If there's a prejudiced Christian shopkeeper who refuses to sell things in the store to a gay customer, that bigot deserves punishment and rebuke. And so does a prejudiced gay store owner refusing to sell to devout Christians or Jews who believe gay marriage is a sin.

But how best to punish and thus deter future occurrences of such intolerance? Should the heavy boot of government enforcement be brought to bear to impose fines and, eventually, a jail term? Market forces can punish much more swiftly and finally. Few of us will patronize stores owned by hateful people. If the so-called Westboro Baptist Church family ever ran a business, they'd be boycotted and bankrupt in days. Ditto for any retail business enterprise owned by the infamous Pentagon bomber Bill Ayres.

Courts agree that government may only substantially burden the religious expression of a person or organization if government has a "compelling interest" to do so. Bureaucrats must use the "least restrictive means possible" to further that compelling interest. There's ample court precedent to help clarify. For example, only someone with a "sincere belief" in a religion can advance a religious freedom defense to a government enforcement action. That means someone grasping for the handy shelter of a church as a ruse to avoid a penalty would be, literally, without a prayer in court.

America was founded on religious freedom. The very first words we declared to the world included the bold assertion that our rights come from God. That's why it's proper to mediate these disputes with respect for religious freedom. We shouldn't require an observant Muslim male massage therapist to provide massages to women customers or force an Orthodox Jewish caterer to provide the food at a pork barbecue down at the neo-Nazi clubhouse. Sincerely held religious beliefs — not bigotry or hatred — ought to remain free from unnecessary government intrusion.

CHAPTER 25

Gag order request shows prosecutor's biased motive

As I discussed in two earlier op-eds in this book, not long after the racial cacophony in Ferguson, Missouri, a black man in police custody in Baltimore wound up dead. He was arrested after fleeing police, who suspected he was a drug dealer.

The death of that man, Freddie Gray, caused a few tense days of dangerous and volatile rioting in the angriest corners of Baltimore. The local elected prosecutor reacted viscerally, bringing serious criminal charges against every police officer involved in the arrest and transport of Mr. Gray, even as nearly everyone else was still trying to discern how the death occurred.

Her infamous press conference (which can be viewed online in full at http://tinyurl.com/MosbyPresser) evoked vigilantism rather than vigilance and prejudgment instead of precaution. I've prosecuted serious criminals including rapists and a serial killer. I've also conducted countless news conferences. Ms. Mosby's actions in that setting so affronted my sense of professionalism and fair play that I felt compelled to write this op-ed, which ran in Maryland's largest newspaper.

Note how I draw parallels to a previous Maryland case that, once fully understood, underscores my argument that the Freddie Gray case prosecutor was acting unethically.

PUBLISHED: *The Baltimore Sun* — May 26, 2015

T he searing spotlight of media scrutiny fell upon a Maryland state's attorney, a rising star in Democratic politics. After a high-profile beating death, the young prosecutor convened a well-attended news conference to announce murder charges, detail the evidence, and insist that the public's desire for justice had finally been achieved.

If you think I've just described Baltimore State's Attorney Marilyn Mosby's actions surrounding the death of Freddie Gray, you're only half right. Nearly the exact same situation occurred a dozen years ago in Maryland. In that case, the politically ambitious state's attorney was Doug Gansler. And, in a sharply-worded judicial opinion that my law students study because of its landmark holdings, Mr. Gansler was publicly reprimanded and disciplined by Maryland judicial authorities.

Most Marylanders know Doug Gansler as the former attorney general who ran for governor and lost. But in 2000 and 2001, he was the state's attorney for Montgomery County. While serving in that important role and amid three highly-publicized murder cases, Mr. Gansler used televised news conferences to grandstand in a manner that the Maryland Court of Appeals later described as "improper." The judges then concluded that Mr. Gansler's media performances *"dangerously jeopardized the foundational principles of our system of criminal justice."*

It was the first time a Free State prosecutor was legally disciplined for attempting to use the news media to unfairly prejudice a trial. But the clearly-stated precedent of the Gansler case now binds every prosecutor in Maryland. The holding is so well known in legal ethics circles that I spend much of a 2-hour class discussing it with my law students. But the subject of what prosecutors may say publicly is more than an academic exercise for me.

As a prosecutor, I've spoken to the press on many occasions. When I was the deputy attorney general of Ohio, it was part of my job to discuss complex and controversial legal issues with journalists. And early in my career, when I was the spokesman for the federal prosecutors who were bringing police brutality cases, I briefed hundreds of news media outlets. Yet, in each of those press encounters, I reminded myself of the special ethics rules that apply when prosecutors speak to the news media.

Simply put, using the words of the legal ethics rules applicable in Maryland and elsewhere, a prosecutor is more than just a lawyer advocating for a legal position. A prosecutor is, and must be, a "minister of justice."

The fact that State's Attorney Mosby is now asking a judge to issue a gag order against defense lawyers in the Freddie Gray case is more than just troubling; it shows a misunderstanding of ethics rules on pre-trial publicity. These rules provide that when one side in a case (typically a prosecutor) has so completely exploited the charges in the press that the other side's attorneys (here, those representing the officers) must be allowed to be even more aggressive with public statements than pre-trial publicity limitations would typically permit.

Ms. Mosby's first misstep was to showboat, using rhetoric more suitable for a candidate seeking votes than an officer of the court seeking justice. From her over-caffeinated statements at her initial news conference to the other national news interviews she leapt into, her tone was remarkably strident. But her second, and more serious, misstep was to strive to silence defense attorneys who are still trying to unwind their clients' prospects for a fair trial from the numerous prejudicial statements the prosecutor already made.

Had Ms. Mosby taken the time to read and reflect upon the opinion in the Gansler decision, it's likely she would have taken a more thoughtful, even responsible, approach. After all, no attorney wants to face disciplinary charges that could lead to disbarment. It appears that the legacy of the Gansler ethics case went unheard in what someday may be called the Mosby ethics case.

Whether Marilyn Mosby will be disciplined along the lines of Mr. Gansler remains to be seen. But she already shares the most troubling common denominator of the Gansler case: the willingness to abuse media relations and the prosecutor's authority just to brighten her political horizons.

We trust ministers to do the right thing and to be guided by higher principles. From a minister of justice, we should expect no less.

CHAPTER 26

In time of crisis, be careful about over-reassurances

It's easy to forget that, if you draw an organizational chart of American government, the people belong at the top of the chart — not the bottom. The politicians and bureaucrats work for us. They should stand up when we enter a room, not the other way around.

This crucial American tenet came to mind one Sunday morning when, during the early stages of the Ebola virus scare, a White House spokesman told a TV interviewer that the government was going to stop the virus from coming into the U.S.

Anyone with even the most basic knowledge of how viruses work and the nature of international travel will immediately identify this statement as laughable. Worse yet, it's an example of over-reassurance by someone who works for us and must think us dim-witted. The spokesman's TV claim made me recall a similar example of zealous over-reassurance from a bureaucrat that took place during the deadly scourge of the great influenza virus that killed as many as 100 million people worldwide.

Immediately, I noticed other similarities. In helping my clients communicate better in speeches and written essays, I often encourage them to use the parallel construction of connecting two seemingly random events that, upon closer inspection, have much in common. This allows the persuader to offer a lesson that obviously applied in the well-known example as one that also exists in the more recent example.

I used that technique to begin this essay. When trying to decide what newspaper to submit this to, I chose Philadelphia because I was born there and that city was the epicenter of the 1917 deadly influenza pandemic.

I was pleased when the Inquirer — one of the widest read newspapers in America — agreed to publish this op-ed. Another major daily paper in Iowa featured this piece as well.

PUBLISHED: *The Philadelphia Inquirer* — October 10, 2014; *The Des Moines Register* — Oct. 14, 2014

Nearly a century ago, in 1917, America was weary from a recent unpopular war and Americans were living in the second term of a controversial "progressive" president who'd made bold promises in his re-election campaign that he would ultimately be unable to keep.

Violence among nations far across the sea was beginning to seem less like the conflict of one continent and more like a world war. Russian forces had invaded Ukraine with an eye toward further expansion. And the American president promised that there would be no U.S. boots on the ground to respond to these clashes.

The bulletins of that era sound eerily like today's news. And there may be one more similarity. The major event of that decade, perhaps more important than America's eventual entry into World War I, was the outbreak of the worst virus in modern times.

It was influenza, specifically the strain now known as H1N1. And when it was done ravaging most of the world, it would claim as many as 100 million lives, 675,000 in the United States alone. For a quick comparison, we lost about 58,000 — less than ten percent of those 1917-18 influenza victims — Americans in the Vietnam War.

Now our nation watches and wonders whether the similarly deadly Ebola virus might become a comparable pandemic. It's far too early to tell, but the mistakes and lessons of the influenza crisis of the early 20th century must be reviewed and heeded now.

I've spent much of my career speaking for government agencies in times of turbulence. I've been a spokesman for a police department, a state attorney general's office, and the United States Department of Justice in Washington. Through three major universities and in seminars across the country, I train government officials about how to credibly and persuasively inform the public when lives are at risk and information is hard to confirm.

The work experience of conveying government action to the news media informs my teaching. Which is why I tell those who act as government spokespersons to avoid the strong and natural temptation to over-reassure the public, particularly when unforeseen and uncontrollable factors are involved.

I thought of this lesson last week, as I watched White House spokesman Dan Pfeiffer being interviewed about the Ebola virus. When directly asked by one TV interviewer if the Ebola virus could engulf an entire Navy ship of U.S. military personnel — much like the influenza did to Navy ships in 1917 — Mr. Pfeiffer responded, "we'll make sure that doesn't happen," and "we're very confident of the procedures we have in place."

Let's pray he's correct. But Mr. Pfeiffer's rush to reassure brought me back to 1917-18 and brought to mind Wilmer Krusen.

Mr. Krusen was director of public health for the city of Philadelphia, where the influenza was slaughtering city residents by the thousands. As the public's fears grew and panic began to boil over, Krusen took to the news media to calm those concerns. One day, when the daily death toll hit 254 in the city, Krusen and his colleagues released a public statement claiming, "the peak of the influenza epidemic has been reached." Over the next few days, the daily number of deaths increased but, each day, Krusen continued to reassure that the worst was over. Even as the deaths per day topped 600, Krusen was still over-reassuring, warning the public not about the dangers of contact with the infected, but rather of the dangers of being "frightened or panic stricken over exaggerated reports."

But citizens were no longer listening to a government they didn't trust. They instinctively knew the official line was more like the official lie. Bodies of influenza victims wrapped in bed sheets stacked up on the front porches of that city and many other towns as families were decimated. Authorities couldn't or wouldn't dispose of the corpses.

To be clear, this is not to say such a horrific fate is in store for us now that Ebola has found its way to our shores. Rather, it's a cautionary tale. We must weigh carefully the statements of leaders who seek to quell the torrents of fear that naturally arise when news reports show hundreds dying in Africa and people forcibly quarantined in Dallas.

The medical system and public health officials in this country are second to none. But every human enterprise is fraught with human error. And even a single mistake could be the falling domino that triggers many more to follow.

I will leave it to others more educated in this area to suggest the appropriate levels of medical precaution, limits to travel, and quarantine. But as an expert in the distribution of public information amid fast-changing factors, I can say this: The tendency of government to over-reassure is ever present. Citizens should know that skepticism and preparing for the worst could be life-saving measures.

CHAPTER 27

Ruling on false speech lets voters decide

No one likes a liar. And few people like politicians. And when politicians are liars, they can expect boos and brickbats from every corner. But, in political communications, what's true and what's false is often a blurry bit of business. "Senator Bob Blowhard voted to raise taxes," is a likely attack you might hear. In reality, the senator voted to place an issue on the ballot where the voters could raise taxes. So, is the attack against Bob Blowhard true or false?

No matter how you answer that question, I hope you'll agree with the premise of my op-ed below. It's that voters, the shareholders of government, ought to be the people in charge of the truth squad — not government regulators. Note my use of alliteration to add to the rhythm of the language. When done sparingly, alliteration can make a powerful passage positively persuasive. If you know what I mean.

PUBLISHED: *The Cincinnati Enquirer* — July 7, 2014

History impels us to remember that America arose from a political dispute with Britain. Colonists loyal to the crown and those agitating for independence volleyed truths and falsehoods in a political war of words preceding the real battles to come. Those calling for a new country won the day, and we celebrated the pronouncement of that independence this week.

But before, during, and after the American Revolution, one of the strongest weapons of our founding fathers was their political speech. Now, a unanimous decision of the U.S. Supreme Court has opened the door to what might mean the end of an Ohio law that regulates political speech — the ban on false campaign statements. A historical perspective can enlighten this dispute.

In 1775, Thomas Paine anonymously penned *Common Sense* and ignited a firestorm of dissent against British overreach and overrule. Many still loyal to the king clamored to learn who wrote the tract so they could press for charges of treason. But Paine held fast to his belief that, in the discourse of political speech, it's "the doctrine, not the man" that matters most.

Anonymous political communication to advance policy continued through the publication of the *Federalist Papers*, wherein authors James Madison, John Jay, and Alexander Hamilton (mostly Hamilton, by the way) obscured their identities by employing the pen name *Publius*. They wanted the focus to fall solely upon the essence of their ideas — not their personalities.

Even today, courts protect purveyors of potential unpopular political speech from the byproducts of outrage. In 1995, the U.S. Supreme Court ruled that a Westerville, Ohio, woman who anonymously circulated fliers opposing a school levy was protected by the First Amendment despite the fact state regulators found she violated a state law requiring her to disclose her identity.

As with her founding forerunners, it was the doctrine, not the woman that won the day.

This is why it's foundationally American that the merit of political speech is best judged on its own assertions.

Government intrusion to referee this process is both unnecessary and unconstitutional. Some among us clamor to divert from this direction and weigh down political actors with additional government regulations circumscribing who can speak, when, where, and how.

With good reason and as they did this week, our nation's highest court has largely declined these invitations, even when lawmakers and regulators have been unable to resist.

The court's recent decision arose from a Cincinnati case, but it could affect every state in the nation. The Supreme Court was supremely piqued at the Ohio law.

The justices, who rarely rule unanimously in high-profile matters, hinted that laws, such as Ohio's, that empower government regulators to rule on the truth or falsity of political speech, may well run afoul of the First Amendment.

If this result comes to pass, no doubt the self-anointed defenders of that easy-to-praise-but-hard-to-define concept of "good government" will thunder, sputter, and lament this decision as the spark of infernal ruin. They'll predict the reign of deceit, deception, and doom in elections.

Yet courts, if they do eventually strike down all false campaign statement bans, will leave undisturbed the ultimate judge of political speech: the voters who take the time to do their homework ahead of Election Day.

A well-informed citizenry can surely be credited for the rise of this nation and a poorly informed electorate will rightly be blamed for any future demise.

Simply put, nearly all voters have at their command the ability to discern campaign fiction from non-fiction. With the ability to conduct basic internet searches and the multitude of fact-checking enterprises underway, the truth of a candidate's claim can be uncovered easily enough.

In court, we trust laypeople on a jury to sort out which side is telling the truth. We instruct those jurors to use their common sense to determine which witnesses have a motivation to lie, which scenarios are most plausible, and which advocates are trying a bit too hard to deny the obvious. Voters, like jurors, can do the same with claims made by politicians and interest groups.

Ballot box decisions matter — a lot. When voters overly-consumed by cultural tripe, hobbies, or sports cast ballots, the resulting quality of government suffers. Surely the choice of who should make, judge, and execute our laws deserves as much time from us as our avocations and other recreational pursuits.

As Americans, we have searched mightily for the sentinels of our democracy and they, to borrow a phrase, are us. And the fact that our nation's highest court has begun to unravel laws against false campaign statements won't ever change that.

CHAPTER 28

History may haunt the George Zimmerman trial

When a town watch volunteer in Florida confronted a young man who the volunteer thought was acting suspiciously in and around private residences, the encounter became a deadly one. While it took weeks for him to be charged, George Zimmerman's shooting of Trayvon Martin quickly became a catalyst for a national discussion — more like an argument — over race and self-defense laws.

Reading and watching the news coverage day after day, I saw the metaphorical tent posts of a media circus going up outside the courthouse. Because I teach a law school class on how media scrutiny can undermine a fair trial, I wrote this essay that outlined my concerns. As I've done elsewhere, I used the opening of the piece to compare the current controversy with one from the past. More so than in other op-eds that employed this technique, I described the past incident in detail. My goal was to help readers see the importance of stopping history from repeating itself.

PUBLISHED: circa June 2013

T he man was blamed for a cold-blooded murder. His alleged crime was the talk of the entire nation. Special interests and the media clamored for his arrest. Defenders and accusers squared off and hotly argued the purported facts of the killing.

Critics said the police bungled the investigation and should move quickly to take the suspect into custody. Weeks passed. Finally, only when the public outcry built to a roar, did prosecutors bring charges and the suspected killer was hauled away in handcuffs and charged with murder.

If you think I've just described the recent controversy in Sanford, Florida, involving George Zimmerman and the slain Trayvon Martin, guess again. These are the precise facts surrounding the case of Sam Sheppard, a Cleveland-area doctor accused of brutally slaying his wife in 1954. The case sparked one of the biggest media circuses of the last century and spawned a TV show and subsequent movie, both entitled *The Fugitive.*

What should all of this mean to those observing the Zimmerman case some 58 years later? Simple — stunningly unfair pre-trial publicity is a grievous wound to Lady Justice. Once convicted of the crime, Sheppard appealed his case, literally, all the way to the U.S. Supreme Court. The justices heard arguments from two of the most renowned legal figures of that era: then-Ohio Attorney General (and later U.S. Attorney General) William Saxbe and nationally prominent defense attorney F. Lee Bailey.

In a landmark opinion that changed the way prosecutors and police handle high-profile cases even today, the high court overturned Sheppard's murder conviction and set him free. The justices recounted in detail the histrionics and media frenzy that preceded the arrest. The county coroner, an elected official, held an inquest in a high school auditorium, with every seat in each bleacher filled by a gathering mob. The coroner drew a loud standing ovation when he directed police officers to frisk Sheppard when he entered the room. When Sheppard's defense attorney simply asked to introduce some evidence into the proceeding, the coroner did more than object — he ordered the lawyer be physically removed from the building. The crowd was overjoyed; one woman ran down to where the coroner was sitting and planted a kiss on him.

Later, a plethora of newspapers competed with one another to scream loudest for Sheppard's arrest. The cacophony culminated in a rarely seen front-page editorial with the large headline: *Why Isn't Sam Sheppard in Jail?* Mere hours after that edition hit the street, the prosecutor, who was up for election that year, promptly complied and ordered the doctor arrested. Media coverage in the months before the trial dominated TV, radio, and newspapers not just in Ohio but also throughout the nation.

In ruling that there was no way Sam Sheppard received a fair trial amid that tumult, and with a nod to a previous reference made by the Ohio Supreme Court, U.S. Supreme Court Justice Tom Clark wrote in his majority opinion: *"In this atmosphere of a 'Roman holiday' for the news media, Sam Sheppard stood trial for his life."*

None of us will ever know whether Sam Sheppard killed his wife. But no one can credibly claim that Sheppard got the fair trial guaranteed to every American by the Sixth Amendment.

George Zimmerman now stands charged with second-degree murder, the same charge on which Sheppard was convicted. Jurors must presume his innocence but millions of Americans, already swayed by what passes for evidence in the court of public opinion, have rendered their verdict — guilty.

Sam Sheppard clashed with hundreds of reporters and braved a jungle of cameras and microphones. Yet he never had to contend with the existence of a Facebook page dedicated to the memory of the victim in the altercation where (as of this writing) 214,909 people had "liked" the call for "Justice for Trayvon." Sheppard couldn't have even comprehended the notion of hundreds of thousands of people discussing his case in 140 character messages in an activity we know now as tweeting.

Early in my career, I briefed national reporters on high-profile national cases as spokesman for the U.S. Department of Justice. I saw firsthand the difference a press conference can make as a criminal case moves to trial.

Shortly after moving to Ohio in 1995, I began teaching a course at Ohio State's law school where I train future lawyers on the rules that govern how prosecutors and police can ethically interact with the media while protecting the rights of defendants and victims alike. We study the Duke lacrosse case, the O.J. Simpson case, and — yes — the Sam Sheppard case.

History calls us to learn from the mistakes it lays bare. Here's hoping that the lessons learned from high-profile criminal cases like that of Sam Sheppard can light our path and inform our deeds as we await the trial of George Zimmerman.

CHAPTER 29

Mayor's courts bring local justice to citizens

Ohio's judicial system includes mayor's courts, where misdemeanor crimes and traffic offenses can be heard in a local setting, rather than a distant city court. Some jurisdictions have abused mayor's courts, allowing non-attorneys to preside in an often-clumsy attempt to handle difficult evidentiary issues and more complex cases. Other municipalities have used these courts as little more than a way to bring money into the city budget.

Because I've been a magistrate in mayor's courts for many years, when the daily newspaper in Columbus, Ohio, featured a prominent article criticizing them, they printed the following op-ed in response.

When trying to place an op-ed, you will increase your chances if you write a piece that responds directly to the work of a given newspaper. This is especially true when the article was a major story that the newspaper featured on the front page.

Another reason why this piece was more likely to be published is my familiarity with the issues raised. And, given that my experience was local to the newspaper, it gave my submission a leg up on others who might have had the same opinion but lacked the background.

PUBLISHED: *The Columbus Dispatch* — circa 2012

T his week's news coverage brought needed scrutiny to Ohio mayor's courts, but there's no need to abolish them. Minor reform can resolve nearly every concern raised by critics.

In 1999, then-Chief Justice Thomas Moyer appointed me to the Supreme Court Futures Commission, which was making recommendations for changes in the state judicial system. Among other topics, we heard from supporters and opponents of mayor's courts. While listening to the testimony, my initial concern was that mayors have an inherent conflict of interest when they are permitted to determine how much income their budget receives from fines the mayors themselves impose in court. The chief justice asked me to address an Ohio mayors conference on this concern. I received a polite reception but was spurned nonetheless.

Later, with no reforms in sight, I was appointed to serve as a magistrate in a local mayor's court and over the last decade, I've presided over two other mayor's courts. After seeing the value local courts have for many Ohioans, I now advocate for reform rather than elimination.

While handling the cases of thousands of people charged with traffic violations or crimes, I've heard people appearing in court express relief at avoiding difficult parking, long waits, and the bedeviling-bureaucracy that often exist downtown at municipal court. Those who live far from the city typically prefer to handle traffic cases or zoning disputes in a nearby venue with local officials, who many perceive as more accountable.

When drivers cited for speeding through a local school zone come before me, I typically order a monetary fine and a requirement to write a letter of apology to the parent teacher organization of the affected school. I'll sometimes require someone found guilty of littering in a certain neighborhood to spend an afternoon picking up trash there. Local touches like this are less likely in a distant, more harried, municipal court.

There's also a safety impact that would accompany elimination of mayor's courts. In Columbus suburbs, police officers who've issued citations must remain near the court session to testify about those cases. If the cases are held in downtown Columbus, those officers must travel there and sometimes wait hours before even being called to testify. This puts those officers far from where they patrol and unavailable to respond to emergencies that arise. Since most mayor's courts are conducted in the same building as the police department, police officers can work nearby while waiting to testify in the courtroom that may be just down the hall.

There's more. Every person appearing in mayor's court can appeal a judgment to the local municipal court, where the entire case starts over again as if the mayor's court conviction never occurred. Few people do so, suggesting a preference to resolve these mostly minor disputes locally.

But no reasonable observer can deny the flaws of the current system or the handful of municipalities that abuse it to direct more money into their respective budgets. It's a fair concern and one that deserves a fair response. A few basic structural changes can eliminate these problems.

First, lawmakers should limit mayor's courts to villages or cities with at least 3,000 residents. Nearly every "speed trap" out there will vanish if this is done.

Second, mayors must be prohibited from personally presiding over these courts. Instead, the mayor should be required to appoint an attorney with court experience to serve as magistrate. This guarantees that the person presiding over a hearing is minimally competent, having already passed the Ohio bar examination and handled trials using the various Ohio rules of evidence and procedure. Under this model, the person setting the fines (the magistrate) would also have no role in that municipality's budget process. No more conflict of interest. The use of magistrates is already common in most of the larger Central Ohio mayor's courts.

Next, every mayor's court should be equipped with an audio recording system with recordings available as a public record. Any magistrate who abuses a litigant or fails to provide due process would have to do so on tape, which would allow the Office of Disciplinary Counsel to bring charges that could result in that magistrate losing the right to practice law. This would be a powerful incentive for model behavior. Current law encourages, but does not mandate, such recordings.

Finally, the Ohio Auditor of State should be permitted to make a finding for recovery for any salaries paid to mayor's court staffers who fail to file required paperwork with the Ohio Supreme Court. This would bring about nearly perfect compliance.

If you get a traffic ticket and want to have your day in court, visit your local mayor's court. You may see the value of a more expedited experience administered by people from your community.

CHAPTER 30

Faulty interpretations could aid rise of tea party

Reading this piece years later, the one thing that stands out most for me is my prediction that infidelity to the U.S. Constitution on the part of certain politicians would fuel the anger of what was then a relatively small group — the TEA Party, which stands for "Taxed Enough Already."

Looking back, the growth of the TEA Party and the election of President Donald Trump six years after I wrote this op-ed may well have been sparked by exactly that constitutional infidelity. Indeed, my last sentence here foretold an "uncommon uprising."

A common feature of my writing is the injection of historical perspective and other foundational principles that were once taught with gusto in civics classes. This includes one of my most persistent peeves — a widespread misunderstanding of the First Amendment. The founding fathers who worried about central government (anti-Federalists, largely) insisted on adding some amendments to the Constitution before it was ratified. Their concerns fueled both the text and the context of the first of those initial ten amendments, which we now call the Bill of Rights.

Throughout this piece, I continued the primary work of my career: taking complex legal principles and translating them into prose that can be understood by those who, unlike me, were smart enough not to go to law school.

PUBLISHED: *The Newark Advocate* — July 7, 2010

As President Obama's nomination of Elena Kagan winds its way through the U.S. Senate, many Americans have tuned out of the debate, viewing the high court's work as far too arcane or academic to affect their lives. That's too bad, because many, if not most, of the court's decisions have a great impact on the rights and responsibilities of citizens. One such judicial ruling was handed down by the justices last week and it's worth a full understanding.

If you've ever made the choice to join a church, club, or another group of people who share your beliefs and values, you'd probably deeply resent government regulators ordering you to appoint a group leader who opposes everything your organization supports. But the U.S. Supreme Court recently did just that, and a head-shaking misunderstanding of the First Amendment paved the way.

The decision was called *Christian Legal Society v. Martinez*, and it started — this won't surprise you — in California. At a public university, a campus Christian group welcomed all students, no matter their beliefs or practices, to participate in club activities, but it required group officers and voting members to pledge their commitment to the society's core Christian beliefs.

One of the core beliefs of this group was to not participate in or advocate for "a sexually immoral lifestyle," whether homosexual or heterosexual. These beliefs are neither odd nor novel — they are spelled out rather clearly in the Old and New Testaments and they govern the lives of billions of humans on the earth. Based on the group's decision, the university (acting as a state agency) revoked their official recognition.

Can it really be unconstitutional for a Christian group to be led only by professed Christians? The Court, in a decision authored by Justice Ginsburg, said precisely that. To understand how such a nonsensical result arises, a review of history helps. It starts and ends with the tension between freedom *from* religion and freedom *of* religion.

By its own language, the First Amendment only prohibits Congress from establishing (or, to be precise, "respecting the establishment of") a religion. At its inception, it didn't even prevent states from establishing a religion — just the federal government by a vote of Congress. Only later did the Supreme Court extend that prohibition to state governments.

Contrary to what many people believe, the phrase "wall of separation between church and state" is nowhere in the Constitution. It came from a letter written by Thomas Jefferson years after the ratification of the First Amendment. While Jefferson was the primary author of the Declaration of Independence, he had little influence over the drafting of the Constitution. He was overseas during the Constitutional Convention and later served as leader of the political party largely opposing ratification. A Supreme Court decision in 1878 borrowed Jefferson's offhand expression to make a point, and the phrase "separation of church and state" became a mainstay of American colloquial legal lexicon, much like "it's a free country" and "ignorance of the law is no excuse."

The First Amendment also protects freedom of religion. Scholars call this the "Free Exercise Clause" and the restriction against an established religion the "Establishment Clause." Over the years, justices have differed on how to balance these two competing clauses. Straying too far toward either can create a real wall of separation — between courts and common sense. Which brings us back to the decision this week.

Imagine a Jewish student group at a public university whose purpose is to remind people of the horrors of the Holocaust. Such an organization can now be required to accept anti-Semites or Holocaust deniers as leaders. The same is true for a campus atheist group, which can be required to accept devout Christians, Jews, and Muslims as officers.

Beyond these troubling legal ramifications, this case could also cause more trouble politically. Americans who are supportive of the TEA Party movement are on the lookout for infringement of what they believe to be the core protections of the Constitution. This perceived lack of commonsense interpretations of our founding document makes people want to rise up and fight for change. Since most public polls show about a third of Americans support the goals of the TEA Party, the court's decision will only add fuel to this political grassfire.

America was founded as a haven for those fleeing government dictates about religion. The First Amendment was forged as a mighty shield to protect that refuge. So it can only be called ironic that bureaucrats in California, aided by five Supreme Court justices, are wielding that amendment as a mighty sword to undercut the rights of citizens to organize a private campus group according to their beliefs.

If Solicitor General Kagan wants to become Justice Kagan, she'd be wise to agree that it's time to restore some of the balance between the founders' dual goals of freedom of religion and freedom from religion. The country is already up in arms with the president and the Congress. And when Americans think all three branches of government are untethered from common sense, an uncommon uprising might be in the works.

CHAPTER 31

Polanski should be treated like any other child rapist

In 1977, Hollywood director Roman Polanski notoriously raped and sodomized a child. He was charged by prosecutors and convicted but fled to Europe to escape going to prison. In 2009, Americans were debating whether Polanski's alleged skill as a director was reason enough to allow him to return to the U.S. and avoid the jailer's grasp. Many people who would have otherwise called for a harsh sentence for a child rapist seemed to be blinded by their affinity for Polanski and whatever talent he has making films.

Many of these famous Hollywood Polanski defenders would later speak out loudly and with passion against the 2016 election of President Donald Trump, who — no matter what anyone thinks of his politics or personality — is not a convicted sex offender in the vein of Polanski.

In my work as a prosecutor, I've spent too many tearful moments with child sex victims to stand by and watch wealthy celebrities shower praise on a convicted pedophile. So, I was angry enough to take to my keyboard and pound out my discontent. I was grateful when the major daily newspaper in Atlanta published my fiery op-ed on this topic.

PUBLISHED: *The Atlanta Journal-Constitution* — October 8, 2009

Famous movie directors such as Woody Allen, David Lynch, and Martin Scorsese have presented us with many fine works of fiction over the years. This week, they joined with other film-industry luminaries to offer up one very bad work of fiction: *The Child Rapist Who Never Hurt Anyone*. They support director and international fugitive Roman Polanski, even though he raped and sodomized a child some 30 years ago.

As a father of a teenage daughter, I'm greatly troubled by this latest Hollywood production. And as a prosecutor who has brought several child rapists to justice and sent them to prison, it causes me to worry for the future of our judicial system.

The rape of a child is one of the most despicable crimes imaginable. Only rarely does a young victim completely recover from the physical and emotional damage involved. In this case, the victim appears to have overcome this and now wants mercy for Polanski. While we can respect her desire to move on, a victim's preference is but one factor in ensuring justice.

The larger question is one of public protection. More so than most other classes of criminals, someone who sexually assaults a child is likely to do it again and again.

The California prosecutors seeking to bring Polanski back to face his punishment know this all too well. Indeed, the Justice Department's Bureau of Justice Statistics reports that sex offenders are about four times more likely than non-sex offenders to be arrested for another sex crime after serving their time in prison.

We may never know whether Polanski continued to sexually assault children after he fled the United States. But we do know he'll be unable to hurt another child while imprisoned for his original crime and for the serious offense of fleeing from justice.

Polanski's Hollywood pals will try to use their substantial fame and fortunes to bend public opinion in his favor. No doubt they'll offer up

Polanski's life of hardship and his achievements in film. Some may even deny that a crime occurred. Don't think so? TV host and actress Whoopi Goldberg was quoted this week as saying the crime was not really a "rape rape," whatever that means. I remember, while prosecuting a sexual assault case, hearing the same argument from the defense lawyer representing a man who raped his two-year-old daughter.

The rush of prominent apologists for this sexual predator is, sadly, just the latest episode of misplaced sympathies. All too often, child sex victims are cast aside in favor of a victimizer posing as victim.

One of my most memorable prosecution experiences occurred immediately after the sentencing hearing for a man I had prosecuted for sexually assaulting his granddaughter.

Over the course of an hour, a courtroom full of relatives queued up to testify in favor of leniency for the grandfather. None of these people — nearly all the adults in the child's life —spoke in support of the child. She had been shunned for reporting the assault and placing her grandfather in jeopardy.

After the judge properly sent the man to prison, I left court. One of the relatives followed me into the hall and called my name. I turned and braced for some sort of protest for having helped put the man behind bars.

Instead, the woman — one of the relatives who didn't testify — thanked me "for being the only person in that courtroom willing to speak for that child." Prosecutors don't do the job for the thanks, but we get some simple satisfaction from giving voice to the voiceless.

Unfortunately, in that noble quest, prosecutors and other child advocates just can't compete with the volume and vigor of celebrities whose every utterance is potentially newsworthy. But we must try.

The lesson from this case is plain to see. We have a moral duty to treat Roman Polanski like any other person who raped a child, was convicted, and then ran from the law. Academy Awards may glitter and glow, but their luminance ought not distract us from an honor truly worth collecting — protecting the defenseless from those who've shown themselves willing to enact the very essence of evil.

CHAPTER 32

Obama's view of racial dispute offers insight into nomination

As Barack Obama was beginning his presidency, he suffered through a hailstorm of political criticism when he hastily commented on a minor dispute between a black professor and local police who were responding to a 911 call at the professor's home.

I used this op-ed to make a nexus between Mr. Obama's use of empathy as the measuring stick for deciding what causes he supports and who should sit on the U.S. Supreme Court.

The portion of this piece I'm proudest of is the switched perspectives of who deserves more empathy. Hasty judgments on who the underdog is in a certain dispute might lead to some erroneous conclusions. People are often quick to place facile labels on characters in a public morality play while the truth may be more elusive.

Read for yourself as I test out an early argument for what I now teach in my crisis communications classes as the theory of the "underdog swap."

Despite my best efforts, I can't locate which newspaper ran this op-ed. I stored it in my computer files of published work, so we only have the date it ran.

PUBLISHED: July 2009

At his news conference last week, President Obama showed admirable candor when he acknowledged he didn't know all the facts regarding the recent arrest of a black Harvard professor. But the president showed poor judgment when he nonetheless went on to criticize the police, despite his unfamiliarity with the facts. He later retracted his comment after it sparked an inferno of criticism.

Only those at the scene really know what happened and even those eyewitness accounts vary. If the matter ever goes to court — threats of litigation arose — a jury will decide who did what to whom. That's why our legal system makes jurors finders of fact and judges finders of law. The centuries-old process of both sides submitting to close questioning of their respective accounts before a jury has a remarkable tendency to expose the truth.

So, let's not take sides in the media-heated saga of the professor vs. the police. It's not particularly momentous for us as a nation and, more importantly, it's a no-win exercise. All heat and no light burns us all.

President Obama's failure to initially grasp this notion provides insight into something more important: the direction of the U.S. Supreme Court. While the media churned about whether Cambridge police were racist or the professor was unruly, the U.S. Senate was weighing the appointment of Supreme Court nominee Sonia Sotomayor.

Mr. Obama famously — or infamously, depending on your viewpoint — promised to appoint "empathetic" federal judges. As someone who served as spokesman for the key official recommending Supreme Court candidates to President Reagan, you might expect me to line up with the "anti-empathy" crowd. Nope. My mother raised me better than that. While I'm not willing to serve as its president, count me as an active member of the empathy fan club.

Empathy is a wonderful quality in a friend but how can judges determine which party in a court case deserves empathy? Mr. Obama glibly suggests empathy should accrue to what he calls "the little guy." But there's a problem.

Both the 5th and 14th Amendments to the Constitution require courts to give all persons *"equal protection of the laws."* And every Supreme Court justice must swear an oath to *"administer justice without respect to persons and do equal right to the poor and to the rich."*

But even if judges inclined to violate that oath could somehow properly handpick outcomes favoring underdogs, another very real problem emerges. Which underdog to help? Which little guy should a referee throw the game for?

Take the fictional case of elderly widow Brown vs. gigantic Alpha Corp. We all think we know — and President Obama surely does — who the underdog there is, right? Maybe not.

Widow Brown could be a vexatious litigator who sues everyone she dislikes. And Alpha Corp isn't some faceless entity; it's no more than a group of citizens who've pooled their savings or pensions to help fund a particular business enterprise. Indeed, many of these stockholders are likely elderly widows themselves — living on Alpha's stock dividends.

Back to the original query: Which elderly widow deserves empathy? The one who brought the lawsuit or the one who must pay the damages?

There's more. In a criminal case, there might be mugger Michael who claims a childhood of abuse led him into his misunderstood misdeeds. He deserves empathy, some might say. But what of his victims, working class people, perhaps members of racial minorities who are disproportionately the victims of crime? These "little guys" deserve empathy, as well.

Having a judge with empathy at the top of her skill set won't help resolve those questions, unless the real goal is to favor one set of underdogs for racial, social, or dare I say, political reasons.

In the case of the police vs. the professor, who was the underdog? Mr. Obama and others will say a black citizen is always unmatched against an officer of the law. Police union leaders, many of them black, will say officers are frequent targets of deadly violence and disrespect. Both are classic underdog arguments.

Whether it's a Supreme Court justice or a president favoring one "little guy" over another in the name of empathy, the entire endeavor moves us further away from a nation of laws where, to paraphrase the great Martin Luther King Jr., you ought to be judged not by the color of your skin, but the strength of your case.

CHAPTER 33

Unsolicited advice to former mayor Rudy Giuliani

One of the key concepts I use in the most difficult communications challenges is proactivity. Clients often hire me in the hopes that I will help them hide their dirty laundry or bad report cards. While there are ethical ways to do that, my preferred approach is to convince them to air that laundry and discuss those grades before others get the chance.

On more than one occasion, when I encourage clients to quickly release their own bad news, their reaction is something akin to "Wait — we're paying you for this advice?!" Indeed, they are. And, eventually, they write the check with a smile on their face. That's because the practice of using the theories of primacy and cognitive dissonance to proactively release negative information has a way of building credibility and averting disaster. Learn more in this essay.

PUBLISHED: Online, 2008

Sometimes in politics the right answer to a question is counter-intuitive. It's human nature to keep our weaknesses to ourselves. But in the case of a well-known problem, the elephant in the room just sits there, obvious to all. Yet no one wants to discuss it. Or smell it. Or be squashed by it.

When it comes to running winning political campaigns, however, it's often necessary to acknowledge and deal with any pachyderms that might crush a candidate. Especially in the party of the GOP elephant.

One year ago, Rudy Giuliani was the biggest name on the speaking circuit. He was invited to share his views as an expert and he was lauded as "America's Mayor" by papers and pundits from Los Angeles to Long Island and everywhere in between.

Today he's locked in a battle for the Republican nomination for president. Now that he's viewed through a more partisan lens, he's been forced to deal with plummeting popularity and more political slap shots than a goalie for the New York Rangers. The recent indictment of Giuliani's former police commissioner has made matters even worse.

But most deadly is the notion that his more liberal policies on abortion, gay marriage, and gun rights will be disliked by Republican primary voters. Similarly, his two divorces may raise concerns for some values voters.

Such political obstacles are nothing new to any strategist who's ever been involved with a truly competitive political campaign. Every candidate has weaknesses. The key to success is how those issues are addressed.

For Rudy Giuliani, there are two primary options — he can frame his weaknesses himself or he can allow his opponents to use those weaknesses to define him. Putting your own weak points into context on your own is nearly always the preferred approach. Rudy must deal head-on with his family issues and perceived liberal stances on certain issues.

This is where politics mixes with psychology. There are two big ideas here — primacy and cognitive dissonance.

Primacy is the idea that the first thing an unbiased listener hears is the most credible. Cognitive dissonance is the concept that shows how new information in line with a listener's beliefs is accepted, while contrary new information is rejected as unharmonious or dissonant. Once a mind is made up, it's hard to change it.

With these two notions in mind, Rudy Giuliani should manage these issues before his opponents have the chance to do it for him.

For example, take the 2000 presidential election. Republican nominee George W. Bush failed to deal with his drunk driving conviction, allowing opponents to use it against him at the last minute. It nearly cost him the election. Proactive management of that issue would have inoculated the campaign against the attack early on, thereby preventing damage in the final hours.

This appears to be what Barack Obama is doing with his past cocaine use. Although no president has even acknowledged using cocaine (a felony in most states), Obama offered the damaging information on his own terms, framing the felonious activity as the product of a mixed-up youth.

Whether it's a good idea to have a former cocaine user in such high office is a debate for another day. But the success of the inoculation strategy Obama is employing is hard to dispute — the national news media have given him a pass on the issue.

So, what should Rudy Giuliani be doing?

In a Republican primary, it's never a bad thing to invoke Ronald Reagan. In Rudy's case, however, he might use an unorthodox approach — perhaps by reminding voters there were those who said Reagan would never be elected because he'd been divorced. Let the voters know that he's felt the sting of such criticism and, like Reagan, he won't let it deter him.

On social issues, where Rudy may have differences with other Republicans, he should adopt a position that won't compromise his principles. Consistent messaging can help convince swing voters to accept Rudy despite a difference of opinion on certain issues.

Some message points he could use include:

- Respectful disagreements in the party can be good and help make us stronger.

- Ronald Reagan said that someone who agrees with you 80 percent of the time is a friend, not an enemy.

- On the issues that matter most, we agree.

- For the topics on which we disagree, I won't change my position just because a pollster tells me to (unlike the infamous posturing of Bill and Hillary Clinton).

- Leadership requires steadfastness. Facing the problems of our nation requires leadership. I'll be honest and steadfast in my beliefs, just as I'll bring leadership to this country.

Here's the bottom line for Rudy: His strengths will resonate with voters, but in a primary process that rewards conservative values, he must deal with the elephant in the room before his primary opponents seize the opportunity to do it for him.

CHAPTER 34

Unsolicited Advice to teen star Miley Cyrus

History likely won't remember that I once briefed famous comedian Joan Rivers before she met reporters following her seclusion in the wake of her husband's suicide. But that's about the only Hollywood advice I've ever given.

This disclaimer is apt for this chapter, wherein I advised Miley Cyrus that she would be unsuccessful if she continued to tart up her act. For the most part, she was able to avoid the calamities I predicted. While my advice on branding remains relevant for most brands, the success of this young singer who now loves to shock shows that, in limited cases, it's possible to cross over from one target audience to another.

We can (and I do) lament the lowering of public morals as evidenced in the more recent career of Miley Cyrus and others. But we ought not predict that our own moral compass will point in the same direction as the larger culture (a miscalculation I made here).

PUBLISHED: Online, 2008

I magine it. An American icon of home and hearth, a living representation of appropriate behavior and wholesomeness — is convicted of conspiracy, obstruction, and making false statements. And then sent to prison. Not hard to imagine, is it? It's the unsavory story of Martha Stewart.

In the blink of an eye, Stewart found her homemaking empire at risk because of a lapse in judgment. Beyond the financial costs of her mistake, she faced significant reputational risk associated with a direct hit to her brand that was, perhaps more than anything else, upstanding.

As with everything else, there are very real costs to building a brand. One of those costs is defending the brand when it becomes challenged by a scandal.

I spend a lot of time teaching effective communications strategies to businesses and non-profit groups. In my presentations, we talk in detail about what it means to be "newsworthy." And one of the characteristics of newsworthiness is prominence.

Prominence means that something routine and otherwise uneventful becomes newsworthy because of an external factor. The last time you fell off your bike, no news cameras came running. But we all remember when President Bush fell off his bike and injured himself. People fall off their bicycles every day, but it becomes newsworthy when the president does it. That's prominence.

Similarly, unknown people are convicted every day for all variety of crimes. But because Martha Stewart represented wholesomeness, her story became prominent and thus, newsworthy.

Let's look at another story straight from the headlines — the recent semi-nude photo spread by Miley Cyrus (a.k.a child star Hannah Montana) in Vanity Fair magazine.

Consider the brand: Miley Cyrus has built a billion-dollar brand on family values. Her character Hannah Montana is 100 percent pure Disney, another G-rated brand. In a recent article published in a Christian magazine aimed at parents of kids, she was quoted as saying "I'm a Christ follower for sure. Live like Christ and he'll live in you. And that's what I want to do."

Clearly, her brand is one of innocence and purity. And that brand has convinced millions of parents to invite Miley into their homes, through her hit TV show and bubble gum music.

It's not hard to see why a story about her posing semi-nude would make the headlines — the juxtaposition between breaking her brand and the published photos lend prominence to a story that would otherwise receive little attention.

Miley Cyrus now faces a real public relations crisis. This story not only threatens her earning power as a wholesome, family-friendly act, but it has ramifications for the Disney brand as well.

Unfortunately, this is not uncharted territory. There seems to be an established expectation of child actors crashing and burning in this country. Disney-to-mainstream act Britney Spears has made for regular tabloid fodder with her less-than-wholesome antics. Cable entertainment channels create entire documentaries that explore the sad stories of child-actors-gone-bad. But there's no "child-star" curse here, just a record of bad decisions. And it's not a one-hit wonder; it's a double album of greatest hits.

Miley Cyrus now can either make good decisions or she can make further bad decisions and descend a path where she will cross the line from famous to notorious.

Prominence works both ways. She can use her platform to do good. She could produce a public service announcement aimed at young girls. She can make more uplifting public statements at concerts and alert the media to not only directly respond to the situation, but also to earn goodwill toward future appearances.

She needs to quickly grasp and accept that what happens in Hollywood salons isn't the norm in Heartland saloons. Teenage celebs in skimpy clothes may fly in some parts of the culture, but it — and those who revel in it — will be grounded elsewhere. She'd do well to apply the W.W.O.D. test to future opportunities: What Would Omaha Do?

Despite what her agent or public relations advisor might say, not all news coverage is good coverage. Sure, she might still get that invite to The Surreal Life or Celebrity Survivor, but the only path to a good, long-lasting career is to repair and maintain the brand that has paid her dividends to date.

Branding is big business. A well-planned branding campaign can help companies break into the public consciousness, but along with brand comes responsibility. Going against the brand, whether it's the conviction of a homemaking icon or semi-nude photos of a wholesome personality has costs. There's a right way and a wrong way to repair the damage.

Few will argue that the one-time chart-leading Britney Spears has chosen the right path. Martha Stewart, on the other hand, has successfully rebuilt her brand. She resolved to embrace her experience. She played upon her strengths to generate positive, even humorous, news coverage while in prison and today continues to build her thriving business as a wildly successful domestic diva.

CHAPTER 35

Unsolicited advice
for candidate Mike Huckabee

We all have pet peeves — minor things we allow to annoy us. We enjoy being annoyed by our peeve and we revel in describing this bothersome bane to all who will listen.

One of my pet peeves is middle-aged people playing in rock cover bands. You could say I let this pet peeve get the best of me. When I observed a middle-aged politician playing bass guitar on TV, I took to my blog to air my grievance.

And, since I enjoy music as well as politics, I found the occasion to mix the two. One good lesson from this op-ed is that you may be more effective — even more persuasive — when you set out to write about something that moves you personally. That's what I did in this essay about then-candidate Mike Huckabee.

PUBLISHED: Online, late 2007

How many times have you heard someone say, "old enough to know better," when asked how old he is? Unfortunately, not everyone is old enough to know better — even when they're running for president and surrounded by legions of image and media consultants.

As a teenager and throughout college and grad school, I played guitar in several rock 'n' roll bands. We had loads of fun practicing, playing gigs, and hoping our musical prowess would make us popular with girls. Perhaps we should have thought of the girls a bit more when we named one of the bands "Chef Eddy and the Food." I digress.

I made some treasured memories during those rock 'n' roll years. So why am I no longer lugging amps and electric guitars into beer-soaked dives? You guessed it. I'm old enough to know better. And Mike Huckabee should be too.

It's hard to determine whether Huckabee is running for the presidency or trying to reclaim his youth through playing the dulcet notes of "Born to be Wild." It's so ironic, especially since his interview style suggests he was actually born to be mild. I digress further.

And while it's mildly reminiscent of Bill Clinton's saxophone tour during the '92 campaign, it's markedly different. Clinton didn't play gigs — the saxophone was a gimmick to reach the MTV generation. Huckabee's bass guitar thumping isn't endearing him to any group of voters except perhaps those who like aging rockers. The Rolling Stones and the Eagles already have that demographic sewn up.

The bass-playing is a symptom of a fundamental problem with the Huckabee candidacy. Huckabee is probably the best candidate on the Republican ticket to advance the "compassionate conservative" label. He lives it in his pronouncements and he comes off as sincere — in the Reagan mold — when talking about it.

There are, however, behind-the-scenes warning signs that Huckabee must acknowledge and deal with if he wants to maintain his valuable political capital as the sincerest candidate in the field.

I was lucky enough to have directed President Ronald Reagan in a television show. It was immediately clear to me what made him so effective — he was the same person on screen as he was off screen.

Huckabee hasn't established that same level of sincerity, and as a result, he's treading a fine line between maintaining credibility and losing the advantage of making a gut-level connection with people because he seems insincere. And plucking the bass guitar to decades-old hits doesn't help.

One troubling sign is Huckabee's relationship with pollster and former Clinton strategist Dick Morris, the face of what's wrong with Washington politics.

Morris's actions suggest he will do and say anything to get ahead. He plays both sides of the aisle — perhaps against themselves, and in doing so he reveals that he has no core beliefs. Morris' kind words about Huckabee might make for a nice sound bite on cable news, but there is another consideration. A Morris/Huckabee partnership allows the Clinton comparison to extend beyond "a guy from Hope, Arkansas." That doesn't work in a Republican primary or a general election when the big tent of Republicans must be united.

Here's the bottom line — the people a candidate works with matter. That's true now more than ever with cable channels and blogs galore to dissect the inner-workings of the campaign. When a candidate surrounds himself with people who are at odds with his own public image, it only serves to undercut that image.

Mike Huckabee had one of the best one-liners from the debates when he said (paraphrasing) "Democratic congressional spending is worse than John Edwards in a beauty shop."

John Edwards' 28,000-square-foot house and $400 haircuts are at odds with his work as an advocate for the working class, and it undercuts his image.

Barack Obama has worked to create an image as incorruptible. Dirty land deals with Illinois lobbyists, however, don't help that image.

Mike Huckabee is an example of a candidate who has overachieved against low expectations. However, as we near the Iowa caucuses and New Hampshire primary, Huckabee's higher poll numbers will mean increased scrutiny.

Bachman-Turner Overdrive recorded the immortal song "Taking Care of Business." Huckabee should absolutely take care of business — he just shouldn't play it.

CHAPTER 36

College shooting is a reminder to prepare for crisis

The mass shooting on the Virginia Tech campus was one of the earlier active shooter crises in modern America. Now we see violent attacks like this even more frequently. Because no organization is immune from this threat, I spend much of my time preparing government agencies, universities, and private businesses for the communications challenges that come with crisis.

This op-ed spells out some of the basic touchstones of effective crisis communications. I wrote this before the era of social media but in my current sessions and consulting, I advise using social media channels to assist with these high-stakes and high-speed communications imperatives. More thoughts on this topic also can be found in the final chapter of this book.

I could not find a newspaper where this op-ed ran so it's possible it was part of my online blog I used at the time.

PUBLISHED: April 16, 2007

Last week's massacre at Virginia Tech isn't just a wake-up call to universities. The leaders of any organization — government, business, or academic — can come to work one morning and find themselves awash in crisis. And the way an organization handles that crisis can strengthen its brand or crush it.

Look at the disparate cases of Johnson & Johnson and JetBlue. Each faced a crisis that overnight threatened their existence. In 1982, J&J's leading product Tylenol was responsible for the deaths of seven Chicago-area residents who unknowingly ingested the drug laced with cyanide. Two decades later, JetBlue passengers were trapped on idled planes for hours and hundreds of flights were canceled throughout a five-day period, leaving passengers stranded.

In both cases, the company was not directly responsible for its crisis. Tylenol confronted a murderer who tampered with its product; JetBlue confronted a weather system that overwhelmed its air traffic plans. But the differing approaches of the two companies resulted in very different outcomes.

Johnson & Johnson's company credo was to place consumers first. This was reflected in swift decisions to remove all Tylenol from shelves and then reintroduce the product with so much protection that even CIA code crackers have a hard time opening a bottle. Today, Tylenol remains one of J&J's premier sellers.

The verdict is still out on whether JetBlue's new approach and "Customer Bill of Rights" is enough to win back brand loyalty after weeks of bad headlines and worse analysis. Now, even months after their crisis, the brand name "JetBlue" brings just one thing to mind for most Americans — the airline that stranded its passengers for hours.

Why do some companies face a crisis with deftness and grace while others stumble, damaging their reputation with each passing hour?

The answer is found in preparation. No one likes to think about a crisis. Even fewer want to plan for one. But like insurance, good crisis communications planning can prevent a disaster from destroying a business financially.

No responsible executive would manage a company without insurance to replace buildings, equipment, and inventory when disaster strikes. But there's no insurance to repair a damaged reputation.

Unfortunately, too few companies are prepared to protect their reputations. When a crisis hits, there may be no time to prepare. In this age of instant information, the news media can air unfavorable information about a company worldwide in a matter of seconds. That's why forward-thinking organizations plan — and train — for crises before they happen.

"Prepare, prepare, prepare for a disaster" should be the motto of every company, small business, government agency, and nonprofit organization.

By its very definition, a crisis is an unplanned event. The timing, nature, duration, and intensity can't be forecasted. Yet early planning can shed light on certain foreseeable factors and save valuable time to handle the unforeseen.

Preparing to effectively communicate during a crisis involves several critical steps:

- Organizations must take stock of current situations and envision worst-case scenarios. Does a crisis communications plan exist? Is there an identified crisis response team? What are the worst and most likely events that could thrust your organization into a negative light?

- An effective crisis communications plan must be in writing. It doesn't need to be long, but it must be concise, practical, and user-friendly. It should be easily referenced in hard copy and on your company's intranet. (Today, I advise placing these plans on cloud services such as Dropbox or Evernote in case of a complete system failure. This also makes them available via smartphones and tablets.)

- Appropriate training must be provided to the crisis management and communications team. Thoroughly brief those who are most likely to deal with a crisis on the plans and have them participate in practical simulation exercises. Executives and associates dealing with the press and public should attend media training.

JetBlue leaders had many facts in advance to prepare a plan: they run an airline; airlines have customers; planes are impacted by weather; customers might be stranded; pilots, flight attendants, and other employees could be unavailable; re-routes are necessary. It didn't take a rocket scientist or PR expert to realize JetBlue hadn't spent much time in crisis planning, let alone understand how to communicate effectively during a crisis.

How do we know? Thousands of JetBlue passengers were stranded and the company was blistered in media story after media story. Far fewer of their competitors' passengers faced a similar fate.

Planning helps organizations navigate during the storm. During J&J's crisis, management kept their eye on their consumers, articulated a concise consumer-protection message and communicated often to protect this prized possession. In short, J&J withstood the crisis due to sound preparation and effective communications.

The best outcome for crisis planning is for no crisis to happen. But when the unexpected does occur, crisis communications planning may mean the difference between a company's existence and demise. Proper planning and training on the scale appropriate for the potential problems provide the type of insurance needed to protect the one thing money can't buy back: your reputation.

CHAPTER 37

Judges gone wild:
It's time to cancel this show

While I've been a magistrate in a local court, I've never been an elected judge. I've legally represented judges in many cases and disputes. I know hundreds of judges and even teach judicial seminars on ethics. So, when a judge steps out of line, I have a rather low tolerance for it. My view is that judges should live by a higher standard than others. When they fall short, they must be held accountable.

Sadly, many judges in trouble are too blinded by power to submit to oversight and are quick to blame others. I remember writing this piece on an airplane flight after I'd just read about a judge in a high-profile custody case involving the baby of a recently deceased tabloid star. Perhaps you have your own favorite story of out of control judges. This column presented some of mine.

PUBLISHED: *The Columbus Dispatch* — February 2007

S ome of my best friends are judges.

That may sound like the set-up to a bad joke, but it's true. But even as I enjoy the company of some jurists, I cringe at the public display of bad judicial manners by others, both locally and around the nation.

I was abruptly reminded of this just last week while watching the Florida probate judge presiding over the Anna Nicole Smith sideshow (the judge insisted it wasn't a "circus," so I take him at his word).

If you didn't see the clips on the 24-hour news shows, you might have caught them on the late-night comedy shows. The judge regaled a packed court with topics like his choice for lunch, advice from his wife, and stories of his youth. Such homey patter might go over well at a cocktail party, but it's clearly out of place in a court of law.

But that was the least of the judge's judicial sins. He called one woman attorney "beautiful," and refused to address the others by name, instead calling them by the state they hailed from. And he blubbered and sobbed as he read the judicial order concerning who would decide where the deceased tabloid princess would be buried. The judge, whose job it was to be dispassionate, was anything but.

It's hard to blame him. News reports suggested he was auditioning to be a TV judge. This variety of judges is the most troubling of all. Led by Judge Judy, who's famous for berating litigants, insulting them with wisecracks, and screaming, "shut up," TV judging is more than just a poor example of how judges ought to act; it's a perversion of the sober-minded ideal of how justice is meant to be dispensed.

If the judge in Florida wants to join that crowd, that's his prerogative. But his theatrical display in a case already plagued by theatrics was an embarrassment.

He's not alone. A tiny minority of judges in Ohio and elsewhere bring ridicule and derision to our judicial system.

Not long ago in Columbus, a judge dismissed a felony rape case simply because a witness was running a little late. Another Franklin County judge had her law license suspended for routinely screaming at lawyers and staff, forcing defendants to plead guilty by threatening them with jail, and requiring Jewish attorneys to appear in court on the most sacred of Jewish holy days.

And remember the Delaware County judge who observed a car take a quick shortcut through a gas station to avoid a red light? The judge followed the driver, ran the license plate through the state criminal computer system, ordered the man into court, and then lectured and threatened him — all with no case pending.

Indeed, just last year, a local family court judge was investigated for running a courtroom where chaos was the rule and justice for kids an afterthought. In one terrifying instance, a young child who was the subject of a custody dispute was preparing to leave the courthouse with one of her parents. Unexpectedly, the judge ran to the elevator, robes flying, grabbed the child and pulled her away.

Luckily, none of the judges I've discussed here still wears the robe. That's because two powerful entities often step in when judges sully the court system. The first is the Ohio Supreme Court, acting through the Board of Commissioners for Grievance and Discipline. The removal process typically takes several months and allows for several levels of review and appeal.

The other — far more powerful — group is the assembled voters of Ohio. When they learn of judicial stupidity, they often take note and rule quickly. After reviewing the evidence, they make their decision in one day — Election Day. And there's no review or appeal.

Many people with noble intentions would like to change Ohio's system and remove this power from the voters. They want judges to be appointed, not elected. These people make some excellent points in defense of this notion.

But, for this attorney who chafes at judicial arrogance and abuse, the idea of keeping the wrath of voters as a judicial discipline option makes sense. It doesn't always work, but when it does, it's poetic justice. And it gives great voice to the ultimate vindicators, the people themselves.

And to the weeping judge in Florida, I offer this advice. If you want to be a TV judge, go to Hollywood. But if you want to be a judge who citizens can look up to and respect, can the antics and play it straight.

CHAPTER 38

Unsolicited advice to candidate John McCain

As George W. Bush was winding down his second term as president, several of his fellow Republicans lined up to replace him. While Senator John McCain would eventually become his party's nominee, he faced a rocky road during the early days of his campaign. So, I offered this unsolicited advice on what communications strategies could revive his effort.

PUBLISHED: Online — 2007

My firm is often hired by high-profile clients to help them through difficult challenges. The advice we give those clients is confidential. But, in this forum, we offer unsolicited advice to political people in trouble who haven't hired us. Who knows? Maybe they'll listen.

Earlier this year, John McCain was considered the frontrunner to get the Republican nomination for president. Today, he's gone from the anointed to the disjointed. Now a middle-of-the-pack candidate, he faces increasing financial woes. And as these problems mount, he's lost much of his top-level staff.

But the Iowa caucuses and early primaries are still months away. There's still time to reverse course. Remember, Howard Dean was the hot summer hit of 2004, only to be frozen in the snows of Iowa by John Kerry. The Hawkeye state gave Kerry the chance to jump-start his failing campaign and bounce back. He did, and won the nomination.

John McCain needs to shake up the chess board. He can't continue to play the role of Washington insider. Not only is this a bad election cycle to play that villainous part, it's directly opposite to how he was viewed by many voters during his 2000 presidential bid. The McCain "Straight Talk Express" bus tour through primary states was a brilliant tactic, used to underscore his image as a maverick. The result? A 19-point victory in New Hampshire over presumed nominee George W. Bush.

So, what can McCain do to keep from disappearing into a political blip? First, he must fix his fundraising problems. Without money, he won't be able to get his message out. He must find a way to accrue higher receipts with sharper personal asks. If he wants motivation, he ought to remember that these will likely be the last set of national requests he'll ever make if he doesn't change things fast. As more money comes in, he must ensure that the life blood of donations don't bleed out. Someone with a sharp eye and a quick ability to rebuff bad ideas must begin to scrutinize every campaign expenditure. Then, to keep people involved in the outreach efforts, the campaign must motivate the savviest volunteers into the empty desks of the now-gone paid staffers.

He'll also need to use his enhanced fundraising efforts to get better press. Luckily, in politics, fundraising and earned media opportunities aren't mutually exclusive. A great example of this is Mitt Romney's innovations. He's made his fundraising a significant slice of his earned media plan. At the end of June, Romney held donor events at Fenway Park and the Boston Garden. They not only helped him raise much-needed cash, but they were heavily covered in the news and on political blogs.

Once the finances even out, McCain should use the power of the press to show voters how angry he is at the status quo. Voters are angry, and McCain can channel that with them. He won't be able to afford many ads, so he'll have to forego most paid media and heavily emphasize earned media.

Everywhere he goes, McCain should point out the people in Congress who are slowing progress and abusing earmarks. That means naming Democrats and Republicans offenders alike. During the last several months of campaigning, one of McCain's best public rants involves what he'll do as president when a pork-barrel spending bill is sent to his desk: "I will veto it and make its authors famous," he tells crowds.

It's a good line, but why wait? Imagine what would happen if McCain started naming names tomorrow and using the knowledge of how Congress really works to expose wrongdoing and show himself as an advocate for the average taxpayer.

McCain is known for a violent temper and a short fuse. But rather than hide that anger, he could tap deep into it and express passionate opposition to all the things voters hate most about the snakes, weasels, and hyenas in the D.C. zoo. It may be counterintuitive to suggest McCain take on powerful members of his own party on Capitol Hill, but given his sinking position, it may be just what's needed to change his political fortunes.

McCain's situation is not unique to his campaign or even presidential campaigns in general. Here are two takeaway points that are important considerations for any flagging campaign — from township trustee right up to the president of the United States.

First, when making changes, do it quickly. If serious campaign financial problems persist, restructure the organization immediately and announce it all in one press event. Fix the problem and announce the remedy in one news cycle. If staff size must be reduced, don't allow the changes to trickle out. Tear off the Band-Aid in one quick tug. It'll hurt for a moment but be better in the long-run.

Try a new approach even if it's risky. A campaign doesn't have to follow the same strategy — or budget for that matter — and use the same tactics the last candidate did (yes, even if that candidate was successful). Indeed, a change is often necessary.

Chinese General Sun Tzu wrote "The Art of War" — the world's oldest treatise on military strategy — 600 years before Christ was born. He realized that even the best strategies may have to change. *"Just as water retains no constant shape, so in warfare there are no constant conditions. He who can modify his tactics in relation to his opponent and thereby succeed in winning, may be called a heaven-born captain."*

Can McCain, scion of Navy giants, become a "heaven-born captain?" We'll know soon enough.

CHAPTER 39

Michael Jackson case proves jurors need more education

Like many Americans, I enjoyed the music of Michael Jackson yet wondered about his odd offstage behavior. When he was charged with child molestation, the evidence against him seemed overwhelming. The fact that a star-struck jury acquitted him left many, perhaps most, people agape with wonder.

Unfortunately, I knew what was likely the cause — jurors who have difficulty separating emotion and bias from the facts of a case. I had previously ghostwritten an op-ed on the similarly shocking O.J. Simpson acquittal (published elsewhere in this book), so drafting the Jackson op-ed was familiar territory for me. The substance of what I included in this op-ed is now a standard part of the topics I cover when I'm asking questions of potential jurors in the criminal cases I prosecute. I want to reduce these sorts of biases wherever possible.

PUBLISHED: *The Columbus Dispatch* — June 20, 2005

Despite the recent jury decision to acquit Michael Jackson on all charges, I remain a big fan of the American jury system. In the history of civilization, no other procedure is better at discerning truth and ensuring justice. But the haphazard way jurors often make decisions sends a troubling message of danger to potential crime victims like me and you.

In the Michael Jackson acquittal, the jurors found the pop star not guilty of all charges — even those not reasonably in dispute, such as the misdemeanor counts of supplying alcohol to minors. In a press conference after the trial, one juror told reporters her verdict was based largely on her personal dislike of one of the prosecution witnesses, the mother of the alleged victim. "I disliked it intensely when she snapped her fingers at us," the juror said. Other jurors agreed.

Message to jurors: Please decide cases on facts and credibility, not the annoying habits of a witness testifying in a stressful situation few people will ever encounter. As a prosecutor, I've handled several jury trials, including those involving child sex abuse. During that time, I've noticed a disturbing trend where the likability of a victim or a witness has a direct effect on whether the jury convicts or acquits. Talking to jurors after cases, they've told me that. And talking to fellow prosecutors around the state, I've heard the same thing.

I respect the right of juries to judge the reliability and truthfulness of each witness, but a child who is raped is entitled to justice, even when the mother who discovered the evidence of the attack is an annoying or difficult person.

And sometimes, juries can't relate to the problems of the victim. Colleagues have often remarked to me that predators who target a mentally challenged or unruly child for abuse often wind up with a "get out of jail free" card because juries are distracted or put off by the mannerisms or attitude of the victim. Often, the insolent or disconcerting display is a direct result of being victimized.

The Jackson jury foreman told CNN this week that he and his fellow jurors wished there had been some other witnesses to the alleged acts. Citizens who serve on juries should remember (or be reminded by the judge) that we, as prosecutors, don't get to pick our victims or our witnesses. The person who committed the crime did the choosing. We're just presenting the best facts available to us.

Sadly, the inclination to favor likable witnesses and victims and disfavor others isn't the only problem with modern American jurors. Another major problem stems from their choice of television shows.

For the last several years, high-tech TV crime dramas like *CSI* have been among Americans' favorite viewing choices. In less than an hour, a crime occurs, detectives investigate, and whiz-bang computer technology allows prosecutors to gain a conviction from some small detail like an eyelash the killer left at the scene. Before the credits role, the guilty party is sent off to prison.

Such fantasy makes for good entertainment and bad juries. Most prosecutors I know now include a question in their jury selection presentation that involves crime shows in general or *CSI* in particular. Jurors must be reminded that most criminal trials don't involve DNA evidence, computer-enhanced imaging, or even fingerprints.

Indeed, most criminal cases come down to eyewitnesses and tangible evidence like a gun, journal, or what the defendant said to investigators. Even when technology is used in a criminal case, it rarely boasts the impressive abilities seen on TV. A photo taken from 100 yards away simply can't be enhanced to show a small birthmark or tattoo on someone's neck. NASA can't do it and neither can your local crime lab. But many jurors expect it because it happened on TV.

As the magazine *US News* recently reported, some juries aren't even impressed when there's a direct DNA match. An Illinois prosecutor presented a case where DNA that a rapist left on his victim was linked to a gang member arrested for the crime. The match was strong, clear, and unmistakable. On top of that, the victim identified the defendant as the man who raped her.

The verdict? Not guilty. The jurors hesitated to convict because they worried that "debris" found in the victim was never tested to see if it was soil from the park where the attack occurred. "They said they knew from *CSI* that police could test for that sort of thing," the prosecutor told *US News*. "We had his DNA. It's ridiculous."

It is ridiculous and it's all too common. There's only one way to prevent these types of injustices from recurring. It's high time for pre-trial education of jurors, conducted by the court system in language that's easy to understand but underscores the importance of setting aside personal biases and pre-conceived ideas and focusing on facts.

Currently, judges try to do this by reading lengthy jury instructions at the end of the trial. Despite valiant efforts by some very smart people who write these instructions, most jurors appear dazed by the legal terminology used and the written-by-committee mishmash that often results. Perhaps a pre-trial video played while potential jurors are waiting could help alleviate many of these problems. We know that people like watching TV, so using that same approach to juror education could build a firm foundation for more informed verdicts.

So as Michael Jackson moonwalks his way back to Neverland Ranch, let's use the attention from his case as a catalyst for discussion and action. People need to know that no prosecutor can prove guilt "beyond any possible doubt." The American standard is "proof beyond a reasonable doubt." Similarly, bad people can be victims of crime and good people can commit crimes. We have trials to sort that all out.

Premises like these are crucial and bear repeating. Nearly all jurors are good people trying their best. But with the right education, their best can be a whole lot better.

CHAPTER 40

President Reagan is gone but my memories of him live on

My life intersected with Ronald Reagan's in a few ways important to me but undoubtedly less momentous for him. I helped organize youth support for his re-election effort in my home area in 1984. And I was honored to be appointed by him to serve as a spokesman for his Department of Justice in Washington. But, when I directed him in a 1993 television special, I met with him, interacted with him, even gave him some direction and advice on how to more effectively present on camera. He probably didn't need it, but he accepted my guidance with humility and humor.

People often ask me what Ronald Reagan was like in person. I tell them he was exactly what you saw on television. He was genial, kind, and not overly impressed with who he was or what he'd done. One anecdote from the filming tells all anyone needs to know about his down to earth demeanor. Prior to directing President Reagan, I had mostly directed amateurs and novices — people who'd never been filmed before. I was adept at explaining how the filming process works to get them ready and ease their nervousness.

On the day of filming Reagan, I was the one who was nervous. So nervous that when President Reagan sat down in front of the camera and was preparing to start, I hastened into my normal pre-filming monologue. I looked at the man who had starred in dozens of movies and reminded him: "When I say action, that means start. And when I say cut, that means stop."

In an instant, I realized I had just explained to this veteran actor something that he knew far better than I did. Many politicians I've worked with (they will go nameless here) would have thrown a fit and loudly reminded me how important they were and how many filming sessions they've been involved with. And I might have deserved such a rebuke.

But Ronald Reagan, the 40th President of the United States just smiled and said "OK." He didn't feel the need to embarrass me for my nervous mistake. He knew who he was and nothing anyone else said would change that. Perhaps that's one of the reasons he'll be remembered as one of our greatest presidents.

When he died, I wanted to share my interaction with him, so I quickly drafted this op-ed. It was likely accepted for print because I was a local person with a unique perspective on a recent national news event. This is a common and effective way to get an op-ed printed.

My files don't reflect which newspaper printed it, but it was likely The Newark Advocate.

PUBLISHED: June 2004

It was a moment I'll never forget. In 1988, I was standing in the first-floor hallway of the United States Department of Justice, talking to a high-ranking official who was offering me a job to act as a spokesman for the department.

I was rather unsure, as I had my full-time job and fourth year of night law school waiting for me back in Pennsylvania. I was leaning toward rejecting the offer, because a move to Washington would've been a great personal upheaval in my already-busy young life.

The official looked me in the eye with the look of someone about to impart guidance that could alter a career. And then he said one thing that changed my mind.

"If you take this job, you'll forever be credentialed as a member of the Reagan Administration," he said. "We're making history here, and you'll be part of it."

That was all I needed to hear. I said yes.

Here I am in the Justice Department
media briefing room. Yeah, I know -- the mustache!

The prospect of working as a presidential appointee to Ronald Reagan was exciting for me. And throughout the rest of his administration, I enjoyed every minute of that work.

Day after day, I worked in his name, pursuing his policies. When I left the Justice Department the next year, my prized possession was a personalized letter from the president, thanking me for my service to his administration.

After that, I thought my brush with the 40th President of the United States would never be repeated. But I was wrong.

A few years later, in 1993, as a communications consultant in Washington, I was hired to write, produce, and direct a television special highlighting the work of the Horatio Alger Association — a charitable group that gives scholarships to poor teens by honoring the achievements of Americans who achieved greatness despite a childhood of poverty.

The association had a long list of famous people who could be asked to host the program I was producing, including luminaries like Oprah Winfrey, Bob Hope, and Carol Burnett. As my eyes scanned the impressive roster of personalities and world-class leaders, I stopped on one and said, "Ronald Reagan, let's ask him."

We were unsure if the former president would be willing to devote the time necessary to host a half-hour television program, but we agreed to try. Within several days, we got the word — Ronald Reagan had said "yes."

The weeks of preparing for the taping were a blur, but the most rewarding part was writing the script. I had seen and read hundreds of Reagan speeches, so I knew his style by heart. And as I wrote the script, I did my very best to give it that Reagan panache.

When I arrived at President Reagan's office in Los Angeles to tape his portion of the program, I was nervous. But as soon as he strolled into the room, he put me and my entire crew at ease with his easy-going style and brimming humor.

As he began to read my script, I watched him on the television monitor, even though he was sitting just four feet away from me. For a moment, I was transfixed. His delivery was near-perfect and the heart and emotion of his delivery made the words I had written dance and dash with extra meaning. I was truly in awe.

But beyond his talent on camera, I was taken in by his genial, even humble demeanor. I was no one special to him, but he gave me the greatest deference and kindness. Sadly, all too often, people who achieve high positions become rude or surly with those around them. But Ronald Reagan was a shining exception to that rule. He was a genuinely decent man.

When I left his office that day, I knew right then that I had reached the single pinnacle of my professional career. It was unforgettable.

For years, the signed photo of that event has occupied a special place in my office and hundreds of visitors have admired it. In my career advising elected officials and serving in government, I've found myself reaching for the touchstone of Reagan's philosophies. I've attended hundreds of events where his achievements were remembered and feted.

And, as the man in the Justice Department had predicted, I'm still active in the Reagan Administration Alumni Association.

When I learned of President Reagan's passing, my heart grew heavy. Although he has been mercifully released from the bonds of his Alzheimer's disease, there is no escaping the fact that our nation has suffered a great loss.

As I told my two small children about the passing of this great man, I wanted them to understand what he meant to me, what he meant to all of us. My ungainly words didn't inspire them much, but it's my fervent hope that, eventually, President Reagan's legacy will.

The more that's written about our 40th president, the more we see his wisdom and his innate sense of goodness. For much of his career, he wrote his own speeches and those sentiments show his mastery of the nature of the American spirit, as well as his steadfast faithfulness to his core principles.

Though his deeds have now ended, his spirit endures. His words and ideas ring across the nation and the world, inspiring new generations straining the yoke of government overseers.

Simply put, Americans believe in Ronald Reagan because he believed in them.

In a 1983 speech, President Reagan told us: *"I believe in you, and I believe if we work together, then one day we will say 'we fought the good fight. We finished the race. We kept the faith.' And to our children's children, we can say, 'We did all that could be done in the brief time that was given us here on Earth.'"*

Now, 21 years later, those words remind us of the great debt we owe to this great man. He fought the good fight. He finished the race.

He kept the faith. And he did all that could be done in the brief time he was given here on Earth.

CHAPTER 41

20 years later, let's remember the victim of this horrific crime

In the late 1990s, as the Deputy Attorney General of Ohio, I dealt with many cases involving the death penalty. This brought me and our office much press coverage, given that Ohio hadn't executed anyone since the early 1960s. Indeed, on the night of the first execution, I had to be at work until well after midnight. The public scrutiny on my role as the face of the Attorney General's office and one of the state lawyers involved led local authorities to put a police watch on my house that night, as my wife and young children were home alone and potentially at risk.

Although I became familiar with more than 100 murderers then on Ohio's Death Row, there was one case that stuck with me. That's why I wrote the op-ed below. After the major daily newspaper in Akron published it, the sheriff who investigated the child's murder wrote me a personal note thanking me for keeping the victim's memory alive. I still have that note and will always treasure the role I played in helping the child's family reach some level of closure.

PUBLISHED: *Akron Beacon Journal* — July 17, 2002

I n a few months, people all across Ohio will know the name Robert Buell. His execution is set for September. People on both sides of the death penalty issue will invoke his name to make their respective points. What a shame.

216 • MARK R. WEAVER

At least today, we should all remember Krista Lea Harrison.

Twenty years ago, Robert Buell stalked a neighborhood park in rural Wayne County and saw his prey — 11-year-old Krista Lea Harrison. She was in the park just across the street from her house, collecting aluminum cans for recycling.

The details are too horrible to recount, but the evidence clearly proved that Buell kidnapped, brutally raped, and then strangled her. Thanks to the hard work of local police and prosecutors, he was found guilty and sentenced to death.

I served as Deputy Attorney General during the first term of Attorney General Betty Montgomery. In that job, I often dealt with death penalty appeals. I worked on many different cases, but the tragic death of this innocent schoolgirl has stayed with me more than any other.

Over the last several years, the brutal violation of little Krista Lea has been eclipsed by the whines and excuses of her murderer. After his conviction, courts gave him the benefit of the doubt and reviewed his repeated legal claims. Then every single court dismissed those frivolous appeals.

All too often, such legal maneuvering has nothing to do with guilt and innocence and everything to do with gaming the system and buying more time. The defense attorneys who oppose the death penalty point the finger of blame everywhere — except where it belongs.

As a result, dozens of Ohio death row inmates have cases that are literally stuck in the court system — not moving an inch for two years or more at a time. In many of these cases, the killers have spent thousands of days on death row, chuckling as their case files gather dust in court filing cabinets.

Although I learned the legal concepts of the death penalty appeals system years ago, the practical reality of it became real to me in 1996 when I toured Death Row.

Deep inside Ohio's maximum-security prison in Mansfield, I walked down long hallways and was buzzed through several locked doors. Eventually, I was ushered into one of the five Death Row pods.

Each prisoner is locked down in a single cell. The cells feature a thick steel door with a small window at eye level.

The warden escorted me into one of the pods and invited me to walk around. Since each door was locked, I decided to peer into one of the many cells before me. Choosing randomly, I walked toward the cell closest to me, and as I approached, I felt a slight chill.

There was a name stenciled in black paint on the cell door. Robert Buell. I had spent many hours going over his file. I knew his crimes well.

I continued forward and peeked in the window. In the muted shadows of the tiny cell sat a small, frail man reading a magazine. He looked up at me for a moment. Our eyes met.

Every detail of his crimes flashed through my mind in an instant. I turned away.

For the rest of my tour, I was subdued. The run-in I had with Buell seemed strangely coincidental to me.

As I left the prison, I accidently took a different route on the way home. Since I had never driven that road before, I was somewhat surprised to see a sign pointing the way to Marshallville. That's because Marshallville was the little hamlet where Buell began his deadly deed. I'd never been that way and never seen the town before. But fate set me on the precise roads Buell must have driven on the day of his horrific crimes.

Marshallville is a small rural town. The homes sport friendly front porches and hand-painted signs that proclaim the identity of the local high school athletes who live there.

I took the turn for Marshallville and drove quietly past the park where Krista Lea saw her last few moments of peace. As I drove home, I was saddened recalling that her parents still lived across the street from that park and can see it from their front picture window.

Becoming so familiar with cases like this was one of the hardest parts of the job.

Law school taught me to understand the arguments on both sides of the death penalty debate. But Krista Lea Harrison and Robert Buell taught me the real lessons.

The death penalty appeals process has become a sham. It's a system that rewards creativity of defense lawyers who, time and time again, concoct outrageous reasons for yet another meritless legal motion.

Every convicted criminal has an absolute right to appeal. We all must respect and defend that right. But the process has gotten well out of hand.

Death penalty cases should be scrutinized carefully so an innocent man is never put to death. That's called due process of law, and our Constitution requires it.

But due process requires action. Any legitimate questions about a case should be examined and then resolved. And once guilt is no longer in doubt, the death penalty must be carried out.

Such is the case with Robert Buell.

Whether you agree with the death penalty or not, you certainly must agree that our system loses credibility when we fail to follow through on the sentences meted out by courts.

And all of us — death penalty supporters and opponents alike — ought to take a moment today to remember the person behind this tragedy — Krista Lea Harrison.

CHAPTER 42

A citizen's guide to uncovering government information

As a lawyer, I practice in many areas. One main focus is the law surrounding what records citizens can review at their local or state government office. I've written several handbooks on this topic and have taught the subject to thousands of government leaders.

An Ohio magazine asked me to write an article that might help people understand how this area of law affects them. This piece seeks to explain complicated legal concepts in a way that people who are unfamiliar with the topic could easily understand. This requires rethinking what words to use, finding analogies that might make sense, and remembering that jargon is the sworn enemy of clear communications.

PUBLISHED: Ohio State Bar Association magazine — October 2002

There's a lot of interesting information you can obtain from state and local government — if you know how the public records law works.

Want to know how much your child's teacher is paid? No problem.

Interested to find out the names and addresses of the registered sex offenders in your county? Easy.

Would you like to peruse the publicly-funded cell phone bill of your local elected official? Piece of cake.

The key to unlocking access to this information and more is Ohio's Public Records Act. But before you learn the details, a little history lesson is in order.

When our founding fathers separated from Great Britain, one of their concerns was the way King George blocked access to government records. By drafting the Declaration of Independence and the Constitution, our original leaders intended that government information would be owned by the people and accessible to the people.

Two centuries later, Ohio's government leaders still subscribe to this important principle of democracy. State lawmakers gave us a law — the Public Records Act — that allows citizens to inspect or copy most state and local government records. The federal government has a similar law, called the Freedom of Information Act. But it allows much less access to information than Ohio's law.

Simply put, Ohio's law defines a public record as "a record held by a public office." It could be in any form — paper, digital, a photo, a tape recording, etc. To meet that definition, the record in question must be stored on a fixed medium, created, received, or sent under the jurisdiction of a public office, and document the organization, functions, policies, decisions, procedures, operations, or other activities of the office.

When seeking access to a public record, a citizen has two basic rights. The first is the ability to promptly inspect public records and the second is to be able to receive copies of public records within a reasonable amount of time.

Here's an example of how that works.

You're interested in learning more about the people who've applied to be the police chief in your city. The resumes of these people clearly meet the definition of a public record. Just go to the city building and ask to look at or get a copy of each resume.

By asking to inspect, you won't have to pay anything. By asking for a copy, you can be charged for the actual cost of making the copy — and no more. For example, any copy cost of more than five cents per page is suspect. Asking for records to be sent electronically also can save time and money.

You won't always get access to records immediately, but the law requires the city to provide them to you promptly if you asked to inspect the records or in a reasonable amount of time if you asked for copies.

Be aware that while most records are open for review, there are some records the law keeps confidential. For example, investigation files, trade secrets, medical records, and information within the attorney-client privilege are all kept confidential. There are other categories of information that can't be accessed either.

But here's the good news for citizens — the law puts the burden on government to show that a record is not public. If you decide to challenge a government's decision to keep you from seeing a record, the government will have to show in court what law allows it to withhold the document. And in some cases, if you win, the government may have to pay your lawyer's bill.

There's one guideline that will help you discern what may or may not be available. Ohio courts have consistently ruled that records reflecting how government spends tax money are public records. It's your money and you have the right to track how that money is used.

Interested in learning more about how to access public records? The Ohio Attorney General's office publishes a helpful guide to this area of the law. The "Yellow Book," as we call it, will provide you with an easy-to-understand explanation of the law, as well as a summary of many court cases that interpret the laws.

No government official enforces the Public Records Act. If you want to bring a lawsuit, you can start by filing a Petition for Writ of Mandamus in your Common Pleas court, Appeals Court, or the Ohio Supreme Court. It's best to get a qualified lawyer to help you with this, but many people do bring these cases on their own.

Few people ever bother to seek out government information. If you decide that you want to try, the Ohio Public Records Act gives you much support. The key is to know your rights, be persistent and allow a reasonable time for the government office to respond. Good luck.

CHAPTER 43

Parents who leave kids alone in hot cars should go to jail

After reading too many articles about parents leaving their children to die inside hot cars, I decided someone ought to step forward and say what many people think but are afraid to say to grieving parents: If you forget your child in a hot car and the child dies, you need to spend some time in jail. It sounds heartless at first but, like drunk driving, sometimes being tough is the only way to get people to be much more careful.

Several major daily newspapers around the nation published my op-ed, typically after a local tragedy involving a kid suffocating in a car. Because of the multiple publications, this piece may well be the most widely-read op-ed I've ever written. It also contains one of the better word imagery I've concocted in these forums: "the liquid hiss of sprinklers quenching lawns and gardens."

PUBLISHED: *The Philadelphia Inquirer* — August 15, 2002 (as well as newspapers in Minneapolis, Atlanta, Los Angeles, and others)

Across America, the traditional sounds of summer are all around us. The sharp crack of a baseball hit right down the middle. The liquid hiss of sprinklers quenching lawns and gardens. The jangle of an ice cream truck making its rounds.

But amidst the chorus of these happy summer sounds, comes a terrible plea for help — the muffled screams of babies and toddlers begging to be relieved from the suffocating, hot death of an automobile interior.

A frightening prospect, to be sure. But these horrors happen again and again every summer. At least 21 children have died this year after being left in overheated cars. There have been as many as 125 heat-related deaths of children left alone in vehicles since 1995, according to Kids 'N Cars, an advocacy group dealing with issues of child safety in automobiles.

A study in the Journal of the Louisiana State Medical Society found temperatures can reach 140 degrees in vehicles even when the windows were left slightly open.

And, horribly, many more will die before the heat subsides.

In case after case, the same shocking situation occurs. A parent claims to have "forgotten" about the child in the car. Or they left the young one "just for a minute." Everyone involved calls it a "tragedy."

Tragedy, yes. But entirely preventable.

Not long ago, a similar fate befell a little girl in Philadelphia.

Local papers called it "a tragic mix-up" when the toddler was locked in her family's minivan on a hot summer day. Her parents had been out late the night before and had taken their three other children into the house and put them to bed. Little Angelika Gaines was somehow left behind overnight.

Strapped down, unable to move to save herself from the next day's unbearable heat, her screams went unanswered for hours. Her parents slept soundly. She died alone and in agony.

A family friend was quoted as saying "I don't think it was neglect. They definitely weren't that kind of people."

I disagree. Cases like this are negligence, perhaps criminal negligence.

In the law, the term negligence describes a careless act that causes injury. Typically, negligence can result in a civil judgment — meaning the careless person will have to pay money to the injured party. But there are times when negligence can be criminal in nature. Forgetting to remove a child from a simmering car may be such a case.

There's a Latin phrase used by lawyers to describe one type of negligence. *Res ipsa loquitur*, which literally means "the thing speaks for itself." In my view, that means there are some things which are, by their very nature, negligent.

A child bakes to death because a parent is distracted. *Res ipsa loquitur*.

Being a parent is the most demanding job in the world. Most people who become parents have little idea of how difficult things will be. Particularly with young children, parenting requires constant vigilance.

Forgetting your small child for several hours is by no means a reasonable action. No matter how tired a parent is, no matter how distracted by other events or problems, the top priority of a mother or father must be the physical safety of their children.

This concept seems to be lost on those who view these deaths as mere accidents. This is tragic, considering the fact that this happens more than most people could ever imagine. A search of a computerized database of news stories shows more than five dozen children who died after being trapped in car seats inside hot cars. And that's just over the past few years.

In each of these cases, the children died horrible deaths. The coroner reports describe a level of unspeakable suffering that makes one weep to even contemplate. One little girl tore her own hair out with clenched fists as she died in the misery of 130-degree heat.

This is shameful neglect. How a parent can forget where a helpless toddler or infant is for hours at a time — as if the child were a set of keys routinely misplaced — is beyond any rational understanding or explanation.

Even if the temperatures aren't high enough to create a danger, an unattended child in a car is a target for a multitude of evils.

In the shadow of our collective concern for school shootings, child safety has rightfully taken center stage. But school shootings are infrequent events, difficult to prevent. Children are being left alone in hot cars every week. And every one of these deaths is preventable.

After a decade of experience as a practicing attorney, I've seen state laws change to offer more protection for children. That's good news in a setting normally tinged with sadness and horror. And as a parent of two young children, I take heart from that news.

But more needs to be done. While none of us can save the children who were so cruelly left to die, all of us can remain vigilant. We can speak out and take appropriate action to save a child.

Here are some points each of us should remember:

- Don't leave a young child unattended, out of your eyesight, in a car — even if it's just for a few moments.

- If you see a young child unattended in a car, call the police.

- If your child is asleep in the car when you arrive home, bring him inside immediately — even if you're concerned he might awaken.

- Keep your car locked when it's parked — many children die each year when they sneak inside to play and are overcome by heat.

- Finally, be observant for the neglect of others. If you suspect any sort of child abuse or neglect, call your local child welfare office.

People who aren't willing to give laser-like focus to the physical well-being of their children simply shouldn't have children. And those who seriously neglect their children should go to jail.

CHAPTER 44

No help on the way to end Ohio's "judicial emergency"

I've written before about how federal judgeships are filled. And the issue of leaving judicial vacancies unfilled for too long, without good reason, is one worthy of debate. In the early days of George W. Bush's first term as president, there were judicial vacancies in Ohio that slowed the pace of federal appeals. I decided to use my experience at the Justice Department to lend a different perspective to the debate about moving those nominations. I also felt moved to write because one of the nominees (Jeff Sutton) was a friend and colleague of mine in the Ohio Attorney General's office.

Successfully pitching this op-ed required timing the submission to relate to the peak of the public discussion. I've often had to move quickly to write and submit something to a newspaper before the issue grew stale or before another op-ed writer made the same point in the target publication.

PUBLISHED: *The Newark Advocate* — September 24, 2001

Former U.S Attorney General Bobby Kennedy reminded us that "justice delayed is democracy denied." Unless the U.S. Senate acts quickly to confirm the 11 men and women appointed by President Bush to serve on some of our nation's highest courts, Kennedy's words may prove to be true. And, here in Ohio, we are particularly at risk.

Two Ohioans — former State Solicitor Jeff Sutton and Ohio Supreme Court Justice Deborah Cook — were nominated to serve on the Sixth Circuit Court of Appeals. This is Ohio's only federal appeals court.

According to the agency that helps manage federal courts, Ohio's federal court of appeals has been under "judicial emergency" for several months — because there aren't enough judges to hear the cases already waiting. In fact, it's gotten so bad that the chief judge of our federal appeals court must regularly call judges from far-away states and plead with them to volunteer their time to hear Ohio cases that are backlogged.

It doesn't have to be that way. Mr. Sutton and Justice Cook are extremely qualified and ready to serve on this court, but they are still waiting to be confirmed by the U.S. Senate. The president nominated judges who will focus on interpreting the law accurately, respect the appropriately limited role of the judicial branch and practice judicial restraint.

Justice Deborah Cook is one of the Ohio Supreme Court's most outstanding scholars. After serving as the first female partner of Akron's oldest law firm, she served with distinction on the Ohio Court of Appeals. Since being elected to the state Supreme Court in 1994, she has emerged as a thoughtful and well-reasoned justice.

Former Ohio State Solicitor Jeff Sutton is one of the best-known appellate litigators in Ohio. He's argued several cases in the United States Supreme Court and is best known in Ohio for representing the state in the landmark school funding lawsuit. His skills in legal writing were honed in one of the most prestigious legal assignments in America — as a law clerk to two different U.S. Supreme Court Justices.

Now that they've been nominated to serve on the Sixth Circuit, these two exceptional attorneys ought to be sworn in as soon as possible — to help remedy the inexcusable backlog of cases. But unfortunately, that's unlikely to happen anytime soon.

Over the last several years, the confirmation process for federal judges has been over-politicized and more focused on partisanship than statesmanship. All too often, the confirmation hearings have little to do with the merits of the person sitting before the committee.

America saw that exact problem on display 15 years ago, when the Senate rejected the nomination of Robert Bork to the high court. Experts on both sides of the political spectrum agreed that Bork's academic and judicial credentials were stellar, but many Democrats didn't agree with some of the results of Bork's judicial decisions. They used the political process to demonize Judge Bork and his nomination was doomed. Because of that embarrassing spectacle, the process for judicial nomination has become little more than a political food fight.

That national problem has a real-life impact on Ohio. That's because when the inside-the-beltway crowds begin their petty political games, the cases and crimes heard in our federal courthouse grind to a crawl.

Each of us is entitled to our day in court. But because of the judicial emergency in our federal appeals court, Ohioans are more likely than residents of other states to see their cases delayed. That makes the stalling of the nominations of Mr. Sutton and Justice Cook even more troubling.

It's my hope that speedy senate review and confirmation of these respected legal scholars will allow backlogged and delayed cases to begin moving through Ohio's federal court of appeals.

"Vacancies cannot remain at such high levels indefinitely without eroding the quality of justice," Supreme Court Chief Justice William Rehnquist wrote three years ago.

The chief justice's words remain true today. Each of us is affected when one of our courts is in a judicial emergency. Let's hope the U.S. Senate will respond to our dire need with prompt action.

CHAPTER 45

Technology and politics
— a 'Net gain

It's hard to believe it today, but the internet was a new thing to politics in 2000. Because I was teaching a graduate course in Advanced Campaign Management, I was aware of what were then the latest in technologies used by political campaigns. The daily newspaper in Dayton, Ohio, agreed to publish a column explaining some of that early technology.

In this essay, you'll see how I adapted the use of less formal, shorter sentences to impart a more modern feel to the topic. This is a good reminder that it's OK to break some of your eighth-grade English teacher's writing rules. Particularly in a more creative piece, these diversions from the norm can help the reader understand your point better.

Also, note my use of "camel case" for web addresses. This allows readers to see and remember the URL. For one word addresses like apple.com, it's not really needed. But as more domain addresses take the form of two- and three-word combinations, capitalizing the first letter of each word is preferable. The letters go up and down like the humps on a camel's back, hence the term "camel case."

The example I often use for my students is the need for camel case for Pen Island, a company that sells pens. With camel case, their web address is PenIsland.com. Without it, it's penisland.com. With that offbeat example bouncing around your head, maybe you'll remember why camel case is so important!

PUBLISHED: *Dayton Daily News* — 2000

Most Ohioans are enjoying their summer days with little thought of the electoral season looming ahead. But now that the political parties are beginning their nominating conventions, hundreds of campaign operatives are sequestered indoors, hunched over computers, hoping to secure your vote in November.

Make no mistake about it — if you resist the tug of new technology, you might be relegating yourself to membership in the new American Know-Nothing Party. If you insist, you can still struggle to obtain information about candidates, campaigns, and congressional cash through the tried and true ways of old.

But those who rebuff techno-phobia and accept new media will become more informed, more quickly. And more informed voters can only lead to better self-government.

You can start on this journey right now.

A website called PseudoPolitics.com will have "you-are-there" cameras located throughout the meeting halls at both major party conventions. Internet users will choose what camera angle they want to see at any time, giving them full control over what they see and hear. As voters realize the potential or tech like this, politicians won't be far behind.

Candidates now realize that grassroots campaigning must include outreach to the millions of Americans on the internet. According to a University of Pennsylvania study released last month, more families now have some form of internet subscription (52%) than a newspaper subscription (42%).

As a result, entire warehouses of political data are now available to anyone with a willing mind and a working modem.

Want to find out whether your congressman is taking money from corporate polluters?

Click. Gotcha.

Want to watch an entire U.S. Senate hearing on campaign finance reform? Click. Click. Zzzzzzzz.

Want to donate to the candidate of your choice?

Click. Click. Click. Ka-ching!

The wealth of detailed political data available for use by campaigns is stunning to consider.

Go to OpenSecrets.org and you can find out which presidential wannabe has the most donations from Dayton zip code 45423 (Bush, by a two-to-one margin).

Go to OhioCitizen.org and you can uncover the largest political donation in Ohio history ($515,000 from the Ohio Democratic Party to 1998 gubernatorial candidate Lee Fisher).

Go to SmartVoter.org to review the background and experience of your local candidates.

Indeed, the political information available on the internet will have increased significantly — just by the time you're finished reading this newspaper!

More information requires more citizen scrutiny. And inattentive voters (a rapidly growing species that flourishes in the current American political habitat) must change their observation habits or their habitat will become endangered and representative democracy may become extinct.

The next generation understands this. And they are already building the campaign infrastructure of tomorrow.

I teach a graduate course in Advanced Campaign Management. Each year, I end up devoting more class time and additional readings to internet campaigning.

Recently, I assigned these graduate students the task of building an entire functional website for a fictional political campaign. They had to build it from scratch, fill it with effective and persuasive content and make it look professional. The students were initially apprehensive at such an intimidating project, as many of them didn't know a mouse from a modem.

Lucky for them, an innovator in internet politics, CampaignOf-
fice.com, donated a website to the class. Choosing from dozens of different designs, and tweaking the user-friendly controls, my class soon
built an extensive and attractive political website. The students didn't
have to write programming code, understand HTML editing, or have
any advanced computer skills. The easy-to-understand interface let
them concentrate on adding features that would attract and persuade
potential supporters.

The result earned them an "A" and reminded me that the internet
will only grow as a political force. A company like CampaignOf-
fice.com allows campaigns at every level to have a professional-looking
website. As a result, more and more candidates will choose the internet to communicate with voters.

Websites such as these allow candidates to communicate 24 hours
a day, sign up volunteers electronically, and even raise money without
making a single phone call.

And this burst of digital democracy doesn't have to be lacking in
fun.

Political websites also can be a source of humor. One South Carolina candidate's web page suggests that he's "not your typical politician." To prove his point, his home page offers a downloadable web
poster of himself, pictured with his young child, noting that he
"changes diapers on command" and "takes out the trash if reminded
by his wife."

As creative internet applications like this increase, so too will the
relevance of cyber-campaigning. What does this mean for the average
voter? For those who partake, it means better information about candidates, enhanced access to government officials and an unparalleled
ability to build truly democratic coalitions.

Those who ignore this trend will someday be remembered as the
21st Century Flat Earth Society. Because, from now on, elections will
be virtually unprecedented.

CHAPTER 46

A peek behind partisan lines in the political wars

Advising politicians has given me the chance to know them well. During the years of Bill Clinton's presidency, America was debating the morality of politicians and I thought it was an opportune time to draw back the curtain and let voters know more about the foibles of candidates. While I started the op-ed with a look at some of the less scrupulous examples of politicians at work, my final point was that people in politics are probably no better or worse than any other profession.

My files do not show which newspaper ran this piece. I still chuckle when I read the line: "Our car ride to the television station was a little bumpy, but the real jolts were just ahead."

PUBLISHED: Circa 1994

A s a media consultant, I often accompany clients to TV appearances, suggesting strategies for communicating their chosen message. One day, I was advising a candidate on the way to a live television interview.

This officeholder was quite vocal in his opposition to "dial-a-porn" telephone lines. He'd made quite a name for himself, railing against the telephone company's policy of providing pay-for-sex phone lines. Our car ride to the television station was a little bumpy, but the real jolts were just ahead.

"Who else will be on the show with you today?" I asked, as we neared the station and began searching for a parking place. "Well, I wanted to talk to you about that," the candidate replied slowly.

"The producer told me a phone company representative will be on the show to argue the other side of the issue," he said.

"Super!" I retorted. "It should make for great live television."

We had just squeezed into a parking spot when he dropped the bomb. "Do you think the phone company keeps records of people who call phone sex lines?" he asked, avoiding my gaze.

I told him I wasn't sure. Then it hit me.

"Why do you ask?" I asked.

This guardian of public morality stammered out a sordid tale involving some late nights when he had called phone sex lines. And he wasn't researching the issue. The public opponent of phone sex was an avid consumer in private.

After removing my jaw from the sidewalk (I was a little less jaded then) I recovered and helped him dream up some possible responses in case the ticklish subject was raised. I settled on some vague counter attacks which would accuse the phone company spokesman of violating the right to privacy. We held our breaths and walked into the studio — him looking a little relieved, me feeling a little stunned.

Lucky for him, the subject was never raised, and afterward, he stopped highlighting his stand on the phone sex issue.

This wasn't an isolated incident. I've advised politicians with all kinds of peculiar behavior.

One was often befuddled as to which way to vote on certain legislation and would call me at all hours to ask for instructions.

Another drank so much that his participation in our late-night strategy meetings became little more than barely coherent tirades against our opponent.

I'll never forget one government wannabe who took me home to meet his wife, then a few hours later, at a neighborhood bar, casually introduced me to his two girlfriends.

One politician whom I knew (but, thankfully, never worked for) was so drunk at a public meeting he thought nothing of urinating against a wall adjacent to the building's exit while people left.

Are all politicians like this? Absolutely not. Most are rather normal. Many are the same upstanding citizens they appear to be.

I once advised a war hero who spent six years withstanding deprivation and torture in a North Vietnamese POW camp. He also earned the Medal of Honor for his air to combat heroics before he was captured. And he offered an inspiring positive outlook in his political campaigns. With him, there was no sign of any of the shenanigans for which other politicians have become notorious.

Some politicians are good. Others, not so much. But you knew that already. The larger question is, as the personal lives of politicians receive more scrutiny by the media, does the public have the right to know about the personal peccadillos of political candidates and office holders?

As someone who's worked in hundreds of political campaigns and advised officials at every government level, I've concluded that while there may be a limited right to know some things, that focus is all wrong.

The problem lays more in voters' perceptions than it does in the failings of candidates.

It's been written that each voter has a portrait gallery in his head — each featuring portraits of good guys, bad guys, trustworthy people, untrustworthy people, and other such broad-brush caricatures. Unknowingly, voters compare political candidates to these pictures in an attempt to categorize them.

Thanks in large part to media stories about Bill Clinton's well-documented womanizing, George H.W. Bush's son's legal troubles, and Ross Perot's reported penchant for hiring private investigators, voters have become disenchanted with our nation's electoral fare. This tendency is a natural reaction, yet it's part of the problem today. Voters are eager for someone who doesn't fit the profile of a sleazy politician.

This is one reason why there's an increase in interest for women candidates this year. Voters compare women candidates with their various portraits in their mind and don't find an easy match. Thus, women candidates appear more change-oriented — whether it's true or not.

I've advised several women candidates and, as a rule, they're no better or worse than men candidates, so this game of subconsciously matching candidates to preconceived notions is ineffective.

Political candidates typically don't have any more skeletons in their closets than pipe fitters, stockbrokers, or even lawyers. But since candidates use such extended rhetoric and hard-sell tactics to sway voters, people expect a lot out of them. Then they are ultimately disappointed and become cynical when flaws emerge.

The most often heard argument to this point is that "politicians should be held to a higher standard." However, this viewpoint is incongruent with the political system envisioned by our founding fathers.

These men believed in government tended by citizen legislators. Just plain folks. They asserted that when officeholders use government funds or act on behalf of the people, they should be held to a higher standard. But the examples I cited before are from their private lives. Requiring a private life standard for politicians higher than that which we set for ourselves is moralistic, self-defeating, and downright stupid.

People who live in glass republics shouldn't throw stones.

Rather than looking for some prurient personal problem when sorting out candidates, it's far better to look for someone who believes in something.

Ronald Reagan is a perfect example. He believed what he said. Whether people agreed with him or not, they didn't question his devotion to his ideology. In fact, a perceived lack of a clear philosophy is one of the underlying causes of the defeat of President Bush in 1992.

When looking over candidates for this year's election, look for a core belief in a philosophy matching your own. If this doesn't work, try to identify significant changes in a candidate's position made for obvious political purpose.

We all change our mind sometimes. But a politician four square in favor of something at one point and in full reverse later merits closer scrutiny.

Don't rush too quickly down this path, or you'll be fooled. Media gurus often produce "flip-flop" TV ads that purport to show how an opposing candidate has switched his position. The alleged flip-flop is usually just a contrast between two votes on two different versions of a given proposal. To really find a flip-flop, voters should look past such commercials and examine trends in the candidate's voting record.

Rejecting the scandal approach so often put forth by the media is the first step toward rational voting decisions. The next step is learning more about the real candidate — not the person you see for a few moments on TV each night.

After a while, you'll stop thinking the worst of politicians. You'll realize some are scum. Some are harmless blowhards. But it's likely there are just as many personal scandals on your block as there are in Congress. The increased focus on personal problems is an unhealthy trend that we can beat if we try.

CHAPTER 47

President Clinton should know better

As a Justice Department spokesman, I conducted high-profile media interviews, defended the work of the attorney general and federal prosecutors, and took an average of 50 press calls a day. The work was challenging, high profile, and required me to think on my feet.

I have great memories of working there and, as a result, I feel a sense of loyalty to the department as an institution. That's why I still defend the department against those who seek to unfairly undermine its mission.

Shortly after Bill Clinton was elected president, he hastily chose two poorly qualified people for the job of U.S. Attorney General. Seeing these appointments as something that could hurt the prestige of the Justice Department, I wrote this op-ed to make my feelings known. I was not the only one to speak out on the weakness of these two nominees, and President Clinton was soon forced to withdraw both nominations.

In this op-ed, you'll also note my use of a colorful metaphor — "the Flying Wallendas," a well-known family of high-wire acrobats at the time. A well-chosen metaphor can add punch to an essay or speech. Finding one that's not overused can take time, but the effort will be worth it.

My files don't show which newspaper ran the piece but it was likely The Newark Advocate.

PUBLISHED: February 1993

Bill Clinton may still believe in a place called Hope, but for thousands of career prosecutors and law enforcement officials in the Justice Department, there's little hope that Clinton's new attorney general will be anything other than a hastily chosen payback to the special interests that helped elect him.

During the campaign, Clinton constantly told America that if we only had the "courage to change," things would get better in Washington. The selection of federal Judge Kimba Wood as his attorney general designate de jour proves that little courage — and even less change — is emanating from the Clinton White House.

Judge Wood's nomination was halted late last Friday after it became apparent that — like Zoe Baird before her — she too failed to learn the basics of immigration law while attending law school. Wood clung to a technicality to explain away her hiring of an illegal alien, but the appearance of impropriety stuck.

Many Americans don't remember that Clinton had promised us "the most ethical administration in the history of the republic." The overall ethics of his cabinet selections to date have been questionable, but the process Clinton is using to select the person who will lead all federal prosecutions and oversee the FBI, Drug Enforcement Administration, and Immigration and Naturalization Service has been the political equivalent of a bad "Saturday Night Live" sketch.

In the context of this unraveling Clinton embarrassment, it's helpful to remember that soon after President George H.W. Bush appointed Clarence Thomas to the Supreme Court, the Democratic drumbeats of dissent began. "This is not the most qualified person for such an important job" was the mantra heard from Democrats as well as most liberal-leaning pundits.

Fast forward several months later. With Bill Clinton now in the White House, the standard of searching for the most qualified person has suddenly changed. Because Clinton promised feminist groups he would name several women to cabinet positions, he opted for expediency over experience and pander over preparation.

While several women are qualified to serve as attorney general, few legal experts would have placed either Baird or Wood at the top of the list. For reasons known only to Clinton, he bypassed those more qualified and instead chose two relative neophytes to oversee federal law enforcement.

But the advocates for qualifications and merit of 1991 are noticeably mute in 1993. There's little or no public debate about the fact that Clinton's Justice Department choices wouldn't make anyone's "most qualified" list.

Clinton wouldn't have had to look very far to find a top-notch woman. In fact, several top career prosecutors at the Justice Department are women. To name just one, Civil Rights Section Chief Linda Davis is one of the toughest prosecutors in the department — she or any other leading career prosecutor would have made a better choice than Baird or Wood. And at least current Justice Department officials have already passed the scrutiny of an FBI background investigation.

By limiting the choices for this key domestic policy post to only women, Clinton cheats the Justice Department as well as the country. Americans don't like quotas and if Clinton is truly in touch with the people, he should know that. At a time when crime rates are rising, drug use is proliferating, and Americans are demanding more from law enforcement agencies, the attorney general needs to be the best person for the job and not the person who will fulfill whatever partisan debt Clinton might owe.

Clinton's political promise reveals his disdain for the Justice Department and its historic role as the one federal agency where senior officials are chosen more for their legal ability and less for their membership in a particular interest group. Not since Lyndon Johnson's appointment of Ramsey Clark has such little disregard been shown for our country's top legal post.

President Clinton's credibility has already worn thin in many areas. A poll commissioned by NBC News recently found that more than a third of Americans don't think Clinton can live up to his word.

Since November, Clinton's political flip-flops have made the "Flying Wallendas" look like amateurs. He changed his stance on the Haitian boat people. He promised, and then quickly forgot his 100-day legislative plan. He faked toward normalizing relations with Iraq, then button-hooked away from the idea. And he quickly abandoned his much-heralded middle-class tax cut. These persistent missteps and blunders only add to his credibility gap.

On the fifth floor of the Department of Justice building, just down from the attorney general's office, portraits hang displaying the people who've led the department. But a few portraits can't be found there. To see Watergate-era Attorney General John Mitchell and the aforementioned Ramsey Clark you must go to the furthest reaches of the building. Their discredited reigns relegated them to an out-of-the-way corner that reporters dubbed "the hall of shame."

President Clinton has the opportunity to appoint an attorney general destined for a rightful place in the main hall. But if he continues with the process he's already started, it's likely that Mitchell and Clark will have some company in a few years.

My advice to the new president is this: If you want to instill confidence among the Americans who expect the Justice Department to be above the normal political fray, limit your attorney general choices to men and women who have been career prosecutors at the state and federal levels. Don't administer litmus tests. Pick someone who knows how to manage, lead, and prosecute.

Oh, and one more thing. Find someone who took and passed immigration law.

CHAPTER 48

Despite his passing, legacy of this community leader remains

One of my earliest clients was Jon Fox, who went on to several elected positions, including United States Congressman. The office where Jon and I worked was in the office pavilion named after the Fox family. In fact, many of the prominent places in my community had been touched by the Fox family. When the patriarch of the Fox family died, I wrote this op-ed as a tribute to him.

Other than learning more about someone who led an interesting life, this piece can help you understand the emotional writing style that can enliven an account of someone's life. Listing accomplishments and citing to dates of service comes off as clinical and rather pedestrian. Each of us lives a life of wonder. When you're recounting the highlights of that wonder after a loved one's passing, ponder the impact beyond the statistics. Who was better off because this person walked among us? How was the world different? Using that prompt and reviewing this essay may help you draft a send-off that will give the rest of us a brief yet bright glimpse of the soul that has moved beyond our view.

PUBLISHED: Montgomery Newspapers (Pennsylvania) — 1990

I t seems disquieting to see the bright lights that adorn the trees in front of the Fox Pavilion in Jenkintown and know that Bill Fox is no longer there to light them.

William Laub Fox, the creative force behind that and many other well-known area structures, a man who truly loved life, died last week at the age of 75.

He lived life to the fullest as an attorney, real estate developer, and broadcast pioneer. And he recorded it brilliantly as an accomplished oil painter.

Bill Fox often said, *"Never miss an opportunity to do a good deed or say a kind word."* And he never did.

In large part, I owe my career as an attorney to one of the many good deeds Bill Fox performed. Despite my longtime association and friendship with Bill's son, Jon, it was Bill's encouragement that crystallized my desire to attend law school.

After four years of working two jobs during the day and going to law school at night, the dream Bill Fox helped spark in me was realized: I graduated and became an attorney.

Bill Fox was a success at nearly everything he did. And as he did with me, he gave people the ability to believe in themselves; enough for them to be successes, too.

His magic worked for me. His advice will live with me always. The example he set will serve as a beacon of sustenance.

Those of us who were lucky enough to know Bill Fox could only hope to emulate his example. But those who didn't know Bill Fox can still appreciate his legacy.

Next time you enjoy a television program on channel 29, think of Bill Fox. He founded the station.

Next time you're listening to FM radio and you appreciate the music or conversation happening at 103.9 on your radio dial, think of Bill Fox. He started that radio station and hosted a broadcast on it for 25 years.

Next time you visit the Abington Art Center or the Cheltenham Art Center and enjoy the works on display, think of Bill Fox. His devotion on behalf of those places helped make the inspiration and beauty of art more attainable to so many people.

Next time you're shopping in the Fox Pavilion and you notice the detail and uniqueness of the design, think of Bill Fox. He planned and built that building, as well as the Benson Manor Apartments, the Benson East Apartments, the Foxcroft Square Apartments and the old Lord & Taylor building.

And finally, next time you read about state Rep. Jon Fox, or admire a deed he did, think of Bill Fox. Jon is Bill's son, and Bill was Jon's role model.

These accomplishments will be with us for many years to come. And the spirit of Bill Fox will stay with the thousands of people whose lives were touched by the divine ways of this quiet man.

Bill Fox inspired me in more ways than just encouraging me to go to law school. The law requires each new lawyer to have his bar membership moved by someone who is already an attorney. Traditionally, each graduating law student chooses a lawyer he admires to move his bar admission. Last year I was proud to be admitted to the Pennsylvania Bar on the motion of Bill Fox.

As I visited with Bill and his wife, Elainne, after he admitted me that day, I listened carefully as Bill gave me timeless counsel.

"You're an attorney now," he told me. "And you'll be able to do many good things. But don't lose track of what's important."

He paused for a moment to let his words sink in. And as the late afternoon sun poured into Bill and Elainne's apartment, surrounded by the many oil paintings Bill had created, I noticed Bill beaming at his baby granddaughter as she gurgled at him with a look of glee. His hand reached out and held Elainne's.

I knew just what he meant.

CHAPTER 49

Preparing for the most feared news interview: The ambush

Much of my work involves preparing government leaders, university presidents, and business executives for news interviews. Through the years, I've worked with tens of thousands of people on this topic.

Most of my clients approach media encounters with great trepidation. What frightens them most is the rare but dangerous "ambush inter-view," where a TV reporter pops up unannounced and starts pelting them with hostile (and sometimes unfair) questions. Everyone who deals with the news media needs to be prepared for this most difficult of encounters.

Because many of my clients are police chiefs, I wrote this piece for a magazine tailored to them. My file does not show a publishing date but this would have been around 2009.

PUBLISHED: Ohio Chiefs of Police Magazine

T housands of years ago, Cro-Magnon Man experienced the rush of "fight or flight" adrenaline when he noticed a saber-toothed tiger ready to pounce. He quickly learned that, in a few seconds, the quarry's instincts make all the difference between living to see another day and ending up as a predator's lunch.

Luckily for corporate executives and public figures in the 21st century, there are no more saber-tooth tigers out there. And dying from a carnivorous attack ranks pretty low on the probability scale. But there's another predator stalking the lobbies and parking garages of America — the rabid, sweeps-crazed TV news reporter.

Four times a year, this species goes on the hunt for allegedly crooked politicians, incompetent public officials, and evil company executives. The goal: take a premise that casts some poor downtrodden person as a victim, blame someone in authority as the villain, and trumpet the TV news team as the vindicator. All of this melodrama is then aired during the "sweeps" months where TV stations promote salacious stories to boost their ratings so that they can charge more for future advertising spots.

To be sure, some of this journalism is righteous and meritorious. But many other efforts are out and out smear jobs — either intentionally or due to journalistic incompetence. Either way, when you or your organization is in the crosshairs of a potential ambush interview, your reputation hangs in the balance.

Former presidential candidate John Edwards found this out when the National Enquirer ambushed him in the halls of a California hotel where he'd been visiting his mistress. Locking himself in a washroom wasn't the best response.

And several Wall Street CEOs learned this lesson recently, as well. Not long after the corporate and banking scandals of 2008, TV news hounds began stalking CEOs who had permitted lavish expenditures on conferences while stock prices plummeted. As they ran away from the camera, their credibility meter ran down to zero.

While the ambush interview is one of the rarest media encounters, it's certainly the most dangerous. In that respect, it's a lot like a shark attack. Most people will never experience one, but those who do need to know how to react or things will get real painful real fast.

PR trainers can teach the concept behind the response techniques to these impromptu encounters but there's simply no substitute for simulating the experience. Whenever media training lasts a day or longer, arrangements should be made to bring in a mock news crew, along with a camera, lights, microphone and an over-caffeinated reporter.

By starting the day with a mock media crisis scenario and allowing participants to create and practice possible messaging points, lunchtime or an afternoon break is an opportune time to stage the ambush. Later, video can be played back and critiqued by the instructor.

The principals who survive these types of interviews tend to have one thing in common — they were prepared and had practiced. It's important to note that success doesn't necessarily hinge on the organization having clean hands in the alleged scandal; just that the person ambushed appears to be reasonable, credible, and concerned about a resolution to the issue.

Training on these high-stress encounters should start with a thorough lecture and discussion of the foundation of the causes and conditions of these types of TV stories. The instructor should show several examples of ambush interviews and many can be found with a quick internet search. Local TV news outfits will also feature these stories during the "sweeps" period, when ratings are being monitored to help set advertising rates.

Afterward, allow the class participants to discuss how they feel about the targets of the interviews shown. They will quickly discern that principals who appear reasonable and calm are sympathetic while those who act in a belligerent manner come off as deserving of the scrutiny.

Once the group understands the importance of preparation, participants should discuss what made the person with the favorable encounter look so good or why they appeared professional or unruffled. They may notice little things like the person smiled, was genial with the reporter, agreed to be interviewed later, and didn't act in a way to merit the "villain" label. In other words, the principal looked reasonable.

In fact, the instructor should note that when the interviewee in the ambush situation acts reasonably, the encounter often won't even be aired, because it doesn't make for what news producers consider "good TV." Such a result should be the goal of the interaction — the interview is postponed to a more traditional setting where the spokesperson can be properly prepared.

There are a few basic components of a successful ambush interview response. They revolve around the strategy of trying to appear more reasonable than the reporter.

As soon as you notice the reporter, smile and walk calmly toward him or her and offer to shake hands. This sends an immediate and clear message of openness. It may also confuse the reporter, who's expecting (perhaps even hoping) to be rebuffed.

No one should ever attempt to touch the camera or block the camera lens in any way. And covering your face with a file folder or briefcase is just as bad. These are the well-known dance moves of someone who looks like they have something to hide.

It's also important to emphasize to the principals that they shouldn't ever threaten the reporter in any way. That includes any discussion concerning trespassing or private property.

Instead, remain calm and politely say that you're willing to do an interview at the office later in the day – in a more professional setting. This is a promise that must be kept or it will simply force another more hostile ambush.

Don't respond to any substantive questions, instead again offer to do an interview in a more conducive setting. If the reporter persists, the interview can be ended with this reply: "If you want to conduct a professional interview, I'd be happy to sit down with you. If you don't, then goodbye and have a good day."

During media training, it makes sense to take several opportunities to ambush the participants, even asking them questions they could easily answer at the time. The goal is to replace the impulse of "fight or flight" and replace it with the impulse of out-thinking the reporter as to who appears to be more sympathetic.

Television news reporters typically only use the ambush technique when the principal has refused or ignored previous interview requests or the reporter wants to create a dramatic encounter that will play well on screen.

In either situation, the foremost goal must be to have the principal appear more reasonable than the reporter. Implicit in this strategy is the notion that the principal will consent to an interview in a more controlled and less volatile environment. Principals who are unwilling to offer an interview will almost always fall victim to the ambush scenario.

Throughout the encounter, the principal must appear to be calm and open to inquiry. The visuals and etiquette involved are important, because most viewers will remember which of the two people (the reporter or the principal) was more rational.

In old western movies, the good guy wore a white hat and the bad guy wore a black one. This basic narrative is in play during every ambush scenario. It's important for the principal to remember that it's not enough to be the good guy; it's equally important to act like the good guy.

Most accomplished people have trouble understanding this dynamic because they are accustomed to succeeding through substance, not style. But intensive training with reality-based ambush interviews occurring throughout the day will help the principal achieve a sense of the big picture.

Follow these strategies and the outcome of your next ambush interview will be no surprise.

CHAPTER 50

Behind the scenes: My day directing Ronald Reagan

As I've discussed in a previous chapter, one of the highlights of my career was directing former President Ronald Reagan in what would be his last significant television appearance. This was the essay I wrote for my hometown paper, which devoted an entire page of the paper to the photos and essay.

PUBLISHED: Montgomery Newspapers (Pennsylvania) — 1993

"President Reagan's office called. He's agreed to host your TV program."

As a national communications consultant, I produce a lot of TV commercials. But I also produce features. And one of my clients for such work is the Horatio Alger Association.

Last year, I was hired to write, produce, and direct a video about Americans who've overcome adversity to achieve great success.

We got underway after the Disney Channel agreed to air the production. What had started out as a simple video quickly became a major network television special.

For the host, we considered Charlton Heston, Carol Burnett, Kenny Rogers, James Earl Jones, and many others. But our first choice had always been former President Ronald Reagan.

Here I am directing former President Ronald Reagan in 1993.

A bit of background. In 1988, I was a presidential appointee of President Reagan, as spokesman for the U.S. Department of Justice. I grew to be a great admirer and supporter of the president.

We submitted a request to Reagan; for weeks, we heard nothing. I diligently worked on the script and other aspects of the production and waited. Then came the phone message.

The days before flying to Los Angeles to meet with the president were a blur. I spent hours finding the best film crew and clearing each person with the Secret Service.

I had sent Reagan the script several days earlier and arranged for it to be fed into a teleprompter. Reagan clearly was a master communicator, but a half hour of lines is lot — especially for an 82-year-old man.

At the high-rise building where Reagan has his office, we were escorted by security guards to his top-floor suite, which was empty, given the early hour. I expected high-level security and a long wait to get in, but we were never searched or asked for identification. In fact, until later when President Reagan arrived, there was no sign of the Secret Service at all.

An aide showed me into Reagan's empty private office and left me alone there. It was small and sparsely appointed. There wasn't much more than a desk, some book cases, and a sitting area. I did notice a red button on the wall (to summon Secret Service in case of an emergency) and a direct phone line to the White House.

I grabbed a few props (mostly small framed photos) for the set and headed back to the conference room. I had a large crew and our low-level nervousness buzzed in the air. We checked equipment, adjusted lighting and waited.

Right on time, the former president arrived, Secret Service detail in tow. A staffer introduced him around the room and brought the former president over to me last. "This is Mark Weaver, Mr. President," the aide said. "He's the director."

"Well ... hello," he said.

I suppressed a chuckle, remembering countless times I had garnered snickers from friends and colleagues with my impression of Reagan -- always beginning with a cock of the head and a raspy, "Well..." Apparently, he often begins sentences that way.

We'd been scheduled for a half hour but it was sure to take longer. I hoped we wouldn't be asked to stop before everything was finished. Without his part, the program couldn't air.

There wasn't much to worry about. Although somewhat reserved when the camera was off, Reagan came to life when it was time to begin filming. He looked up, smiled and recited the lines as if he'd memorized them by heart.

He was a little slower and slightly hoarse with age. But it was vintage Reagan.

Between takes, he told a few stories. He didn't interact with us much, due to his hearing problems; he wears a hearing aid in each ear. But his tales drew laughs from the staff, crew, and Secret Service agents.

Early on, I leaned over to him and pointed to a life-size bust of Horatio Alger sitting on the table next to where Reagan was seated. (you can see the bust in the photo on the previous page).

"Mr. President, do you see this? That's Horatio Alger."

He did a mock double-take, paused (with perfect timing), looked at the bust and said, "Well, hello Alger!"

The room broke up.

We were well past 90 minutes when it became a "wrap." Clearly tired of sitting, Reagan bounded to his feet, shook my hand, and started to go. I could see relieved looks from his staff members, who were eager to get him back on schedule.

We engaged in some more small talk, he told a few more well-worn anecdotes and prepared to leave.

Just before he left the room, the president turned one more time to look at me. He cocked his head, gave a little wave, and showed a sparkle in his eye. And then he was gone.

Later that afternoon, I took the same crew to film another celebrity (one of the most famous men in America in his day). We needed his interview to add to the program.

The man was nice enough to me (he made a pass at my wife) but I have little or no memory of that session. Directing Ronald Reagan in what would become one of his last televised appearances was then, and still is today, the most memorable part of that day.

CHAPTER 51

"Character factor" may affect upcoming presidential races

This is the first op-ed I ever published in a major metropolitan daily newspaper, in this case the venerable Philadelphia Daily News. I was an eager consumer of political news and was following the maneuverings of which Democrats would run for president as the years of the Reagan era came to an end. The spark that moved me to write was the hypocrisy of Joe Biden bragging that he graduated at the top of his law school class — when he actually graduated at the bottom. Since I was going to law school at night, this fib struck a more personal note with me. Given that I was in the top 10 percent of my law school class then, I felt moved to write. On top of that, Biden's history of plagiarism in college, law school, and on the campaign trail was also coming to light.

This may surprise some people because, more recently, Joe Biden has developed a more mellow reputation as an elder statesman who has experienced personal tragedies in his life. But at the time of this writing, he was a strong partisan who regularly used his acerbic style to take down his opponents with a tinge of sanctimony.

I genuinely doubted the Daily News would print my piece. They had a stable of regular columnists and the paper rarely ceded space to outside voices. Autumn of that year was a low point in my young life due to some personal disappointments. When this column appeared, my mood and outlook brightened. The rush of having hundreds of thousands of people reading my words and (some of them, at least) debating my ideas was a much-needed tonic.

If you write well and raise interesting points, others will be drawn to your work and your musings may take on a life of their own.

Technology note: This op-ed was written on something called an IBM Selectric II typewriter. Millennials may want to go ask Uncle Google what that is.

PUBLISHED: *Philadelphia Daily News* — Oct. 27, 1987

As the already intense glare of the national news media increases, Democratic presidential hopefuls are quickly wilting one by one. Next fall, long after the "sleaze factor," "gender gap," and other such current presidential predictors have been forgotten, voters will cast their ballots based, in part, on the "character factor."

The emergence of this issue in recent times can best be traced to the failed vice-presidential candidacy of former U.S. Rep. Geraldine Ferraro. She was hailed as the variable that would take America by storm and propel her and running mate Walter Mondale to the White House.

But as soon as Ferraro was chosen from a long line of diverse contenders — including, I think, an Eskimo and an Ancient Aztec — she was being investigated for financial improprieties and possible tax fraud.

To her dismay, it almost got to where her accountant drew larger crowds at campaign stops than she did. As the election neared, it was clear that the Ferraro family character factor blew one last hole in the sinking ship of Mondale's presidential bid.

The Ferraro episode was three years past when 1988 Democratic frontrunner Gary Hart challenged the press to follow him and was discovered in the highly unpresidential posture of having to explain his relationship with a beautiful young model. When the flow of ever important campaign funds slowed to a trickle, Gary Hart exited, stage left.

While pundits argued over whether Hart's actions were the exception and not the rule, a Syracuse Law School transcript was being dusted off, and Democratic presidential hopeful Joe Biden was watching slow-motion replays of a speech by British Labour Party leader Neil Kinnock. Before anyone knew it, every newscast was showing clips of Biden doing his Bobby Kennedy impression, his Hubert Humphrey impression, and a very good impression of Neil Kinnock.

Then, following reports that he plagiarized speeches, law school work, and misrepresented his law school ranking, Biden came to the same monetary conclusions as Hart and stormed off to fight the worst demon since fluoridation of water, the Supreme Court nomination of Robert Bork.

In the post-Watergate political climate, Americans have begun to hold their leaders to a higher standard. They want the people they elect to have a strong sense of ethics and personal values. Episodes like the Ferraro, Hart, and Biden affairs only disenfranchise voters, making them more indifferent to government and more likely to tune out of the process.

The improprieties of some of the leading Democrats will very likely haunt their past, as voter concern over the Iran-Contra affair wanes in favor of the more continual charges of ethics violations involving Hart, Biden, and company. Voters are better able to relate to these several types of indiscretions than to an allegedly corrupt government operation.

From this writer's admittedly Republican viewpoint, 1988 looks to be a very good year for the Grand Old Party. But just to be sure — George H.W. Bush, Bob Dole, Jack Kemp, Pat Robertson, Pete duPont, and Al Haig, do us a favor — if a pretty young model wants to sit on your lap, point her toward Mike Dukakis.

Ghostwriting

GET IN THE SPIRIT, BY WRITING FOR SOMEONE ELSE

CHAPTER 52

Ghostwriting doesn't have to be scary

Some people don't believe in ghosts. But I've seen many myself — ghostwriters, that is. Don't be frightened. These friendly spirits can be helpful, especially to those CEOs, government officials, university presidents, and other community leaders who have a story to tell but are haunted by a lack of time or skill to write that story themselves.

I've spent much of my life ghostwriting. In fact, several times a week, I'm writing for other people. I've written for Hollywood stars, members of Congress, and Fortune 500 executives. And, as you read in a previous chapter, I ghost wrote for President Ronald Reagan.

Writing with your own style and panache is hard enough. But trying to write in the voice of another person can be challenging and, at times, even vexing. Don't worry — I've learned a few of the paddle strokes that can help you navigate the roaring rapids of composing for others.

The most important touchstone in this journey is understanding your subject. This involves more than reading his or her Wikipedia entry or perusing a bio on a website. People are complicated and a few hundred words can barely dent the veneer of the human personality.

Writing for President Reagan wasn't hard because I'd listened to and studied his speeches for years. The same is true when I've ghost-written for friends and clients whom I've worked over a long period of time. Because I know their heart, I know their voice.

When you write for someone you don't know well, it helps to have a lengthy conversation covering the topics of the work you intend to draft. Beyond the substance of the piece, listen for phrases that he or she uses a lot. One of my clients grew up in rural North Carolina and he'll often employ a phrase that hails from his home and has the distinct hallmark of Southern-style common wisdom. It's like barbecue sauce for the soul. If one of his phrases is something others will understand quickly, I'll make it a point to use it when writing for him.

It can be beneficial to ask your subject if there's a phrase or word that grates on his or her sensibilities. Take good notes and refer to them often. Don't risk a reprimand by including something your subject specifically asked you to avoid.

When I was writing for one prominent woman leader, she told me she doesn't like the word "female" as an alternate for the noun "woman." She pointed out, with a smile, that "female refers to animals and humans, woman refers to just humans." I filed that preference away and kept it in mind when I wrote for her.

Another great way to pick up on the tone and style of your subject is to read things he or she wrote. Make sure it's truly self-written because pieces ghostwritten by others will send you in the wrong direction. You can even ask your subject to dictate the answers to your questions and send you the recording. Before long, you'll have a good sense of voice.

Once you think you know your subject's voice, write your first draft. Particularly if this is the first time you've written for this person, insist that he or she take a heavy edit of your work, scratching out disliked phrases and adding language that fits better. Talk to your subject about the draft — what didn't you like about this? How often do you use this phrase that's been added?

To properly calibrate mutual expectations, tell your client that you expect to exchange drafts as many as a dozen times before being ready to finalize the piece. The back and forth will sharpen the work and show you how to capture this person's voice for future writing efforts.

Before you move to a final draft, have a third person proofread and copy edit the work. While your client and you have both been reviewing it, you are the one expected to get it right. Published mistakes will be blamed — probably correctly — on you. None of us is a good editor of our own work — in fact, we can be blind to our own mistakes because our mind knows what we meant to write, so our eyes skip over the words with less of a critical view. Be sure that whoever proofs the piece is within the chain of confidentiality for the project. If you're not sure, hire an editor who works with a non-disclosure agreement to do the final pass. This person should be nimble with words, confident enough to offer constructive criticism, and familiar with different writing style books. There are several online services that will connect you with such editors.

Particularly if you are writing for a high-profile person, you want to run your piece through an online plagiarism detection program. While I'm sure you didn't purposely plagiarize, a quick check will alert you to any negligent appropriations.

Once your ghostwritten work appears in print or is spoken in a public speech, be sure to have an understanding with your subject about whether you can acknowledge your involvement in the work. Some people (like the clients whose ghostwritten pieces appear in this book) don't mind others knowing that they work with a writer. Others prefer to leave the issue unaddressed.

Occasionally, some clients may boast that they wrote the work and even snort off any suggestion a ghostwriter was involved. Such flights of incredibility will raise or (mostly) fall under their own weight. Ignore it, cash your check, and move on with your life. Either way, checking before you take any form of minor credit will save you problems later.

There are legal considerations when you write for someone else, most particularly issues of copyright. While I'm a lawyer, I'm not your lawyer. So talk to an intellectual property attorney if you want to have any ownership interest in what you write. Most typically, people who are paid to write speeches or columns for someone else should expect to be paid for their work but also expect to have no claim to ownership. Ghostwriting a book is a different enterprise and consulting a lawyer is even more important.

So give ghostwriting a try! It's not scary at all.

The next few chapters in this book offer some prominent examples of my ghostwriting.

CHAPTER 53

South Dakota State of the State: Bringing in the Harvest

In April 1993, federal agents stormed a barricaded complex in Waco, Texas, where a cult leader was fighting a standoff. Because the federal action resulted in 76 deaths the event dominated national news that night and for the next few days. Sadly, that same day, my client South Dakota Gov. George Mickelson and seven community leaders were flying back from a trip aimed at keeping one of the state's biggest employers from relocating. Flying in a tumultuous thunderstorm, the small plane lost its way and hit a grain silo and crashed, killing all aboard.

What would have been a national news story on nearly any other day was instead eclipsed by the tragedy of the Waco assault. As most of America watched the constant coverage of the Waco story, I spent much of the night on the telephone with reporters and the governor's senior staff members, as the mind-rattling details came tumbling in, like so many hailstones of grief. In a state with as small a population as South Dakota, these tragic deaths tore a swath of sadness through most communities there.

I was proud to be an advisor to Gov. Mickelson. He was a bear of a man — tall, strong, and with a grin as wide as the prairie. His political future was bright and he was bringing his state out of an economic downturn. I had helped him with speeches while he was alive, so I was asked to help the new governor, Walter Dale Miller, prepare his State of the State address.

The mood in this close-knit state was sad and defeated. Hundreds of families in the state had some connection to one of the many people who died in the crash. My task in writing this address was to help the governor lead the mourning, recognize the loss, and begin the process of starting anew.

I spent a weekend searching for the right analogy to use in this speech and finally found it while paging through a book of farm country photos I found in a bookstore. The book mentioned that farmers have a tradition of stopping their own work to bring in the harvest of a farmer who died while his crops were still in the field. South Dakotans — residents of a state where agriculture is a mainstay — understood this. It resonated with them in a way it wouldn't have elsewhere.

This metaphor, which I used as the anchor of this speech, was one of the most powerful I've ever employed. I've written other state of the state addresses before but none as emotional as this one. My boss at the time, Paul Wilson, co-wrote this with me and it was a sad chore for him, as well. He had known Gov. Mickelson well before I did.

South Dakota State of the State Address
Gov. Walter Dale Miller
Delivered: January 11, 1994
Written by Mark Weaver and Paul Wilson

L t. Gov. Kirby, Speaker Cutler, Chief Justice Miller, members of the Supreme Court, constitutional officers, honorable legislators, and citizens of the great state of South Dakota. Just as my predecessors have done over the past century, it's now my duty and honor as governor of this great state to report to you the events and progress of the past year, as well as my vision for 1994 and beyond.

I've been in this chamber for 27 state of the state addresses. But, this is my first time from the governor's side of the lectern.

There's a tradition in agricultural communities that, when it's time for the harvest, everyone joins in. We realize that months of hard work and dedication to the land will come to fruition in just a few short weeks.

But when a farmer dies or, for whatever reason, cannot finish his harvest, his friends and neighbors will gather to do it for him. It's a ritual passed down from one generation to the next, and one that speaks to the richness of our farming heritage.

I cannot talk to you today about the events of this last year without acknowledging that we are, in many ways, bringing in George Mickelson's harvest. And as we harvest, this legislative session will sow the seeds for our state's future. We must do so with the harmony of cooperation.

Today, I extend my hand to each of you. Man and woman. Republican and Democrat. West River and East River. Urban and rural.

The only way I can be an effective governor is to solicit your ideas, respect your beliefs, and ask for your cooperation. And, I won't badger or threaten. After 27 years as a state legislator and lieutenant governor, I've discovered the truth of the saying: *"What begins in fear, usually ends in folly."*

Now, as this is my first state of the state speech as governor, I want you to know how my background of working with others has shaped my style of government.

I'm a lifelong South Dakotan, born and raised in Meade County. I still live in the same house where I was born.

I was a school board member for 20 years. I know what it means to balance a budget — and look your neighbor in the eye when you are doing it.

I've been in business for many years, which means I've invested in South Dakota.

I served in the legislature for 20 years. I held every leadership position except minority leader — and I never wanted that one!

I served as House majority leader, speaker of the house and lieutenant governor, and I presided over the Senate for six years.

During this time of public service, I learned what it means to find the consensus that will move legislation forward. I know finding consensus requires that everyone has a chance to be heard.

And, I know no party — Democrat or Republican — and no geographical location — East River or West River — or rural or urban — can do it by themselves.

I enjoyed all that public service. But, as Harry Truman once said: *"We can never tell what's in store for us."*

While this speech is about governance, I want to talk for just a moment about politics.

There will be a lot of tension in this Capitol as people feel pulled by one political camp or another. That's to be expected — indeed, that's part of the process. But, I ask you now — here at the very beginning of this legislative session — to help me make the sweet harmony of cooperation.

We will not be judged by the people of this state as Republicans or Democrats or as East River or West River or urban or rural. Rather, you and I will be judged on what we do for South Dakota. What we do for our future.

I'll do everything within my power to make this the most successful legislative session in South Dakota's history. You've shown that you are willing to do so.

After the death of our beloved governor, I want to thank the members of this legislature who joined with me in a special session to deal with the terrible problems we faced.

And to the thousands of South Dakotans who wrote or called or stopped me on the street to express support and offer their prayers, I humbly thank you. I'll always be grateful.

Now, let's turn our attention to the state of our state. I am proud to report to you the state of South Dakota is in excellent condition.

The seeds for this harvest, we all planted together — let's behold this harvest.

Lengthy list of accomplishments not included.

That's a record any governor of any state would be proud of. And there's so much more to do.

I see a state where we can keep our sons and daughters here in South Dakota, or bring them home to stay. That will require jobs. And, we have them. That will require being on the cutting edge of technology. And, we are. That will require an educational system that prepares our children to meet world-class standards, and we can do that.

But, most of all, it will require people who are willing to work hard, who are willing to sacrifice for the future, and who are willing to work together for the good of the community and the state.

At the outset of this speech, I spoke of farmers who join together to bring in the harvest of one of their neighbors who is unable to do so.

The image of that great harmony of cooperation is one which I want to leave you with today. When the farmers are done harvesting, they sit down, side by side, at the dinner table. Some have known each other for years. Others are bound together only by their heritage of helping.

They give thanks for the gifts and bounty that grow from God's good earth. They give thanks for the time together to help one another. And, they give thanks for the time spent with those whose life journey has ended.

Now, given the tremendous loss our state suffered this year, please join me in prayer: Dear Lord, as we strive to serve the people who elected us, please guide our hearts and minds. We thank you for the many bounties of this state. And we thank you for the time you gave us with our friends. Our lives are richer for having known them. Comfort their families in this new year and help us employ the wisdom of these departed men as we see our way through this legislative session. Amen.

Let me now close with words spoken previously in this chamber, but words that nevertheless still ring true today.

In the passing of a century also comes the passing of friends — people who shaped this state — people who shaped our lives. As we remember the personal pain of these losses, let each of us dedicate ourselves to replacing that loss with a commitment to build a better future.

Those words were spoken, from this very lectern, by Gov. Mickelson in his 1990 State of the State Address. My friends, let us begin that better future. The work is at hand. King Solomon, in the Book of Proverbs, said: *"Where there is no vision, the people perish."*

In this session, we must have the vision to complete the harvest and plant the seeds that will determine the future of our state. I invite you to join with me so we can meet these challenges — together.

Thank you. God bless each of you, and God bless the great state of South Dakota.

CHAPTER 54

O.J. Simpson Trial: Many TV shows don't run that long

As the Deputy Attorney General of Ohio, I helped Attorney General Betty Montgomery manage the office. I also supervised all the communications and reputation management work. I took dozens of press calls every week and managed a staff of communicators and lawyers. While I relied on my staff to do most of the writing for the agency and the Attorney General, there were occasions that were so important that I reserved the writing for myself. Such was the case of O.J. Simpson.

Betty Montgomery had spent 11 years prosecuting dangerous criminals. When she was elected attorney general, she focused the office's resources on investigating and prosecuting the worst of the worst. In 1995, as the nation was fixated on the murder trial of football icon O.J. Simpson, we fielded countless press calls asking for her views on the case. She largely remained silent as the trial proceeded but, following the verdict, she told me she wanted to speak out on one particular aspect of the case — cameras in court.

After sharing her views with me, I sat down at my computer, cranked up a Bach concerto, and began to write. I did my best to write in her voice and with her passion. The result was the most commented upon op-ed she'd ever published. In addition to the many calls and letters she received after the essay went to print, one particularly pleased reader had the op-ed reprinted on a golden plate and then affixed it to a fancy plaque. When it was delivered to the office, Betty walked over to my desk and presented it to me.

Writing for someone else won't go well unless you know that person well enough to capture and evoke their personal spark of inspiration. In this piece, I did my best to do that on a topic close to the heart of my boss.

Many of the phrases you will read in this piece came from my conversation with Betty. By including these key statements, I ensured that the final piece would reflect her voice.

By Ohio Attorney General Betty Montgomery
Written by Mark Weaver

PUBLISHED: *The Cleveland Plain Dealer* — October 11, 1995

O J. Simpson is guilty.
   At least if you ask many people in Ohio, that's what you'll hear. At the same time, many feel just as strongly that Simpson was rightfully acquitted of the murders of his ex-wife Nicole Brown and her friend Ron Goldman.

Because of the rapid news media frenzy that surrounded his trial, most Ohioans reached their own verdict even before Simpson's acquittal was announced by that Los Angeles jury. And feelings have been rubbed raw as a torrent of disagreement rushes into personal conversations.

Although my background in law enforcement allows me to sympathize with the prosecution, it's not my job as attorney general to talk about my personal views on this verdict. As an officer of the court, I must respect the jury's verdict. And I do.

What does trouble me greatly is the systematic injustices exposed by the trial. No matter how you feel about the verdict, we should all be able to agree that this case is a symbol of how our nation's criminal justice system has deteriorated. As our state's chief lawyer, it's my job to help propose reforms that will make the system work and bring back public faith in justice.

When I was a county prosecutor, the longest it ever took me to try a murder case was three weeks. Not 15 months, not even 15 weeks. Three weeks. That's how our criminal justice system is designed to work. And it usually works that way when the courtroom isn't flipped into a fiasco, as it was in this case.

No matter what your feelings are about this case, you've probably been angry at how our legal system has handled it. I know I am.

This double-murder trial has been little more than a circus largely because of cameras being allowed in the courtroom. It's fair to ask: Would the trial participants have engaged in pointless theatrics if the world weren't watching their antics on television? Definitely not. But instead, once Judge Lance Ito allowed the news media in the courtroom, defense attorney Johnnie Cochran aimed his arguments toward the television cameras — not the jury. He was making his arguments not to the court of law, but to the court of public opinion.

It was then that "The O.J. Show" began, and lasted an atrocious four seasons. Most bad television shows don't last even that long.

Fifteen months and 15 defense attorneys later (most people are lucky to afford just one lawyer), the public is left wondering if justice truly was served. People also wonder if all the hype encircling the Simpson case has made a mockery of a criminal justice system as a whole. It's a fair question.

But as attorney general, I must tell you this: Don't lose confidence in the judicial system because of the O.J. Simpson case.

The real tragedy of this incident isn't that the judge allowed the press to take over his courtroom. Or that it took a year for the attorneys to present their cases. And it has little to do with the witnesses and attorneys who cashed in on their overnight-star status with book deals and television appearances.

At its core, the tragic shame of the O.J. Simpson case is that two innocent people were bludgeoned and stabbed to death. Their stories deserved the limelight in this trial. Instead, the focus was stolen by the needless sensationalism of the defendant, witnesses, the judge, and even the lawyers.

The courtroom is not a stage, and shouldn't be treated like one. It's a place for fact-finding, not grandstanding. Television cameras don't belong in court. The misery of victims shouldn't become other people's entertainment.

Just above the entrance to the U.S. Supreme Court is the inscription "Equal Justice Under Law." If that motto is to have any meaning at all, we must struggle every day to ensure equal access and fair play in our justice system.

Let's not linger over the fact that O.J. Simpson was acquitted. There's a bigger issue to tackle. Let's resolve to examine our justice system and find ways to recommit to its stated purpose — equal justice under law.

CHAPTER 55

Inaugural remarks of Ohio House Speaker

When I was in high school, I served as the Speaker of the House of Representatives in a Youth in Government program in Pennsylvania. This meant I spent a few days, in the House legislative chamber for that state, presiding over the debates and deliberations of a few hundred youth legislators. After that, serving as speaker of the house in an actual legislature became my career goal.

Years later, I decided that elected office didn't suit my desire to devote most of my free time to my family, and I never pursued the job of house speaker. But I did end up advising a few people who served as Ohio Speaker of the House. One of them — Larry Householder — asked me to write his first speech. Few people knew Larry as an orator and he wanted to make a strong impression. With the speech I wrote, and a dedication to practice, he gave a compelling presentation that brought many positive comments and even good reviews in press accounts.

Larry gave me the freedom to develop this speech based on several things he told me. Foremost in his mind was his desire for the rest of the state to understand the people who come from Appalachia, his home area. You'll see how I tried to evoke the spirit of that unique region in this address. The "Ghost of Appalachia" in this speech is one of the most vivid and memorable passages I've ever (coincidently) ghostwritten.

Inaugural Remarks of the Ohio Speaker of the House
Speaker Larry Householder
Delivered: January 3, 2001
Written by Mark Weaver

Thank you, fellow members, for this honor.

It's with profound pride and a steadfast belief in the greatness of our state that I accept the responsibilities you've bestowed upon me today.

I'm deeply honored to be the leader of this House — the people's house.

I'll try my level best to keep this new position in perspective. The new term limit law has given us all a new outlook. In fact, I didn't even renew my subscription to "Governing" magazine this year. From now on, my advice to all of us? It's safer to buy each issue one month at a time.

Over the last few years, I've traveled across Ohio to meet and listen to the good citizens who've entrusted us with our term in this great House. I've been to nearly every county, given hundreds of speeches, and spoken with thousands of people.

And, to be sure, I learned a heck of a lot along the way.

First, I learned that the political advisors you can trust the most usually have mud on their boots.

Second, I learned that a county fair funnel cake tastes better than the finest filet mignon in Columbus — and it's a whole lot cheaper.

And finally, I learned that only Santa Claus is loved for making a list and checking it twice.

Including me, there have been 93 different speakers of the House since Ohio became a state.

The first was Michael Baldwin from Ross County. Interestingly enough, Speaker Baldwin was the first of seven speakers from Ross County — that's more than any county has ever sent to lead this chamber.

In 1803, when that initial session of this House convened, there were just 30 members. Ohio was the edge of the great frontier. Back east, they saw us as pioneers. And in many ways, we were.

My own family came here in 1802. From Pennsylvania. My great grandfather's great grandfather — Adam Householder — left the home he knew so well for an uncertain future 300 miles west.

He had faith that his sacrifice would lead to better opportunities for his children. So Adam Householder braved those unknown fortunes and traveled on.

The official history of Perry County records it this way: Adam's wife came "on horseback — carrying her eldest son, Philip, while her husband accompanied her on foot — carrying his trusty rifle."

The trip across the great Alleghenies must have been slow and hard, as fields turned to hills and hills to mountains.

But soon after they came down that mountain range they faced their toughest challenge of the trip — crossing the mighty Ohio River. Our family history doesn't tell us whether they found a boat, discovered a foot bridge, or located a shallow section to wade across.

But we do know the Householders stood on the eastern shore and wondered. They wondered what might be next for them.

Yet they had faith that this new territory held promise for their future. And they were right. It did.

They passed that torch of faith down through six generations, to me.

That faith still burns in my heart today.

Just as they then strived to make Ohio a better place for their children, so must all of us now strive to make it a better place for our children.

And with that in mind, let me speak about a topic of academic debate among us — but a real-life concern to the people we represent.

I'm talking about how we educate our children.

Ronald Reagan used to say that "status quo" is Latin for — "the mess we're in."

When it comes to our schools, we cannot accept the status quo.

282 • MARK R. WEAVER

That's because improving the quality and equality of our public schools remains the most important issue facing this new legislature. It represents our best chance — perhaps our last chance — to kindle a better tomorrow for every school child in Ohio.

The civil rights struggle of the last century opened doors to everyone in our state. And the education efforts we make in this century will help everyone walk through those doors — to brighter futures.

That's because a little boy who lives in the most wretched shack has hope — if his school can launch him into a life free from want.

A little girl with no one to motivate her at home can count on a promising future — if she has a teacher who is well-trained, motivated, and ready to teach.

So hear me well, because nothing I say from this platform will ever be so sincere or so serious.

My goal — and my passion — is to assure that every child in this state receives a top-notch education. Not just a diploma, but a passport to unlimited opportunity.

Each of us was sent here for a purpose. In large measure, this is mine.

On this issue and all others, the people of Ohio expect progress, not partisanship. They deserve results, not rancor.

And most of all, they want us to be leaders who listen — to them, to our own hearts, and to each other.

My father always told me, "The good Lord gave you two ears and one mouth, and you should use them proportionately."

As I see it, a good representative listens and takes other people's opinions into consideration.

Meeting those simple to understand, yet hard to achieve, goals will be my foremost aim as your speaker of the house.

You know, the leader of the Union Army Calvary came from my county. Phil Sheridan will always be remembered for plain talk and accepting the mantle of leadership — even when problems were daunting. That's an example to which I aspire.

In fact, my eldest son attends a high school named for General Sheridan. And that school was the first to bring attention to many of the school problems we're committed to resolve. The good general from Perry County would have wanted it that way.

Sheridan's commander in chief, Abraham Lincoln — who addressed this very legislature in 1859 — warned us: *"A House divided against itself cannot stand."*

He was right. Representative democracy can only collapse from within. To prevent that, we must remain united and treat one another with respect and civility.

And we have a good example to help us in that regard. She's a trailblazer whose time in this chamber made a difference for — and to — every Ohioan.

Jo Ann Davidson has been a skilled lawmaker, a respected leader, and an unparalleled peacemaker.

The first woman to lead this House will be remembered for more than just that achievement. Her tenure as speaker enriched this institution and made it stronger. For that, we all owe Jo Ann Davidson a debt of thanks.

Jo Ann taught us that a good speaker always remembers the folks back home.

And where I'm from, our faith keeps us looking above and ahead — even when we feel down.

That's because many of the people I represent have learned to keep a limit on their dreams. To keep their hopes modest. Their outlook is reflected in what I call the ghost of Appalachia.

Just as that spirit shimmers through the backwoods and hollows of our state, it also appears in this great Capitol.

You might not see him — but I can't turn away.

The ghost of Appalachia wears a coal miners hat to light the way through the darkness.

His back is bent from the load of timber he carried to build our homes.

He wears the thick perfume of the oil that heated those homes.

His hands are worn and lined with the clay that made the brick that built our factories.

And his clothes are covered in dust from the coal that fueled those factories.

His eyes squint as they look toward the horizon. And he wonders.

He wonders what will become of his people.

This speaker is a son of Appalachia. That spirit lives in me. You simply can't understand and appreciate the Appalachia of today without understanding the ghost of yesterday.

In Appalachia — as well as the great urban centers — sweat turned to tears. And tears to blood.

During Ohio's first century, children worked 60-hour weeks in treacherous coal mines and factories. Many workers lived just half the lifetime of those whose profits they built. The toil of those Ohioans paved the way for the state we know today.

Based on that history alone, we owe workers — and those brave souls who fought for workers — so very much.

Basic issues of job safety have been addressed over the years. Yet, job security remains elusive for many Ohioans.

Somewhere beyond these marbled walls is a single mother. She's struggling to raise her children in a safe and nurturing way. Yet she clings to a job that pays some of last month's bills, but none of the next's.

To working mothers, working fathers — workers everywhere, we owe an obligation of fairness and attention.

So those who come to the people's House to oppress working men and women or use them as political pawns will find no support here.

That's because every person we represent has an inherent right to pursue his or her job in an environment free from excessive government intervention.

From Cleveland to Cincinnati. From Toledo to Marietta and every city, township, and village in between, we must remember the needs of those whose economic future is unsure.

And I have absolute faith that the members of this House join me in that concern.

Now, let me talk with my friends on the other side of the aisle.

As we've all recently seen in the presidential election, excessive partisanship — by both parties — demeans and debases our representative democracy.

I'm not here to twist your arm or slap your wrist. I want to stand shoulder to shoulder with you, for the common good.

I want to help you reach out and serve the people you represent. And in turn, I'll ask you to do that for all Ohioans.

The river of difference that runs between our parties only appears deep from afar. People who don't take the time to look carefully, think it can't be forded.

But I know it can. Just as my ancestors chanced the Ohio River and went forward to build a better tomorrow, so can we.

I truly believe the common ground between us is plain to see. We all got into government because we believe — that if we do our very best — we can make tomorrow better than today.

All of us — Democrats and Republicans — must do our work in a way that brings honor to us and to this great institution.

But we can't do this without providence.

While helping to draft our nation's great Constitution, Benjamin Franklin addressed his colleagues, saying *"I have lived a long time. And the longer I live, the more convincing proofs I see of this truth, that God governs in the affairs of men. If a sparrow cannot fall to the ground without his notice, is it probable that an empire can rise without his aid?"*

It's with that purpose and divine legacy that I approach this next term.

So allow me to close with a final glimpse of who I am and where I'm from.

Since 1802, when Adam and his wife crossed the Ohio River and built a life on their own initiative, the Householders have been stubbornly self-reliant.

286 • MARK R. WEAVER

In fact, Ronald Reagan and my Dad had similar philosophies in that regard.

President Reagan said, *"governments have a tendency not to solve problems — only to rearrange them."*

Well, my Dad believed in government, he just didn't believe he needed it.

Like him, I tend to tip the balance in favor of individuals. But I recognize that my beliefs may differ from many of you. That diversity of experience is at the very core of our inspired system of governance.

When we first came through that door, we all looked forward to the work ahead. And when we finally leave through that same door, we'll look back on a legacy of public service.

And during the all-too-brief time in between, we're simply guests of this House. The landlords are the people who gave us our lease of leadership.

Each day we meet here, we write another page in the book of Ohio history. It's up to us how that book turns out.

In this new position, my energy and efforts belong to all the people of Ohio. But my heart and my soul remain with those who sent me. I come from a place where a hard-working family and a hundred acres can feed masses far beyond their view.

I come from a place where a newly widowed farm wife doesn't have to bring in the harvest alone. Neighbors join with her to gather that family's reward.

I come from a place where people are far too acquainted with hard times. Yet they remain ever hopeful in providence and grace.

I come from a place where the daily miracles of hard work and survival mean that you don't need to descend the Statehouse steps and look down at the Great Seal to know that, *"With God, All Things Are Possible."*

Now let us go forward with the tasks ahead and let that belief in God guide us as we do the important work of the people's house.

Speeches

STRATEGIES FOR CRAFTING EFFECTIVE
AND MEMORABLE PUBLIC SPEECHES

CHAPTER 56

How to write a speech people won't forget

As children, we were all taught to talk. But most people go through life without learning how to *speak*. And by that, I mean to speak to a group of people with purpose, passion, and perfection.

Part of my job is to coach CEOs, members of Congress, and university presidents to be more effective public speakers. When conducting my training, I often walk clients through the five steps of writing and delivering a memorable speech. I call it "learning the ROPES" — Research, Organize, Practice, Execute, Survey.

This chapter will focus on the R and the O of ROPES, what you probably think of as speech writing.

I've written thousands of speeches for hundreds of people over the years. I've learned to write quickly and with precision. No doubt there are wordsmiths who write much better than I do, taking a great deal of time to painstakingly select each word and shape each idea. These would be your best-selling book authors.

Just as certainly, there are those who knock out quick verbiage on a deadline, far faster than my typical work. Think of a reporter writing breaking news for a wire service such as the Associated Press.

But the area where I've made my mark is writing with the best possible blend of speed and quality. This is a crucial skill for a speechwriter.

Considering the "R" of ROPES, a good speech needs to be researched before the hands touch the keyboard. And that means questions. Lot and lots of questions.

Whether you're writing the speech for yourself or for someone else, the first question you'll want to ask is "who is my audience?"

Speaking to a group of university professors at a professional conference is a much different endeavor than giving a toast at a family wedding. A business meeting calls for a different approach than a talk at a local elementary school's career day.

Knowing your audience will help you determine the best content and the most effective style.

Another early question to ask is "how many people will be in the audience?" This could significantly affect the style of presentation. For example, an interactive presentation will be a lot easier to do with a conference room of 20 people than a cavernous auditorium of 2,000 listeners.

Knowing whether your audience will be seated, standing, eating, or drinking can also help you prepare your speech. It's also important to know how long your speech should take.

Once I was the keynote speaker at the annual dinner of a statewide association of criminal prosecutors. I noticed there was an open bar before the dinner. Ahem.

I also noticed that about seven other speakers were slated to speak before me. It didn't take much cogitation to deduce that the 45-minute speech event organizers had requested from me would be better received in a reduced five-minute form. When I announced to the restless crowd that organizers had asked me to speak for 45 minutes, there was an audible gasp of despair from the mildly inebriated crowd. But when I told them that I had decided to shorten it to less than five minutes, a gratifying ovation ensued.

Other research topics include discerning what level your content should be — beginner, intermediate, or advanced. What topic has this group heard before? What past speeches have been well received? Are there any sensitive issues that should be avoided or handled diplomatically?

Perhaps the most important tenet of the research portion of your speech is the topic selection. Passion for a subject plays a key role here. In graduate school, I was once asked to substitute teach for a professor who was ill. He had a passion for talking about the Treaty of Versailles and Woodrow Wilson's proposed League of Nations. I did not share that passion. As a result, my lecture — part of my job as a graduate teaching assistant — was perfunctory and uninspired. I was working from the same source material and outline as the professor, but not from the same frame of mind.

Pick a topic you care about. I'll bet someone in your life inspired you to be a better person. Delivering a eulogy at that mentor's funeral would likely be a project of passion for you.

However, simply selecting a topic that resonates with you is only half the equation. The topic must also be of interest to your audience. While a polite and attentive audience could theoretically be willing to listen to a speech on almost any topic, you will be much more likely to persuade, inform, and amuse with a theme that connects with your listeners.

When I teach my law school classes, I can see the students looking up from their laptops and devices when I talk about what the practice of law will mean for them in the years to come. They might not have been fully engaged while I outlined the contract issues in a media law case, but they tune in quickly on matters of their financial survival as aspiring lawyers. The difference is not my lecture style. The difference was the choice of topic.

So, if a topic matters to you and to your audience, you're on the right track. Your presentation also will be more interesting if it provides a different perspective than the norm.

A graduation speech that talks about how graduates should "follow their heart" has been done and overdone too many times. Years ago, Supreme Court Justice Antonin Scalia tried the opposite approach. He encouraged graduates not to follow their heart, especially if the desires of their heart are hurtful to others or otherwise evil. It was a logical point that was made from a different perspective than most graduation speakers.

Once you've determined your topic, it's crucial to boil it down to one key takeaway point that can be remembered by the audience. You'll know you've made it simple enough if you can write it on the back of a business card. If your main point has more than you can write on the card, boil it down further.

Imagine one of your audience members going home after the speech and being asked "what was the speech about?" If the answer is a restatement of what you wrote on the back of the business card, you'll have achieved your goal.

You've chosen your topic. You know your main takeaway point. What's next?

An outline. Your eighth-grade English teacher was right — you need to take the time to outline your ideas before you begin writing. The outline doesn't necessarily have to be written. If you can think through the main point, supporting points, and conclusion, you'll have a functional outline.

Another advantage of an outline is that it might become the talking points for your speech. I rarely encourage clients to use full speech texts, unless they are using a TelePrompter. People who write out speeches word for word tend to read them word for word. The result is poor eye contact and a bored audience. A brief outline will keep a speaker moving through the speech but will force the speaker to use more conversational language.

Your outline should have the opening and closing lines of your speech written out word for word. Those are the only parts that should be memorized. The remainder of the outline ought to be short phrases that will remind you what point you want to make.

For example, if your takeaway point is that Americans should cheer more for our troops than for sports teams, you might decide that one of your supporting points is that our nation spends billions of dollars on sports-related booster gear every year.

The outline point for this idea could be written like this:

- Sports fan gear / billion $

That's enough of a reminder to make your point in a natural sentence that comes to mind as you're speaking.

Throughout the speechwriting, pay attention to certain words that you know will come up. Think about whether there are several different words that might be used. In the above example, you could call the people who like a local sports team fans, fanatics, boosters, followers, devotees, supporters, etc. You may decide that one of those words is a better way to describe the people in question. Once you've decided on that preferred word, use it throughout the speech. Word choice — for key concepts in your speech — matters.

Another advanced tactic in speech writing is the use of inspired metaphors. The selection of just the right metaphor can help your audience use a concept they already understand to grasp a more complex or a new concept. I remember speaking to my son's elementary school class about government. I wanted these children to understand the constitutional principle of how the separation of power prevents abuse of authority. For such a young audience, this was a tall order, to be sure.

First, I established some quick credibility with these third-graders. As the teacher (a family friend) introduced me to the students, I gave her the two finger "bunny ears" behind her head. This was an immediate hit, as making a bit of whimsy with the teacher suggests an understanding of childhood fun.

Next, I skipped the opening and encouraged the kids to quickly grab a partner and start playing the game "rock, paper, scissors." The students — delighted to be loudly playing when they had prepared to be quietly learning — leapt into action and played with gusto. After a few minutes, I called the group to order and asked a question.

"Which of the signs — rock, paper, or scissors — is the strongest?" I asked. After a few too-eager responses aimed at defending the invulnerability of rock or scissors, the children quickly understood and agreed that each of the three symbols has a strength against one of the others and a weakness from one of the others.

I winked at the teacher, looked at the students, and said, "Now you understand the separation of powers between the executive, legislative, and judicial branches of government." It only took me another few minutes to extend the analogy with an overview of checks and balances. The kids understood my point. The analogy was apt and it stuck. Can you find an analogy that works for your speech?

Once you've written your speech, start to speak it out loud. See what words go together and which ones don't. See if the clipped phrases in your talking point outline are enough to trigger in your memory the point you want to make. Make changes. Edit. Smooth. Refine.

Once, when helping to write the State of the State address for the governor of Ohio, we finally settled on something like draft 64 for him to deliver. That's how many changes were made over the course of just a week or so. But each new version was subtly better than the last.

Using these principles, you should be able to write a speech like the pros.

CHAPTER 57

Advance the cause Union soldiers fought to preserve

Political speeches are a unique breed. By their very nature, they speak to one set of values and, by definition, oppose a different out-look. Particularly when given to a group of partisans, such speeches are meant to energize and organize.

American history brims with examples of such addresses changing the world. From William Jennings Bryant's "Cross of Gold" speech at the 1896 Democratic National Convention to Ronald Reagan's 1964 landmark speech "A Time for Choosing," the passions of political speech have been the fuel of political upheaval.

I've written many speeches for politicians to deliver to partisan audi-ences. I chose the one below for this book because I not only wrote it, but also delivered it to a group of Republican women. When I was asked to speak to the group about Abraham Lincoln and his role as the father of the GOP, I set out to use both history and contemporary reference to frame my remarks.

Because President Lincoln led the nation through the Civil War and since Ohio's role in the Union victories was so pivotal, I decided to re-search what Union soldiers hailed from the towns near the site of my speech in eastern Ohio. Not only did I locate the precise regiment but I also found a muster list that showed the hometown of each soldier. I then uncovered a soldier/reporter's letter back home to the area, sent in 1862.

Once I had my historical framework in place, I endeavored to find an issue in the news that could be linked to it. Bill Clinton, who was president at the time, had begun to suggest that late 20th century Americans needed to apologize for slavery, which essentially ended at the close of the Civil War in 1865.

My great, great grandfather — Eli Weaver of Lancaster, Pennsylvania — fought in the Union Army for four years, seeing bloody battle at tide-turning destinations of destruction like Chancellorsville and Fredericksburg. Fighting in Pennsylvania's 122nd regiment, Eli wept over 16 of his hometown friends who were slaughtered defending God's promise, as stated in the Declaration of Independence, that all men are created equal.

I believed then and now that the 620,000 Americans who died in a war to end slavery was the ultimate apology for that abomination. Modern politicians who play on racial tensions and ignore that massive sacrifice deserve shame and shun.

That's why I merged these concepts into this speech, delivered — as mentioned above — to both energize and organize. This speech shows how a bit of research can find points of interest between you and your audience.

DELIVERED: Circa 1998

The Republican Party has a proud history and a bright future. And our past gleams with men and women of character, who stepped forward to lead.

Frederick Douglass — the most influential black American of his time, was a Republican. His passion for equality found its home in the Grand Old Party. And, decades later, it was largely a Republican Congress and state legislatures — over Democrat opposition — that gave women the right to vote.

This history is often obscured. More Americans need to know that Abraham Lincoln, perhaps our greatest president, was the father of the Republican Party. Indeed, Mr. Lincoln once remarked: *"We hold the true Republican position. In leaving the people's business in their hands, we cannot be wrong."*

His greatest achievement was preserving the union during a war that would have permanently ripped almost any other country apart. And, though it's hard to believe, issues from that great conflict persist in today's news.

You may have read that President Clinton has suggested that a national apology is now due to the African Americans of the late 20th century, because of slavery in centuries past.

What would Mr. Lincoln say to that?

He might remind Bill Clinton that the people and government of these United States have already paid dearly for the mistake of slavery. Hundreds of thousands of Americans sacrificed and gave of their own flesh and blood to purge our national soul of the atrocity of forced bondage.

Brave men like those in the 76th Ohio Infantry, a regiment organized right here in eastern Ohio. These Ohioans came from places most Americans have never heard of — like Millersburg, Wooster, and Cambridge. And they fought and died at places most Americans will never forget — like Shiloh, Vicksburg, and Missionary Ridge. This regiment overcame great odds led by a son of Ohio — Grant at Vicksburg. And they marched to the sea with another great Ohioan — Sherman in Georgia. In 41 months of service, the 76th lost 325 men.

To be sure, small towns in eastern Ohio, like most communities in America, paid the price. Richard Burt, an Ohioan who served with the 76th, sent war dispatches back to local newspapers. On May 10, 1862, shortly after the battle of Shiloh, where 23,000 men were killed in just hours, Burt wrote home to Ohio. He told his readers: *"Our brave soldiers, who have to endure these hardships and bear these burdens, richly deserve the sympathy of those whose homes and government they are fighting to protect."* Captain Burt, a proud man of eastern Ohio, understood what too many others — even today — do not.

America has already apologized and paid dearly for slavery. The apology was borne in brave deeds — deeds fused in fear, anguish, and death.

A hollow TV sound bite mouthing an apology would do no further justice to any American, living or dead. If our party stands for anything, it must be that actions should mean more than words, that substance must surpass style, and that serious issues like racism can't be truly addressed through a political poll and a pithy quote at a press conference.

Yet that's what we've come to. And the suggestion emanates from a man who, despite the revered trust placed in him as president, sowed sin, and reaped reproach. But rather than silently seethe at the disgrace Bill Clinton has brought to the presidency, we must boldly blaze our own new trail for America. And we must be a party with a positive message.

We must display, for all to see, that we have substantive and meaningful differences with Democrats. And that's where Republican women represented here today come in. That's because you can do for the cause of our party what the 76th Ohio regiment did for the cause of the Union.

It might not seem like an act of bravery for you to help with a political campaign. But, in a small way, it is. Because if that campaign helps elect a leader of character, maybe — just maybe — the person you elect will make a difference on an issue we all care about.

And as we carry out these small acts of bravery — risking scorn from those who would oppose us — we can elect more people of principle.

In 1982 in Ohio, that was a radical idea for a Republican to have. Democrats held state government hostage, dominating every office. But the GOP rebuilt slowly.

And it paid off — Republicans now hold every office at the state level.

Imagine if we can do that at the county level. We have a tremendous opportunity. We can secure a GOP future for decades to come if we build grassroots and technology advantages. And each of you can do it.

You don't need a Ph.D. in political science to talk to your neighbors about what it means to be a Republican. You don't have to have the broad populist appeal of a George Voinovich to build your county party organization to new heights. And you don't have to have the presence and respect of Ronald Reagan to organize your friends in a voter registration drive. We can all do it.

And Republican women can lead the way.

CHAPTER 58

Honor Society Induction: Live up to the principles of honor

Years ago, a teenage neighbor asked me if I was free to attend a school event on a particular date. I didn't ask many questions and marked it on my calendar. A week or so before the date, I called him to learn more details. It was only then that he told me I'd been selected to give the keynote speech at our local high school's Honor Society induction ceremony. I was a bit taken aback, as this is a large and prestigious event. I leapt into preparation.

You'll see my use of a brick wall as a metaphor. This rhetorical device is one of my favorites and it's something of a signature in the speeches I write.

This is the speech I gave, summoning all the best advice I could muster for a group of very bright young men and women who were joining an organization that represents achievement far beyond my forgettable high school career.

Delivered: 2007

To all the inductees, please accept my heartiest congratulations. Your hard work has been rewarded. And, for you and your parents, this must seem too good to be true.

So, what does this all mean?

The National Honor Society was founded in 1929 to recognize high school students who've demonstrated excellence in the areas of scholarship, leadership, service, and character.

Tonight, you join about one million of your fellow students throughout North America who've achieved as you have.

Now that you've attained this great honor, you may feel as though you've finished something. In a way, you have.

But, in many more ways, tonight is more of a beginning than an end.

Think of it this way. Few things are stronger than a brick wall.

No single brick provides the strength. In fact, a single brick isn't all that formidable.

The strength comes from the careful building of one brick laid upon another with mortar connecting them all.

Tonight, you've laid down a pretty strong brick. This is a proud moment.

The countless nights of homework, class projects, along with the endless days of school activities all seem a little more worthwhile.

And while this special achievement is undoubtedly yours, I can think of a few people who helped you build this brick.

Students, let's hear a round of applause for your parents! They deserve that applause.

Because behind every successful student is an exhausted parent.

So now I'll let you in on a secret that your parents and I already know but you might not have learned yet.

No, it's not what you're thinking.

I'm talking about the very grown-up notion that each accomplishment is as much a conclusion to a series of successes as it is a beginning to the next round of successes.

Maybe that's why we call graduation ceremonies "commencements" instead of "finales."

So, you've started building on your brick wall tonight with these elements of the Honor Society. We start with…*Scholarship.*

Being a scholar means more than just getting good grades. A scholar has a hunger for knowledge and a thirst for learning. And a scholar is as much a teacher as a student.

So now that you've joined this prestigious organization, you wear the label of scholar. But wear it well. Impart your knowledge to others and model your joy for learning.

The next brick in your wall is...*Leadership.*

Leadership is an important quality but it means more — much more — than just being in charge. It goes beyond just managing things.

Peter Drucker was a smart man who wrote about management and leadership. Here's what he said, and I'll bet you'll have a better under-standing of leadership when you think about it.

"Management is doing things right. Leadership is doing the right things."

So, as a member of this elite group, you now have an obligation not just to try and be the boss of something. You have an obligation to or-ganize people to do the right thing.

And you all know what the right thing is. It's that little voice in your head that you don't always want to listen to.

Sometimes it sounds like Mom or Dad. Sometimes you wonder if it could be God.

But no matter whose voice it sounds like, each of you knows what's right. And now, the brick foundation you've laid tonight requires you to listen more carefully — and more attentively — to that voice.

The next brick in your wall is...*Service.*

You may feel very important tonight, and that would be under-standable. Yet this element of your new-found honor requires you to swallow that sense of importance and focus on serving others.

And you need not worry if you have what it takes to serve. Just look at the example of Martin Luther King. He was a lot of things but it's rather cliché to call him a civil rights leader.

He helped define this nation in the 20th century the way Lincoln did in the 19th and Madison, Washington, and Jefferson did in the 18th century.

Here's what King said about service. It bears repeating.

"Everybody can be great — because anybody can serve. You don't have to have a college degree to serve. You don't have to make your subject and verb agree to serve. You only need a heart full of grace. A soul generated by love."

That's your goal. Drop your sense of self-importance and find someone who could use your help.

I'll never forget the acts of my best friend Steve when we were your age. On a snow day when school had been canceled, I would sleep in and then head out to go sledding.

Not Steve. By mid-morning, as I was just getting to the sledding hill, he was finishing up shoveling the driveway and sidewalk of an elderly neighbor.

When I asked him how much money he made for it, he looked at me funny. That's because he didn't get paid anything. He didn't want to be paid. Steve just wanted to serve. By the way, Steve was a member of the National Honor Society.

The final brick in your wall is...*Character*.

This is an easy one to understand. Simply put, character means doing the right thing — even when no one is looking.

Admit it -- being honest is easy when your parents are nearby.

Driving the speed limit is pretty basic when there's a police car behind you.

But character suggests you do these things no matter where you are or who's with you.

And you were chosen for this recognition because you have the capacity, indeed the reputation, for doing that.

Now, build on it. Keep it up. Prove the worth of this great honor.

It's a special night. You've started a great foundation; the first level of your brick wall.

Now, build it right and keep it strong.

CHAPTER 59

Remember and grieve our fallen heroes in blue

I like to remind my friend and former boss Betty Montgomery that, long after I'm gone and forgotten, she'll still be in the history books. That's because she was the first — and, to date, only — woman to be elected Ohio attorney general. She later served as Ohio's first woman auditor of state. She'll be remembered more than just for being the first — she was also one of the best. She spent her early career as a prosecutor and local police loved her. She understood cops in a way that made them comfortable around her.

During the eight years she was attorney general, she spoke at the annual state ceremony honoring and remembering those law enforcement officers who died in the line of duty. Betty is a strong writer in her own right, but I took great pleasure in writing this speech for her. The emotional and heartfelt reaction she received from the families of the fallen officers was all the reward she or I would've ever wanted. I've written speeches for hundreds of people but this speech received some of the strongest positive responses I've ever seen.

Note my use of specific examples of the losses a child or spouse of a fallen police officer must endure. These poignant passages gave the speech a particularly strong punch.

This is still one of my favorites.

Remarks by Ohio Attorney General Betty Montgomery
Ohio Peace Officers' Memorial Ceremony
Delivered: May 13, 1996
Written by Mark Weaver

Today is a difficult moment in time for all of us. We stand on the precipice of despair, trying mightily to cast our gaze forward while remaining ever vigilant to the memory of those who fell in the line of duty.

Earlier, as I spent time with the families of the officers we honor today, I got an all too familiar glimpse of each family's private pain.

Every wife, parent, child, sibling, and friend of the officers we honor today remembers the feeling of anguish surrounding the individual circumstances of their loss.

The wives think back to the lost moments of love, found in the squeeze of a hand, or a soft kiss on the cheek.

The children reminisce about past special times with Daddy, being tossed in the air, or working on a homework problem.

And perhaps most sadly, the parents feel the tug of an aching heart. While every loved one of a fallen officer is affected, the burden falls in a particularly painful way on the parents.

The violent and sudden loss of a child is an unnatural, tumultuous event for a parent. The course of nature is such that we expect to pass on well before our children do. There's a certain comfort and sense of order in that understanding.

But the parents of the men we honor today no longer have the luxury of that comfort. They've had the rare, yet painful experience of loving their son from his first day to his very last.

The sadness every family member felt when they first heard the news must have been overwhelming.

But the darkness of those days cannot place a shadow on the remembrance of these officers who will have an eternal shining presence with their loved ones, friends, the law enforcement community, and the citizens of Ohio.

It's difficult for me to bestow the dignity and distinction we owe to the officers we honor today.

Although I'm proud of the work I do, mine is a profession largely of words. Attorneys can accomplish many things through the gentle art of persuasion and rhetoric.

But the noble calling of law enforcement is a profession of deeds. Deeds small and large. Both notable and forgettable. Brave and ordinary.

Every day, three shifts a day, peace officers gird themselves with body armor for their protection.

They strap on powerful weapons for our protection.

And they hold in their heart the spirit of our Constitution for everyone's protection.

Most days pass calmly, quietly.

For many officers, an entire career hastens by and not once are they honored with a medal, a commendation, or by the solemn notes of taps played over a hero's grave. Some never even hear a "thank you."

But there are countless tributes to the work of law enforcement all around us.

Every time we drive to work and arrive without incident or accident is an overlooked accolade to police officers enforcing traffic and safety laws.

Every time we withdraw money from an ATM and walk away unmolested is unspoken homage to officers patrolling nearby as a constant deterrent to street thugs who would otherwise move unchecked into every neighborhood near and far.

Every time we pick up a newspaper and skim past the daily barrage of society's excess is a tip of the hat to the people who devote every professional energy to addressing those problems — so we don't have to.

The career of every peace officer is laden with moments of recognition unfulfilled.

It's sad and a little discouraging that we've become accustomed to affirmatively honoring law enforcers only after extraordinary courage or untimely passing. As someone who's spent an entire career working with the men and women of law enforcement, I'd like to see that change.

Every day, we owe a debt of thanks to the law enforcement officers who stand guard so we may go about our business without a thought for the risks they take.

So, to every peace officer here today, I say thank you.

Today, we honor officers who truly exemplify the meaning of the word hero. Let the names of these men ring out from this place and be heard and remembered from this day forward.

Each officer, in his own way, is indeed a hero.

For the sake of the citizens of Ohio, they made the ultimate sacrifice.

Today we raise these flags and lift our hearts in the memory of these five dedicated heroes who lost their lives last year.

The common thread among these brave officers is not how they died, but rather, how they lived. Indeed, the character that inspires someone to become a peace officer is rooted in the very heart of an individual.

To you, the family members of the officers we are here to honor, a peace officer may be a husband, a father, a brother or a friend.

But to us, a peace officer is someone who stands guard over an increasingly violent society. Every moment of every day. From the first step outside that officer's front door each morning through the solitary footsteps back home each night, the men and women of law enforcement stand guard.

Their quiet dedication brings more pride to an already proud profession.

There is a common bond behind the badge and losing one of our own is a tragedy for the entire law enforcement community.

But we should never lose sight of that bond. And don't think for a minute that these precious lives were lost in vain.

In addition to remembering and honoring these officers, we should also celebrate the lives that each of these officers led and reach out to their family members.

It's something our forefathers hoped for. Something our parents and grandparents lived for. And it's an American ideal that hundreds of fellow law officers died for.

I hope these modest remarks about this American ideal can somehow help the families and friends of these fallen officers pass through the torrent of pain and sorrow caused by the tragic events leading up to their loss.

But to the others who've drawn near to learn more about the officers we honor today, I remind you of the words spoken by British Prime Minister Winston Churchill. He said: *"This is no time for ease and comfort. It is the time to dare and endure."*

After today, let's set aside our want for reflection and grief. Let's recommit ourselves to changing our community with such broad strokes and bold action that there may soon come a day when we have no new officers to bid goodbye in such a way as we do today.

Imagine a year gone by without a single officer killed in the line of duty.

My friends, this can be done.

I am every bit the eternal optimist when I say everyone can find a way to build a place where the lives of those who protect us are not squandered and cast aside seemingly with no purpose or meaning.

It starts with values. Simple values. The word values has taken on a partisan or harsh meaning over the last few years. That saddens me.

Every one of us can agree on some of the most important cornerstones of the edifice we've built for our country. First among these core beliefs is the notion that no one should be sent out to do a dangerous job unless we plan to support them in every way. Let's work to advance that notion.

Perhaps the work we can do will help ease the pain of those left behind.

I sense the heartache of the son whose name will be called out at graduation and Dad won't be there to hear it.

I grieve for the daughter who will walk down a wedding aisle alone, or with someone other than her father.

I understand the anguish of the widow who still wakes just before dawn and reaches across the bed hoping — for just a moment — to find her husband quietly sleeping after working the overnight.

And, as I said before, I weep for the special pain of parents who will spend the last years of their lives without the bright light of the child who so warmed their family environment.

The pain, the anguish, the sorrow seems so much like failure.

But none of it is.

The poet said: *"They never fail who die in a great cause."*

And there is simply no more noble calling than that of the law enforcement officer.

It is unselfishness in its most basic form. It is kindness personified. It is everything we want our children to be.

Your loved one died in the same great cause that the revered heroes of all time are remembered for.

The men of George Washington's army died to spark a revolution that would provide unparalleled freedom to millions yet to be born. Abraham Lincoln died to preserve the unity of the greatest nation the world has ever seen. Martin Luther King died so every person can be treated fairly.

And these fallen officers died for every one of those reasons. Because without peace officers, we cannot be free, we cannot be united, and we cannot enjoy fairness.

These ideals are echoed in every beat cop's footstep on a lonely street. These ideals take shape in every courtroom where an officer steps forward and identifies the lawbreaker for all to see. These ideals are the best of what we can hope to be, as individuals, and as a society. And, to be sure, these ideals are now synonymous with the names of the men we honor today.

Just as we place their names on a wall of granite, the Lord surely commends to a very special honor roll those who act so unselfishly.

Every cop who ever broke down a door to a burning building only to never come out alive is named there. Every sheriff's deputy who intervened in a fight only to become that fight's final victim is named there. Every peace officer who ever pinned on a badge one morning and never came home to take it off is surely named there.

So, on a bright spring day, a humble representative of a profession known more for words than deeds now leaves you with this.

We can never know the depths of your torment. We can only feebly try to bridge the chasm created by your loss. But we can always remember and honor the officers you gave to us.

And we will.

I want the families of the men we honor today to know how proud Ohioans are of the sacrifice of their loved ones.

From North Baltimore to South Point.

From Perrysburg to Portsmouth.

From Upper Sandusky to Lower Salem.

And from Cleveland to Cincinnati ...

... the people of this state stand in reverence of the men whose lives we remember today.

To them, I leave the words of Thomas Moore:

"Earth hath no sorrow that heaven cannot heal."

As the families here today seek to move their own lives forward, working to somehow heal the hurt, I hope that in some small way, my words — or this solemn ceremony — can express the sincere thanks of a grateful state.

We will remember your loved ones. And we will always honor their sacrifice.

CHAPTER 60

A memorial to South Dakota's leaders tragically lost

As discussed in the introduction of an earlier chapter, Walter Dale Miller was sworn in as governor after South Dakota Governor George Mickelson and seven other state leaders were killed in a tragic plane crash. To honor these men, on the state capitol grounds, South Dakota lawmakers erected a giant statue of two stallions fighting. It was a stirring symbol of the beauty, strength, and wild temper of the Dakota prairie. The sculptor was the same man who created the famous 600-foot tall Crazy Horse Memorial in western South Dakota, a well-known landmark in the state.

On the one-year anniversary of the tragedy, the memorial was publicly unveiled in a ceremony attended by thousands and watched on television by countless others. The master of ceremonies was NBC anchorman Tom Brokaw, a college friend of Mickelson.

The keynote speech was given by Miller, who asked me to write his address for him. Given that I'd worked with Mickelson and had a great fondness for him, it was one of the most difficult writing tasks I've ever faced.

I had written Miller's first state of the state address (see earlier chapter) and it had been an emotional challenge for me. But much of that speech was policy-focused, driven by the new governor's legislative needs. The Fighting Stallions Memorial dedication speech needed to be different. I wanted it to be a homily of hope. A conversation of comfort. And a tribute of triumph.

I spent hours crafting it, moving through several drafts. The Governor had only one clear request of me. He wanted to include a stirring passage from the Old Testament Book of Isaiah. Of course, I agreed.

When this address was complete, I was pleased that Governor Miller delivered it in such an inspiring and moving style.

The next day, the newspaper reprinted the entire speech. That newspaper, along with a photo of Gov. Mickelson and I together in the state capitol building, is framed and hanging on my wall. It's the only speech text I've ever had framed.

Remarks by South Dakota Gov. Walter Dale Miller
Delivered: April 19, 1994
Written by Mark Weaver

My friends, one year ago, we came together at this Capitol to mourn and remember eight men who died while building a vision into something real.

On April 19, 1993, South Dakotans shared a song of sorrow. Today, with no less tears and with no fewer pangs of loss, we return to dedicate a memorial that celebrates the dream our colleagues died for. And so we mourn. We grieve. And we remember.

But through our veil of sadness, we must see clearly and remember that as long as this memorial endures, their vision will remain as alive and vibrant as it was when they walked with us.

The Fighting Stallions Memorial, so skillfully crafted by our good friend Korczak Ziolkowski, symbolizes life, spirit, and enthusiasm. It is a fitting tribute to these eight men. George Mickelson, Angus Anson, Ron Becker, Dave Birkeland, Roland Dolly, Roger Hainje, Dave Hansen, and Ron Reed all lived life to its fullest measure.

In the honest prairie traditions of our people, they loved their families, respected their neighbors, and contributed to their communities. So today is a day of many emotions. It's a time to remember, a time to honor, and a time to dedicate a memorial, which, by design, will span generations to come.

Here, in the presence of the families of these men, we dedicate the Fighting Stallions Memorial to their memory. It reminds us of their service and their sacrifice. Their lives left an unforgettable imprint on our souls. They will be forever fixed on our minds because of their unique qualities.

Let us always remember George Michelson's vision, Angus Anson's concern, Ron Becker's loyalty, Dave Birkeland's faith, Roland Dolly's character, Roger Hainje's integrity, Dave Hansen's commitment, and Ron Reed's dedication.

From this day forward, whether we pass this memorial in the warmth of the morning sunshine or the chill of the evening dusk, let us remember what these eight men did for South Dakota. While this memorial is a tribute to them, it also serves as a challenge to us, a clarion call for us to finish the job our eight friends started.

We must carry on their vision, continue their work, fulfill their dreams. Today, let us leave here intent on finishing what they started. In life and sadly, in death — they were bound together in a single purpose. A purpose undoubtedly for our benefit. Their legacy to us is one of great weight.

For now, it is up to us to make sure it's not forgotten. Just as they did, let us preserve what is right about our state, build on our many strengths, and grow from our failings. Just as they did, let us all learn the lesson of cooperation, uniting people of different cultures, regions, and professions. And, my friends, just as they did, let us tirelessly work to craft a future that can match the unspoken promise of this memorial.

There's a Latin saying that translates: "*If you seek his monument, look around.*" Look around here today and you'll see another monument to these men — all of us. Because while the Fighting Stallions Memorial is a monument and a testament to our eight friends, we must be their living memorial.

You see, a true memorial is more than just bronze and granite. It's a challenge to make sure what these great men lived for and died for is carried through to what you and I do each day.

These eight men loved this state. And they died trying to make it a better place. We loved them. And the greatest honor we can pay them — the greatest memorial we can build for them — is not this memorial, even as beautiful and meaningful as it is. The greatest memorial we can build for them is to carry out their hopes for South Dakota, to think of their example and apply it to our lives, and to ask ourselves if our commitment is as strong as theirs was.

And, if you'll allow one personal note in today's ceremony, hardly a day goes by that I don't remember Gov. Mickelson and the example he set for us. In those moments, I mourn again for our loss.

Yes, my friends, we mourn. But this memorial stands as proof we can move past our grief and live the rest of our lives as our friends would have wanted.

I invite you to walk the hallowed path around this great statue and remember the eight men it memorializes. And as you grasp for some shred of understanding of the emptiness we all felt this past year, seek solace in the timeless words of the scriptures — Isaiah 40: "*Lift up your eyes on high and see Who has created these things, Who brings out their host by number, He calls them all by name, by the greatness of His might and the strength of His power; not one is missing. But those who wait on the Lord shall renew their strength, They shall mount up with wings like eagles, They shall run and not be weary, They shall walk and not faint.*"

These words have soothed the souls of countless generations, people who have mourned for friends taken all too soon. Guided by the eternal wisdom of this passage, we give thanks that God blessed us all with our time with these very special people.

In recognition of the spirit displayed in life by these men and in honor of the spirit of South Dakota they embodied, I thank you for sharing this day in their memory.

God bless you and God bless the great state of South Dakota.

Now, let us unveil the Fighting Stallions Memorial.

Book Reviews

LET'S REVIEW: WRITING A DISCERNING BOOK REVIEW

CHAPTER 61

Book reports in school were boring, but in the newspaper they can be fun

I love books. My mother started her career as a reading teacher and she taught me to read to at a very young age. It certainly helped that my childhood bedtime was extended by a half hour if I was in bed reading. I took advantage of this loophole most nights.

Later, in ninth grade, I spent mornings perusing *The Hockey News* or daydreaming in the back of the math class for dummies but, later in the school day, I was thoroughly engaged and even thriving in an advanced reading class aimed at college-level reading.

In law school, where professors often required us to read hundreds of pages of dense legal cases per week, my reading skills sharpened further. And, since most law school classes are graded based on just one final essay exam, I quickly learned that strong reading comprehension abilities and sharp writing skills were the building blocks of a good lawyer. I also learned that reading lengthy court opinions written by judges who found their way onto the bench in ways that don't include writing competitions is why so many lawyers look back at their law school years and shudder.

Throughout my early career, I'd spend as much as 15 percent of my meager salary buying new books to read. I was well aware of the free services of my local library but I also enjoyed finishing a book and keeping it on the shelf for future consultation. Books and I had — and still have — a passionate love affair. At least one modern author wrote a book about this obsession and has coined the term "bibliomania." I would buy his book, but I'm nearing the end of my twelve-step program

Nonetheless, when I was given the opportunity by *The Columbus Dispatch* to write reviews for publication, I eagerly dove into the work. While, outside of work, I was already reading a few books every month, this new assignment gave me an incentive to read even more.

As a consumer of book reviews, I was familiar with the basic format but I quickly realized there are as many ways to review a book as there are to write a concerto. I didn't like writing book reports in high school, perhaps because such an unyielding format was required. I decided I needed to shape my own approach of how to impart to others the essence of a given book.

My first advice in this regard is to only review books you enjoy reading. I prefer nonfiction and biography over fiction and fantasy. So I concentrate my efforts there. I also focus on authors or subjects where I already have a base of knowledge. It's easier to see the seams of a presentation when you know how such rhetorical arguments in a familiar field are made.

Next, I realized that all authors have a perspective and an opinion. Their viewpoint informs what facts they marshal to make a case. That's why I typically seek to decode the author's style for the reader. Knowing that some authors use facts the way the proverbial drunken man uses a light pole (more for support than illumination), my goal is to let readers understand the author as well as the author's argument.

I read a book for review with a highlighter and pen nearby. When I find a key passage, I underline it and make a short note. By the time I've read the entire tome, my notes are enough to start writing the review.

Before writing, I look for a common thread that might weave together the notes I made. Sometimes it involves explaining where this book fits in the larger sweep of the subject. Other times I may select a suitable metaphor to bring together the constituent parts of my insight.

I rarely write a book review in one session. I can get most of it done in an hour or so but I'm never pleased with the result of just one stroll down the keyboard. By visiting and revisiting the piece over a period of days, the message of the author can wash through my head and gel into a more precisely formed impression.

You'll see in the selected book reviews that follow this chapter that my writing style is similar to that of the op-eds I write. I disdain formal writing because I genuinely believe most writing should be like a conversation. On the rare occasion when a more formal style is required, I can enjoy the high art and strong architecture of that pursuit. But, just as a soft pair of worn jeans is a better daily companion than a stiff wool suit, I favor the informal.

Asking someone to read your draft review can help shape the final product. Working with someone who never read the book will allow you to get good feedback on the big picture of your work. Asking someone who has already read the book you're reviewing can be helpful as well, since he or she may be willing to engage in a back and forth that could help remind you of important parts of the book you failed to discuss.

Distilling a complicated book into 1,000 words or less is a challenge. Doing it in a way that is both fair to the reader and author can be even more difficult. But the art of the book review beckons artists with a wide palette of verbal paints and the patience to scrutinize the subject until the essence of truth emerges.

Good luck!

Democracy Derailed: Ballot issues nudging out legislators

Outside of my work advising organizations on crisis communications and practicing law, I sometimes help candidates and ballot issue campaigns win elections. Over the years, I've advised more than a dozen statewide ballot issue campaigns, all of which were successful. In each case, voters were deciding a certain policy issue.

But the notion that states ought to place policy issues in the hands of the voters rather than elected legislators raises a question that, like the drunken party guest pawing over the crumbs at the bottom of the pretzel bowl, just won't go away.

I met David Broder at a Washington luncheon several years before he wrote this book. He was then a well-known political writer for The Washington Post. Presidents and potential presidents alike sought his favorable coverage. During our discussion over lunch, I found him thoughtful and humbler than one might imagine. I'd read many of his columns in the past but not any of his books.

When he wrote this book, I welcomed the chance to review it. You'll note that I used the review to take the issues Broder raised and place them in the larger context of American history. This zoom out process can be an effective way to draw someone into reading the book. I also urged others to avoid the book, as it was a bit more targeted toward political geeks.

Book Review of *Democracy Derailed* by David Broder
PUBLISHED: *The Columbus Dispatch* —Spring 2000

H old on to your republic! That's the warning from veteran political reporter David S. Broder in a new book examining how ballot issue campaigns can concentrate political power in the hands of a few individuals.

Broder is a sensible voice and a thoughtful scribe awash in a sea of yappy national political correspondents who seem to know more about television make-up and pithy sound bites than the *Federalist Papers* and John Locke. This worthwhile book distinguishes Broder even further.

Anyone concerned with the prognosis for representative democracy in the nation that has so admirably established it into the annals of world history ought to pay heed to Broder's warning. There's much to ponder and learn here.

Yet this book isn't for everyone. C-SPAN viewers and political scientists will enjoy it most. Those with only a passing interest in public affairs may be daunted even early in the book. In places, Broder's work resembles a somewhat pedantic graduate course in early 20th century American political history. However, for those who persist, an important discourse emerges.

The early efforts of American populists and progressives were largely aimed at reducing the influence of the benefactors of what left-leaning historians call the "Gilded Age" in the political process. The ballot issue — advanced either by initiative (voters initiate the issue onto ballot) or by referendum (legislatures refer the issue to the ballot) — was one of the primary protective shields employed by the activists of that era.

A century later, Broder persuasively, but with more than a nod toward objectivity, unfolds the sad irony that this shield has been slowly beaten into a sword that is now wielded by millionaires and other moneyed interests.

Although California is perhaps best known for statewide propositions, Oregon leads the nation in such elections. This is appropriate since the device first came into use when a gadfly of a reformer led the effort to pass an amendment to Oregon's constitution in 1902. That activist, William U'ren, kindled what would eventually become a bonfire of ballot issues — an average of 14 per election cycle — in that state. Now 24 states, including Ohio, permit such ballot issues to be put to voters.

The examination of several ballot issue races in the last few years shows that the technique of approving public policy through a direct vote of the people exudes, upon a quick glance, the appearance of American democracy. Yet several people argue that money — and the handful of people willing to spend truckloads of that money — really control these elections.

One glaring example surrounds recent attempts to allow medicinal doses of marijuana to be used for terminally ill patients. Among the support of several groups, Broder found just a few notable people who donated or personally raised millions of dollars to advance their personal belief in such a policy. The tidal waves of advertising and public relations created with this small fortune helped convince voters in five states that permitting the legalization of medicinal marijuana was sound public policy. The most common examples in the advertising focused on sympathetic figures battling deadly illnesses and credible medical professionals who cited the need for access to marijuana in limited cases.

Yet the voters may not have fully understood the broad sweep of the political agenda put forth by the wealthy few who bankrolled these initiatives. For example, in Arizona, the complex ballot language covered much more than just marijuana — leading to the legalization of the "medicinal" use of other drugs such as LSD, heroin, and PCP. It's beyond question that most voters would have rejected this result had they been aware these details. Yet Broder discovered that voter confusion is characteristic of ballot issues.

When one ponders such an extreme and dubious result, it is difficult to imagine that a legislature — steeped in the detailed mechanisms of the legislative process — would have let such a blunder slip by. Yet the cry of those who support ballot issues is "Who better than the people? You want to leave it to the politicians?"

Broder's question is salient. Has democracy been derailed by placing complex and sweeping public policy questions in the hands of a populace more interested in watching *Who Wants To Be A Millionaire?* than determining the details of the ballot questions they are deciding? Chapter after chapter, example after example all suggest that the title was indeed well chosen.

Front and center in Broder's case is the stark difference between the intent of ballot issues (to decentralize power) and the reality (it centralizes power). Broder writes: "*The spectacle of three millionaires rewriting the laws of five states — including Oregon — is a far cry from what William U'Ren had in mind when he imported the initiative process from Switzerland and installed it in Oregon a century ago.*"

Who best to govern? This is not an academic question to Ohioans. As term limits wash over a general assembly facing some of the most complex and pressing issues of our times, ballot issues may become more common. If that occurs, the concerns raised in *Democracy Derailed* will resonate far and wide.

CHAPTER 63

The Drudge Report redefining journalism

Matt Drudge may be the most important journalist you've never seen on TV. He's a bit of recluse, but his "Drudge Report" website gets millions of visits every day. The site now is largely just a launching pad into interesting news links, each denoted with a Drudge-style headline. But in the late 1990s, Matt Drudge was using this popular website to break news that mainstream news organizations refused, or hesitated to, publish. The most notable of these scoops was the story (later proven to be true) that President Bill Clinton had a sexual affair with a very young White House intern, including trysts in and around the Oval Office.

Drudge once hired an unknown but passionate and verbose young man to help edit the Drudge Report content when Drudge was otherwise unavailable. That media upstart – Andrew Breitbart- went on to start his own series of Bretibart-branded communications channels that outlived his early death and continue to affect American discourse today.

Painting in bold, clashing colors, Drudge wrote his self-described manifesto as a clarion call to the journalism world. His main premise of the year 2000 was as audacious as it was auspicious: the internet will quickly change the way news is reported and consumed. He was pilloried and shunted aside from those reporters who didn't quite realize they were slowly becoming the late 20th-century version of buggy whip manufacturers.

I would have read this book even if the publisher had not provided it as part of my review for The Columbus Dispatch. I had already taken a liking to Drudge and his contrarian panache. He often dresses like an old-time print journalist and he clearly has an affinity for the genre of the news gathering profession. I adopted the lexicon of that era in my lede (pronounced "leed" and mistakenly spelled "lead" by many) or opening of the piece.

Note how I purposefully began and ended the piece with the same words. This "bookending" style can be a great way to structure an op-ed or a speech.

Book Review of *The Drudge Manifesto* by Matt Drudge
PUBLISHED: *The Columbus Dispatch* — 2000

E xtra. Extra. Read all about him. Matt Drudge. Protagonist and antagonist of the Drudge Manifesto.

If you frequent the Drudge Report on the internet, you'll want to read the book version of it, appropriately named *The Drudge Manifesto*. A review of it simply won't be enough to quench your thirst for all the Drudge that's fit to print. But if the name Drudge is largely unfamiliar to you, read on and decide for yourself if this manifesto is gospel or propaganda.

In Matt Drudge's own words set the table for this tome: *If I'm not interesting, the world's not interesting. If the Drudge Report is boring, the world is boring.*

When the history of how the internet changed journalism is written, there's one name that will assuredly be highlighted in the textbooks. Only the self-deluded will deny that Matt Drudge will be front and center in that curriculum.

Just as the internet music-swapping service Napster confounds the paragons of the music industry, Matt Drudge drives professional media types batty. He calls himself a "citizen journalist." But that's no hype.

He sports no fancy degrees in journalism or experience learning the news trade, yet Drudge reaches more readers in a day than the newspaper you're holding reaches in a month. Whether he can even be called a journalist is a question likely to spark verbal fisticuffs with your friendly neighborhood scribe.

Not long ago, Matt Drudge was a self-acknowledged D-average high school graduate, working the cash register at the CBS gift shop in Los Angeles. Overhearing conversations, picking through office trash bins, and snooping for tidbits, he learned some of the inside stories of the mighty television network.

Armed only with his personal flair and a Radio Shack computer (bought by his father, who feared a dismal future for his directionless son), from his shabby one-bedroom apartment, Matt Drudge began posting his Television City scoops on the internet for anyone to see. Drudge recalls: *"One reader turned into five. Five into a hundred. And faster than you can say I NEVER HAD SEXUAL RELATIONS WITH THAT WOMAN, it was a thousand, five thousand, a hundred thousand."*

Drudge's mention of President Clinton's infamous lie about his affair with intern Monica Lewinsky is no passing reference here. After scooping Hollywood with trash picked sources, Drudge developed even better sources that helped him break the scandal that led to the first impeachment of an elected president (you'll recall that Andrew Johnson took office upon the death of Lincoln — so he was impeached but not elected). He's quick to remind readers that he beat other media outlets by four days — including *Newsweek*, which had done the initial research on the story but put it on ice.

His drudgealicious scoops have gone well beyond the Clinton scandals. He beats the mainstream media on a weekly basis, and most of the time, he has his facts right. It's that "most of the time" caveat that perturbs his critics. He's often attacked by news industry wags for his refusal to follow the time-honored fact-checking format that mainstream journalism typically uses.

He's not apologetic about it, either. *"I've reported when, how, and what I've wanted. My only limitations have been those I've created. There's been no editor, no lawyer, no judge, no president to tell me I can't. And there never will be. Technology has finally caught up with individual liberty."*

Drudge may not be the best messenger for this news. He's being sued by White House staffer Sidney Blumenthal for a scandalous allegation Drudge posted and later retracted.

The author Drudgingly admits that lightning-quick reporting sometimes leads to errors on his part. But when media sharpshooters target his goofs, he fires back with a well-aimed barrage of references to major media embarrassments like NBC's false allegation that Richard Jewell tried to bomb the 1996 Olympics, CNN's Tailwind fiasco, and the Associated Press' inaccurate report on an Anthrax scare in the Nevada desert. Mistakes, he says, come with the complex enterprise of reporting. Given that reliable and unreliable sources often are difficult to discern no matter what the format, internet reporting is no different.

Whatever the debate over his methods, with a web page that boasts more than a million visits a day, the Drudge Report is now a must-read source for news and politics junkies around the world. The book is the hard cover version of the website.

Written in a clipped, stream-of-consciousness style, The Drudge Manifesto chronicles how his report came to be and, in the best parts, gives the reader a fascinating fly-on-the-wall vantage point of Drudge's travels and travails.

In the worst parts, the prose is tedious and just this side of odd. The middle of the book loses focus, consisting mostly of a rat-a-tat romp through the incestuous world of media mergers.

But throughout, there are some innovative devices that redeem. As Drudge relates events leading to his scoops, he recounts how his cat counseled him, serving as the conscience that critics claim he lacks. His self-deprecating references also dampen the bluster factor in many of the achievements he outlines.

The book is part futurist rant, part techno-haiku. It takes some patience and a high tolerance for jargon and insider lingo to actually finish *Manifesto*. Those who make it are rewarded with a full transcript of Drudge's session in front of the National Press Club. The giants of journalism (Drudge fancies them dinosaurs) peppered him with questions about his accuracy rate, his thin credentials for reporting, and why he has no editor or other barrier between him and his readers. His responses to the brickbat queries are salient, funny, and forward-thinking.

Whether you like Drudge or not, he's dead-on right when he predicts the future of internet journalism in this quote: *"In the same way Gutenberg's Bible hastened the End of The Church's stranglehold on 15th-century Europe, in the same way Thomas Paine rallied troops to fight King George, in the same way Upton Sinclair cleaned up the meat packers with a single stroke, the internet is liberating the Great Unwashed."*

A little dramatic and self-important, but correct.

A decade from now, *The Drudge Manifesto* won't be found on many bookshelves. But the impact of the Drudge Report will be felt as the media Goliaths of today are forced to adapt to the legions of internet-based Davids shouting "Extra. Extra."

CHAPTER 64

America's highest court — a chief's view

I was sworn into the Bar of the United States Supreme Court by Chief Justice Rehnquist. In the Supreme Court courtroom, standing amid a nervous throng of new lawyers, I was in awe of our surroundings. In front of us, just yards away, were the nine justices who lead the judicial branch of our nation. All around us were the artwork and artifacts of American jurisprudence. Later, when I read the chief justice's book about the court, I thought back to that day I took the oath.

That oath was one of fidelity and honor. It doesn't get mentioned much in lawyer jokes, but a commitment to these timeless principles is the foundation of what good lawyers do. We put rule of law above the rule of men. We understand that justice is a process, not a result. And, most of all, we pledge in our oath to conduct ourselves "uprightly and according to law." That doesn't make lawyers perfect or even good. But it does make us accountable to the legal profession and to the courts.

The chief justice wrote a compelling book about the high court and I found it an enjoyable read. This book review was my attempt to entice the newspaper's readers to join with the chief in a walk through the hallways of history and the corridors of constitutional law.

The work of the Supreme Court affects every American and I wanted to make this book accessible to non-lawyers. Here's how I did it.

Review of *The Supreme Court* by Chief Justice William Rehnquist
PUBLISHED: *The Columbus Dispatch* — January 14, 2001

U pon his retirement, President John Adams told others that Chief Justice John Marshall had been his "gift to the American people." Marshall's historic tenure with the court proved that sentiment right. But President Ronald Reagan could also lay claim to that same notion when it comes to his nomination of William Rehnquist as chief justice.

Rehnquist has led our nation's highest court through numerous legal thickets armed with a keen intellect and an ever-present sense of history. Whenever he chooses to retire, historians will likely judge him among the elite of his predecessors.

Of the 16 men who've served at the helm of America's judicial branch, few have had a more unique perspective on law and justice than our current chief justice. Rehnquist has been a top Justice Department attorney, a Supreme Court clerk, an associate justice, and now, chief justice. In his nearly 30 years on the court, he served with six different presidents (soon to be seven) and ruled on everything from *Roe v. Wade* and the Watergate tapes to the latest skirmishes over affirmative action and religion in public schools. Along the way, he was one of only two chief justices to preside over a presidential impeachment and the only one to help decide a presidential election debacle.

It is from this vantage that Rehnquist wrote a history of the court he now leads. This month, that work has been re-released with substantial updates and two new chapters. Anyone who follows the grand history of America's court of last resort will find this book indispensable reading.

He opens with a clerk's eye view of the court in 1952 when he worked for Justice Robert Jackson. This is a good place to start, as the reader quickly becomes familiar with the basic operations of the court as Rehnquist learns his new duties.

At one point, after hearing criticism of the justice he serves, he describes his fellow clerks with commentary that is biting yet self-depreciating: *"It would be all but impossible to assemble a more hypercritical, not to say arrogant, audience than a group of law clerks criticizing an opinion circulated by one of their employers. Their scorn — and in due time it became my scorn too — was not reserved for Justice Jackson but was lavished with considerable impartiality upon the products of all nine chambers of the court."*

This is the author's most compelling voice. Describing the rituals and inner workings of the court — as Rehnquist does early on and again at the end — makes for effortless reading and substantial enjoyment. He also takes great care to explain the personal background of many of the justices, often pausing to insert a choice geographical or family reference. These mentions add character and show the chief justice relishes detail.

But the rest of the book is less inviting. To fully appreciate Rehnquist's lengthy interplay between American history and the many rulings of the court, it helps to have a law degree. Or an extreme fondness for the details of legal history. Only those so situated will savor a 14-paragraph direct quotation from Chief Justice Marshall's most famous opinion.

Even those who skip the drier passages will enjoy much of the legal discussion. From the drama of *Marbury v. Madison* (which established the core principle of judicial review) through the politics surrounding FDR's attempt to pack the court, to the expansion of individual liberties under the Warren Court, the chief justice skillfully interweaves the personalities, legal theory, and public pressures that molded the outcomes of our country's most important cases.

Rehnquist's writing skills go well beyond his primary subject. He artfully details the historical underpinnings of several of the cases at issue. For example, prior to examining the infamous *Dred Scott* decision, he provides a thoroughly readable exposition of the status of slavery in the 1850s. His short summary would do Civil War historian Bruce Catton proud.

The chief justice does more than recount *Dred Scott*, a case that strengthened the hand of slaveholders. He picks the legal reasoning apart with a legal rapier. Yet he stops short of bowing to the view held by some that the decision indelibly stains the legacy of the court that endorsed it. Rehnquist calls Chief Justice Roger Taney's holding *"a serious mistake for the reasons I have earlier suggested, but that opinion should not be allowed to blot out the very constructive work otherwise done in his career."*

That's not to say Rehnquist is charitable to all whom he covers. When the Civil War habeas corpus suspension case was argued, he points out that the attorney who argued in favor of Lincoln's war measure (James Speed) was *"surely one of the nation's least-gifted attorneys general."* Ouch.

Rehnquist's long court tenure and unique perspective give him license to comment on the historic cases he's witnessed. Yet he refrains. His final chapter, "The Court in its Third Century," is notable for its exclusion of any cases since Rehnquist joined the court in 1972. Instead, he pens a summary and retrospective.

In fact, those who read this in hopes of discovering commentary on the recent Supreme Court ruling in the Florida recounts will be disappointed. The book went to print well before that landmark episode was complete.

Yet as the inaugural of George W. Bush approaches, some who opposed his candidacy may choose to shower the Supreme Court with invective for its ruling in the election contest. Without ever knowing how cogent his point would soon be, Rehnquist offers them — and other court critics — valuable insight.

"Opinions may differ as to whether in a particular case the Supreme Court has read the Constitution too expansively or too narrowly. So long as the court is involved, as it has been throughout its more than two centuries of existence, in helping to decide what kind of laws shall govern us, it is bound to draw criticism from those who are offended by its rulings."

In just a few days, as Chief Justice William H. Rehnquist swears in the 43rd President of the United States, his perspective and view from the West Side of the Capitol building will encompass much of Washington's terrain. But in *The Supreme Court*, he has encompassed much, much more.

CHAPTER 65

Internet changing politics in ways Dick Morris misses

The decade of the 1990s will be remembered by many for the "dot com bubble" and the Bill Clinton administration. Dick Morris, something of a slithery political operative working both sides of the aisle, was caught up in both of those phenomena. He was a close advisor to President Clinton, often counseling the president on the phone late into the night and confounding White House staffers with his contrarian advice.

Soon after falling from this prominent position in the wake of a prostitution scandal, Morris sought to use the leverage of the rapidly-forming internet to change politics and advance his own role at the intersection of voting and the web.

We know now that his effort failed. Nor did his book really explore these issues. Although I didn't care for Mr. Morris or his ethics, I thought the topic of his book would be worth sharing. That's why I reviewed his book and gave readers the critical perspective it deserved.

Book Review of *Vote.com* by Dick Morris
PUBLISHED: *The Columbus Dispatch*—February 1, 2000

Dick Morris gained national attention for his ability to help politicians oversimplify points to gain strategic advantage.

In his new book, *Vote.com*, Morris is up to his old tricks. Using more hype than hypothesis, he predicts how internet use will change how we select, interact with, and ultimately judge our elected leaders. On the few occasions when he advances that central thesis, he provides an interesting glimpse at the future of politics.

Yet most of Morris' claims deserve to be found at Overreach.com. In what appears to be largely an attempt to promote his Vote.com website, Morris spends much of the book suggesting that internet political activity in general — and his website in particular — will save society from such ills as special-interest dominance of government, the banality of contemporary political discourse, low voter turnout, and the tyranny of China's repressive government.

That's not to say that he hasn't stumbled upon a few interesting ideas. For example, in the New Hampshire presidential primary today, Vote.com will be running internet voting that will allow pundits and political junkies to compare voter interest nationally with the Granite State results.

Morris also envisions a day when people interested in government will go to his website, register their views on a host of topics and then receive an e-mail as elected officials vote on those issues. This is an excellent use of technology and one that can help our political process.

Another interesting prediction involves a candidate web page of the not-too-distant future. Imagine logging onto a candidate's home page and seeing an area where you can type in a question about the candidate's platform. In just seconds, a video of the candidate runs, answering your question in detail.

This scenario is well within the capabilities of current technology. Morris rightfully points out how this kind of feedback will change how voters obtain information about people running for office. *"It will be, literally, the best way of getting to know him short of actually spending several hours in his company,"* Morris writes.

He can be persuasive. Yet beyond the occasional interesting conjecture about the potential mixture of politics and technology, this book lacks focus.

Morris is obsessed with Bill and Hillary Clinton. Some chapters include more references to Mr. Clinton than they do to the internet. Much of the book is devoted to defending the actions Clinton took while he took advice from Morris. Other passages ridicule Clinton for things done without Morris' guidance.

Unfortunately, readers seeking to learn the full potential of how politics and government will be changed by the internet will be as disappointed as Bob Dole was on election night 1996. The book contains only enough cutting-edge information to fill a good-sized newspaper article.

A warning to the easily annoyed: Morris presumes that the rest of us view the world in the same way he does. For example, he refers to the Clinton impeachment as the "unimpeachment." Well then.

If you studied statistics in college, prepare to be further annoyed. Morris dishonestly glosses over the problems inherent in polls that allow participants to choose to be involved. Because people who seek out such a poll are typically predisposed to strong opinions, the polls are not reliable gauges of overall public opinion. Further, these sorts of polls are vulnerable to electronic stuffing of the ballot box by organized groups that encourage members to log on repeatedly and cast multiple votes.

Morris' self-promotion and unwillingness to cover this subject comprehensively are more than just disappointing. It's duplicitous. Technology will revolutionize politics. But it will happen in many more places than Vote.com and in many more ways than Morris discusses. The true potential of the internet will be advanced by people who want to reform the political process, not those who helped create the many problems we now face.

Writing for grief

THE MOST CHALLENGING OF ALL WRITING TASKS CAN
HELP YOU AND OTHERS OVERCOME A LOSS

CHAPTER 66

Writing for those in grief helps all souls

C S. Lewis knew about grief. Torn by death from his mother at a young age, he was sent away to boarding school by a dysfunctional and despondent father. He was wounded in one world war and took to the radio airwaves to calm his shell-shocked British countrymen in the next.

He was unmarried most of his life, fully expecting that the wonders of romance would be locked away from him forever. Yet, in his older years, he met his life's love and promptly married her. Her name was Joy. From that point on, he lived with Joy and with joy. When death cruelly took her just four years into their marriage, Lewis experienced grief yet again.

A master wordsmith himself, Lewis wrote "A Grief Observed," and, about his own grief, he observed:

"And grief still feels like fear. Perhaps, more strictly, like suspense. Or like waiting; just hanging around waiting for something to happen. It gives life a permanently provisional feeling. The act of living is different all through. Her absence is like the sky, spread over everything."

Most of us have felt death's chill freeze over our hearts and bring sharp shivers to our very shaken souls. Among his many promises and plans, God gives us His hope via friends and family, who help us rekindle the warmth of life when we are grieving the loss of someone.

When I've been asked to write eulogies or memorial speeches to help those who grieve, I'm always humbled and awed by the moment. What combination of words could possibly help salve the profound wounds inflicted by a final passing?

Snarling at death's daunt and chafing at the empty page, I typically turn on a Bach concerto, contemplate for a moment, and start to write. Unlike the drafting of logical arguments aimed at the mind, I've found that writing for the heart is more effective when I eschew an outline and begin to form thoughts and capture them in writing. Later, an outline takes shape as I massage and modify the words left in my passionate path.

I've come to believe that writing something — anything at all — is a large part of the consolation endeavor. Those in mourning can be kindly distracted and often uplifted by reading the thoughts and prayerful encouragement of friends. That's why, as my mother always encouraged me, I write notes to people who've lost loved ones. Not texts, emails, or Facebook messages — handwritten notes.

Writing for a large assembly of those wracked in the anguish of mourning is a steeper climb than penning a personal note. And knowing that the words may be recorded in some form to be heard and reviewed by generations to come adds incline and crevasses to that climb.

Luckily, others have taken this task with success and have left markers along the way. Reading the Psalms, New Testament passages on grief, and even some poetry and songs can help focus my thoughts on what to say.

As I write, I try mightily to avoid phrases that are trite. This is harder than it might seem, given that there are a limited number of relevant and appropriate metaphors available to relate to death and mourning. When writing about military or police deaths, the phrase "the ultimate sacrifice" comes too easily. Wordsmiths engaged in this work are called to find a better phrase. I try to do this but am not always as able as I'd like.

As a Christian, I often fall back on words and themes of my faith to help comfort those who grieve. When consoling people who practice Judaism, the Psalms are always a good resource. When the faith tradition of your audience is mixed or unknown, focusing on the life achievements of the departed can often be an effective enterprise. Abraham Lincoln, in his famous letter to the mother of five Union soldiers who died in the cause, undertook this well. Although he mentions God once (appropriately so, in my view), the remainder of his touching missive shows one of America's greatest wordsmiths at work. He wrote:

Executive Mansion
Washington

Nov. 21, 1864.

Dear Madam,

I have been shown in the files of the War Department a statement of the Adjutant General of Massachusetts that you are the mother of five sons who have died gloriously on the field of battle.

I feel how weak and fruitless must be any word of mine which should attempt to beguile you from the grief of a loss so overwhelming. But I cannot refrain from tendering you the consolation that may be found in the thanks of the Republic they died to save.

I pray that our Heavenly Father may assuage the anguish of your bereavement, and leave you only the cherished memory of the loved and lost, and the solemn pride that must be yours to have laid so costly a sacrifice upon the altar of freedom.

Yours, very sincerely and respectfully,

A. Lincoln

May we all aspire to comfort and honor our own dead in such an uplifting, honest, and respectful manner.

CHAPTER 67

The Wonderful Life of Jon Fox

Jon Fox was a celebrity in my hometown. As a long time officeholder and, eventually a U.S. Congressman, nearly everyone knew him. People recognized him from his newspaper articles, political yard signs, or ribbon cutting ceremonies. He was greeted heartily nearly everywhere. But I knew Jon from a different perspective.

Jon gave me my first job in politics. I was in grad school working on a Master's degree in Political Science. He was running for office and my mother encouraged me to reach out to him and offer my help. As usual, Mom was right. So I did. Within days, Jon invited me to at his Country Club. I only knew exclusive clubs like these from the vantage of an employee – parking cars for wedding guests or teaching members' kids how to swim. The glossy china plates, the crisply folded tablecloths, and the pricey food were enough to throw me off during that first conversation. I ordered the cheapest thing on the menu, presuming I'd have to pay my way and knowing that the only money I had was about eight dollars in change scattered in my beaten and bruised VW.

The lunch went on for more than an hour and ended with him offering me a spot on his campaign team. This was a surprise to me, because I knew the state legislative race he was running had been targeted by House leaders as an important one.

Spending 60 hours a week helping Jon win that race was just the first year of what became three decades of friendship, as I watched him attain great heights and, on a few occasions, stunning lows. We had our share of friendly disputes, but he was always one of my biggest supporters. He didn't just shower praise and compliments on others, it was more like a deluge. He was more generous and effusive than I – or anyone else -- deserved. He had a big heart and he wanted his friends, people like me, to succeed.

When his beloved father died, Jon cried on my shoulder, It was awkward and sweet all at once. He asked me to write the eulogy he would give at his father's funeral. It was my honor to do so. Later, Jon was one of the groomsmen at my wedding. And when he and his wife Judi needed to travel through Ohio to pick up their adopted baby, they spent their first night with him in my guest room.

Despite being several years older than me, Jon was like a brother to me. When I learned he was dealing with a few different forms of cancer, I was crestfallen. He deserved better. Each time I spoke with him and asked about his health, he would deflect. He'd ask about my life, my successes, my achievements. And he repeatedly told me he loved me.

When I first met Jon, I would roll my eyes at Jon's compliments. I'd remind him that he already had my vote and that he should save his flattery for an undecided voter. Sadly, I misunderstood him. In a world of cold-blooded political reptiles, Jon was a warm-blooded wooly mammoth. A big, soft, Republican elephant.

His wife called me out of the blue. Between sobs, she informed me he only had a few days left to live. "Jon wants you to write his obituary," Judi told me. After years of writing things for Jon Fox and his many endeavors, he'd given me one last assignment.

Before I could get back to Pennsylvania to bid him goodbye, late on a Sunday night, Jon passed. I was exhausted and had hours of client work due. But I pushed it all aside and sat down to write.

I had to tell Jon's story for those who didn't know him, while also giving a tearful laugh to those reeling from his loss. There were so many angles and anecdotes, I knew I needed a central theme to bring them altogether. As you'll see when you read on, I used a comparison to the protagonist in the famous movie "It's a Wonderful Life." I knew that people who knew and loved George Bailey would know and love Jon Fox.

When your turn comes to write a tribute, eulogy, or obituary for someone you loved, you may want to consider a similar approach. Choose words that will help us know your friend or family member. Tell us the story that still makes you laugh. Share the trait that you remember most.

Write as many of these as you can and then try to weave them together with connecting thoughts. When you're done, you'll likely have too much material. That's good. From there, force yourself to start removing elements. Sculpt your tribute until only the very best of what you've written remains.

The piece I wrote for Jon Fox is my final homage to him. I first posted it on Medium.com, which is a good place to publish op-eds when you're unsure of traditional print coverage. Later, the piece was published in a local newspaper. I was honored and pleased when the rabbi presiding over Jon's funeral – a man I never met – quoted from my piece as a way to end his eulogy for Jon.

PUBLISHED: *Feb. 12, 2018 on Medium.com.*

This is the new chapter of my book. This is the new chapter of my book. This is the new chapter of my book. This is the new chapter of my book.

Bedford Falls had George Bailey. And Abington had Jon Fox.

Fans of the classic movie "It's A Wonderful Life" remember George Bailey as the Bedford Falls hometown boy who devoted himself to helping others and was ultimately rewarded when his countless acts of love and generosity were returned in kind. Friends of Abington stalwart Jon Fox will remember him in much the same way.

Fox, one of the most popular and durable elected officials in modern Montgomery County history, died Sunday night at the age of 70. He was the Abington-born son of a prominent family who rejected a life of privilege to pursue public service and help others. The people he aided repeatedly flocked to the polls to elect him to office, eventually sending him to the United States Congress for two terms. He met and conferred with U.S. presidents, ambassadors, and famous people from across the globe. Yet he preferred the quiet company of friends and neighbors in Abington.

Most of us know how to spot a typical politician: someone looking over your shoulder searching for another hand to shake, another vote to secure. Many politicians promptly forget the people who supported them, content with the prestige and perks of office. For these office-holders, constituent service is handed off to a low-paid staffer, with instructions to do the bare minimum and move along to the next request.

Jon Fox rejected that ethos. Serving in local, county, state and federal office, he shunned contentious partisan fights, preferring the quiet satisfaction of helping people when government stood in their way. His life, his desk, even his car was a messy mix of papers gathered from people in need who trusted that Jon would come through for them. Despite the collection of clutter, he usually did.

Service to others came early for Jon Fox. As a young man, he served in the U.S. Air Force Reserve for six years, building a brimming sense of patriotism that fueled his fervent belief in American exceptionalism. He soon joined the Republican Party and stood by its leaders in good times and bad.

His first exposure to government was working for the General Services Administration in Washington, D.C. Then, after graduating from the first-ever law school class of Delaware Law School in Wilmington, Delaware, Jon passed the Pennsylvania bar and began working as an Assistant District Attorney in Montgomery County. He prosecuted dangerous criminals, volunteered to help battered women, and built a strong alliance with local police. He later established a private law practice, where—unlike almost any other lawyer—he routinely made house calls, helping local senior citizens and those with minor legal problems right at their own kitchen table.

Jon's first elected office was as a Township Commissioner, representing the Jenkintown and Baederwood sections of Abington. He won votes by sheer persistence and good nature. Once elected, he stepped up his effort to an even higher level, particularly focusing on the needs of local senior citizens. He served two terms and won the respect of leaders twice his age.

In 1984, he earned statewide attention by winning an Abington-Rockledge state legislative seat that had been held by the Democratic Party for several years. In that campaign, he knocked on thousands of doors, worked 18-hour days, and won by a margin of more than two to one. Later, in 1991, Montgomery County residents elected him to be County Commissioner and then, on the second try, he was elected to the United States House of Representatives in 1994, where he served two terms.

He was the son of business titan William Fox, a driving force behind several Abington-area institutions including founding local radio station WIBF, the Fox Pavilion (now known as the Pavilion) and local apartment buildings Benson Manor, Benson East, and Foxcroft. Jon's mother Elainne was the spark of the family and Jon inherited her enthusiasm and flair for relating to others. The whole Fox family, including sister Caren and brother Larry, quickly learned that Jon had a knack for politics and government.

After graduating from nearby Cheltenham High School, Jon went to Penn State University, where he became a cheerleader, urging on the massive crowds that flock to the Nittany Lion football games. He revered Penn State for the rest of his life. While he was always willing to put a Republican bumper sticker on his car, Jon's favorite sticker was non-political. It read "if God's not a Penn State fan, why is the sky blue and white?"

Jon was Jewish but, for many years, he dressed as Santa to bring toys to local children. He had a habit of running late, and one December day, while racing between toy deliveries, he didn't have time to change out of the Santa outfit. Driving down Easton Road, wearing the red hat and beard, he stopped at a red light, just behind a car sporting a Penn State decal. Jon didn't know the driver, but he got out of his car, walked up to the other car and tapped on the glass. The man behind the wheel rolled down the window, mouth agape at the white-bearded visage. Jon leaned in and whispered, "even Santa Claus roots for Penn State."

Jon had one true love of his life, his wife Judi whom he met while she was working for Jon's father in the 1980s. She cared for him like no other and her love and devotion gave Jon the stability to continue his work for fellow Republicans, people who needed legal help, or just about anyone with a problem.

Jon passed away after battling multiple forms of cancer over the last few years. Despite the toll of debilitating treatments, he continued his legal practice, representing clients in local courts even as he grew weaker.

Jon's hope for the future was focused on his son, Will—named for Jon's father. Jon loved Will with the blooming passion of the proudest of fathers. His gentle guidance and doting tenderness encircled Will in an extravagant embrace.

Most members of Congress leave behind a legacy of laws. But Jon's is a heritage of hope. Like the fictional George Bailey, Jon was beloved by his hometown and his success was built by advancing the success of others. His encouragement of friends was boundless, his optimism untamed.

In his seven decades of life, Jon rarely rested. There was always another person to help, another problem to solve, another burden to share.

Now, he rests.

CHAPTER 68

Comforting parents of a child lost to overdose

Although I've chosen to obscure the names here, this is a personal letter I wrote to dear friends whose daughter had died tragically of a heroin overdose. Her death occurred well before what America now knows is a widespread epidemic of opiate abuse and fatality. To shield my friends from intrusion, I've changed the name of the young woman who died to "Mary."

Writing to or for someone who's deep in grief requires a light touch and much forethought. So often we spill out phrases that may hurt more than help. Things like "she's in a better place," or "this was God's will" come quickly but may hurt more than help. We've all struggled with what words to employ when we talk with someone who's hurting.

I typically write notes to people who've lost loved ones and, when doing so, I try to mention some of the attributes of the person who died. I've found that it also helps to give some comfort and context around the passing.

Perhaps most importantly, I also try to remind my friends who are grieving that I'm praying for them. I'm no expert in counseling but I am in earnest to help. For me, that means writing.

I hope that these examples may help you find the words to comfort someone in the grip of grief.

Sent: August 9, 2009

Dear J and K: I wanted to wait a week or two to send this to you, as I'm sure you've been overwhelmed with correspondence about your tragic loss. Although I can't know precisely how you're feeling right now, I'm sure you're still in a haze as you come to grips with the new normal, a world without your sweet departed Mary.

Be strong. [Your two remaining daughters] look to you. They need to know that all you've taught them about God, Christ, and redemption remains true.

I know that any mere words I can offer won't help fill the void left by the loss of a child, particularly one as loved and missed as Mary. None of us wants to face such a day, yet you have done so with great poise, love, and grace.

In my own faith journey of the last decade, I've learned much and found great solace in the writings of Christian writer C.S. Lewis (you may know him from the *Chronicles of Narnia*). In a moment of great personal sorrow, he wrote: *"No one ever told me that grief felt so like fear."* You now know all too well what he meant.

Yet Lewis came to his belief in Christ (and in the resurrection that will bring us all together again with your daughter Mary and with Jesus) and later wrote of the pain that death brings to those left behind: *"Pain removes the veil; it plants the flag of truth within the fortress of a rebel soul."*

The flag of truth is that God, too, lost His child at far too young an age and so He understands your pain more than you'll ever be able to know while locked in the struggles, sadness, and suffering of this earthly sphere.

As you try mightily to move forward from this and provide comfort and some semblance of normalcy to [your two remaining daughters], I hope you will remember how great a life you gave to your first-born daughter.

I was reminded of how close you were to her as I reviewed all the family photos on display at the church. I have no doubt that Mary knew you loved her very much. You filled her life with joy and devotion. She was so much better for it.

And, judging by the number of young people at the service, it's clear to me that she touched many people. Her own influence will be felt for a long time to come.

You made Mary's world better and she made our world better. Twenty-five years is a blink in what might have been a long life, but Mary made much of her time. Her art, her sports, her surfing, her friendships, and her family ties all had a wide reach that you will never be able to fully measure.

The lights of the world are a bit dimmer without this vibrant force of nature. You feel her loss like a gaping chasm that cannot be filled. But I hope you will remember that while Mary has passed from this world, she lives on in the world where we will soon enough dwell. It seems far away, but there will be a time when you are reunited with your sweet daughter and your tears will be wiped away forever.

St. Paul, writing to the church he started in Corinth, specifically addressed what happens when we die. *"So will it be with the resurrection of the dead. The body that is sown is perishable, it is raised imperishable; it is sown in dishonor, it is raised in glory; it is sown in weakness, it is raised in power; it is sown a natural body, it is raised a spiritual body. If there is a natural body, there is also a spiritual body."* (1 Corinthians 15:42-44)

This is the truth you've been taught your whole life. This is the truth you taught Mary. This is the truth you must continue to teach [your two remaining daughters].

You were both important people in my life as I matured and your example as parents was a positive one for me. The love you showed Mary was an inspiration to me then and has influenced my attitude as a father.

God bless you.

CHAPTER 69

Eulogy: Remembering Robert Weaver

My father died in 2013, just a few months after my mother died. Although they'd been divorced for decades and were married to different people and living in different towns, the fact that they died so close in time was odd and difficult. Although I was not as close to my father as I was my mother, I knew I wanted to give a eulogy for him.

Dad was never famous, although he was born of prominent relatives (one of the founders of Philco, Inc., which was one of America's biggest companies in the 20th century). He was an ordinary man who had lived a rather ordinary life. But I felt he deserved to have some final recognition. While puzzling over what to say, I started reading some letters he sent home during his service on a U.S. Navy destroyer overseas. As you'll read, I found inspiration in one of those letters and used it to frame this eulogy.

I also used some light humor to tell the audience about my Dad. After each anecdote, I established a pattern of saying "lesson learned." This kind of structure — particularly when used in groups of three — can provide rhythm to a speech.

Delivered: May 4, 2013

I'm Mark Weaver, Robert's only son. Robert Everett Weaver. His first name was his father's first name. He wasn't a junior, but he and his Dad were both Robert and were both R.E. Weaver. In fact, my Dad liked to use the initials on his correspondence and other things bearing his name. I think it was his small way of paying tribute to his father.

His middle name was Everett. This was a family name, the last name of his famous grandfather, Edward Earle Everett. In fact, my Dad's family and closest friends of his youth called him Everett, which was the way he was addressed at home.

My father was proud of his family's colorful history. His father, Robert, was a successful food broker in Philadelphia. Despite being something of a high-powered executive in his industry, my grandfather was gentle, warm, and he especially loved children. My sisters and I were the beneficiaries of the caring and kindness of the man we called Pop Pop Weaver.

Dad's mother, Edyth, was the only child of a family of great accomplishment. Her mother, Rosemary, was a strong-willed force in the family who, in her final years, lived with Dad and his brother, Richard, in their home on East Mill Road in Flourtown.

But Dad enjoyed talking most about his maternal grandfather, Edward Earle Everett. Edward was an adventurer as a young man, working on a sailing ship and even — in the late 1800s — was captured and later released by pirates. He was an inventor who, despite little formal schooling, had the smarts of a trained engineer and the motivation of a world-class salesman. Edward parlayed those skills into a job as an inventor and designer of a new technology called storage batteries.

Eventually, he became a founding board member of a local enterprise called the Philadelphia Storage Battery Company, which was later shortened to simply the Philadelphia Company. Rosemary came up with a nickname for the company, and it quickly became known as Philco.

Edward was superintendent of the Philco Plant and served on the board of directors.

His success blessed first the Everett family, then later, the Weaver family, with fortune and wealth. Dad's parents traveled the world and although he graduated from Springfield High School, Dad spent most of his youth in private schools

For the younger people here, Philco was an international brand that was to the middle of the 20th century what Sony or even Apple is today.

A child of privilege could have somehow avoided serving in the Korean War but Dad chose to serve nonetheless. He enlisted in the Navy and spent three years sailing the world on the destroyer U.S.S. Lowry. He was a radioman, using Morse Code and voice transmissions to relay messages between ships.

During the last several months, my sisters and I have been combing through old letters, photos, and other things that belonged to Dad. Several of them are posted on the boards in the lobby. If you get a chance to look at them, you'll see many pictures of Dad serving in the Navy.

Dad wrote letters home and kept a journal while in the Navy. In one letter, he chronicled his ship's efforts shooting at communist supply trains headed to North Korea. From the details he gave, Dad was clearly proud of his country and of his shipmates.

He ended that letter to his parents by saying: *"We've worked hard, but we've done a good job and we're proud of ourselves."*

In December 1951, Dad was stationed in Norfolk while his ship underwent repairs. He made a diary entry that's worth repeating and typical of his light-hearted style. He wrote: *"I spent most of my time there going home or saving money. Took girls out in Norfolk — Helen — no fun whatsoever."*

Dad left the Navy but the Navy never really left him. He remained proud of his service and was active in the alumni association of his ship.

Many eulogies concentrate on the work accomplishments of the person who died. But although my father worked his whole life and often worked hard, his work was not his passion. He enjoyed meeting with and talking to people and he chose a job — salesman — where he could do just that.

Dad's real passion was his avocation. Or, to be more precise, his avocations.

He loved playing tennis, pitching quoits, and having friendly conversation. Light-hearted banter and chatting were his stock and trade.

He was no intellectual and didn't want to be one. In fact, in many ways, he was the opposite of my mother, Joanne. My sisters and I often wonder how they ever got together.

His lack of pretense led him to share many stories from his youth that kept our family entertained. And, even when he was the focus of the joke, he took it all in stride and was a good sport. Most of the anecdotes revolved around the theme of "lessons learned" by my Dad.

Like when he was a boy home alone, he found out what happens when you use a lit match to look for something under a couch. The fire trucks come. That's what happens. Lesson learned.

And later as a teen, he found out what happens when you drive your car way down onto the sand at the 34th Street beach in Ocean City. The tow truck comes. That's what happens. Hopefully, before the high tide comes in. Lesson learned.

And finally, there's one favorite story of Dad's education through experimentation. The Flourtown house had a large lawn that Dad would mow with a fancy gas-powered mower. Once, after gassing up the mower he decided to find out what happens when you take a hot match, blow it out and toss it — still hot — into the gas can. You spend the first half of your sophomore year in high school without eyebrows. That's what happens. Lesson learned.

Although he had some crazy run-ins with reality, Dad was handy with tools. These skills were not taught to him by his father but rather by his grandmother's chauffeur, Stanley, who took a liking to my father and showed him how to use tools to fix and build things.

When Dad visited, he was always willing, and — in fact — eager to help with handyman tasks that needed to be done. Dad tried to pass these skills on to me but I am sad to report that his best efforts in that regard failed.

But Dad, like his grandfather, Edward Everett, was an inventor. When I was a child, we spent our summers at 30th Street beach in Ocean City, New Jersey.

I have early memories of laying on my back on a beach towel and looking up into a large beach umbrella that was providing shade to our family. Woven among the spokes that held the umbrella together was some white netting. Hanging within that netting were our valuables like a camera, binoculars, or a wallet.

I just presumed that all beach umbrellas had such a convenient feature. It makes a lot of sense to have a secure place for items that you don't want visible or down in the sand.

But I was wrong. The only beach umbrella in the world that had that netting was ours. Dad had come up with the idea on his own and improvised a solution.

So, in 1979, Dad patented his invention. You can look it up in the U.S. Patent Office, it's number 4,154,255. He called it "Weaver's Web."

Dad tried to market it for a while but he preferred a life of tennis, travel, and time with (his second wife) Alex to hustling his invention — so it never really went anywhere.

The patent still exists and now passes to the next generation. So, if any of the children or grandchildren want to become the chief executive officer of Weavers Web, Inc. — let me know. I'll set you up and maybe you can get rich off Dad's idea.

So, what lesson can we learn from the 83 years Robert Everett Weaver spent with us?

The first one is obvious. Talk to people. Chat them up about their interests and tell them about yours. Life is easier when people can be amicable.

I spoke to one of my old friends last night who knew my Dad and he called Dad "a genial fellow." True enough.

But here's the Bob Weaver lesson I hope my own kids will take from the life of this decent man.

Whenever my sisters or I got a new toy, or a new piece of sporting equipment, Dad was always insistent that we immediately get a permanent marker and write the name "Weaver" on it. Everywhere in our house, there were items of every kind and description with "Weaver" written on them. If you didn't know the name of the people who lived there, you might have thought it was a brand name!

Anyway, Dad told us that we should write our name on things in case they get lost. But I think he may have had something of a deeper motive for this habit of his.

This man was proud to be named Weaver. He came from a proud heritage and an accomplished family. He wanted us to be proud of it, as well.

This is a name worth displaying. This is a family worth noticing. And when your name is on your things, maybe — just maybe — you take a little more pride in what you do with it.

So, let's remember my Dad. Let's remember Bob Weaver. And, like him, let's remember to put our name on what we do and take pride in it.

And — just like Dad said when he finished his long cruise around the world in the Navy — you too can say about your own journey: *"We've worked hard but we've done a good job and we're proud of ourselves."*

CHAPTER 70

Eulogy:
I'm Joanne Weaver's son

Sometimes people ask me which speeches were the hardest to write. I usually tell them that writing speeches come easy to me. But, when my mother died in 2013, I set out to write her eulogy and expected it to be difficult. It wasn't. Rather, my mother's eulogy was the easiest speech I've ever written and the hardest speech I've ever delivered. The speech was simple to write because I had so much material and it all meant so much to me. If there was any hard part involved, it was deciding what to leave out.

My mother was a well-known community leader in our hometown. The local newspaper noted her passing in a front page news story. At her memorial service, the auditorium was filled with hundreds of people who came to remember her life. I wanted these people to learn about my mother in a way far beyond what they already know. This eulogy was my chance.

I rarely speak from a text anymore, as I'm able to use talking points or PowerPoint slides to keep me focused and moving along effectively. But this speech was different. I didn't quite memorize it but I practiced it so many times I was able to give it from a prepared text while maintaining eye contact with the audience most of the time.

If you want to read the most passionate words I've ever written, keep reading.

DELIVERED: March 2, 2013

I can't tell you how many times, throughout my life, people have said to me — "you're Joanne's son."

First, it happened in school. Since my mother was a teacher, administrator, and later a principal, nearly everyone who worked in the Abington School District knew and respected my mom.

So, every new teacher, every new principal, sometimes even a coach would hear my last name, make a connection in their head and then say to me — "you're Joanne's son."

But it wasn't just school.

My mother was an elder and a respected person at our church, so people at Abington Presbyterian often knew me first as "Joanne's son."

Later, as I got to know people in local government and in the Abington community, that was how I was often introduced to people — "this is Mark Weaver, he's Joanne's son."

In fact — most people may not know that as a senior in college, I ran for Abington School Board. It was the first and — trust me — the last time I've ever run for office.

And before the voters had the good sense to elect someone else to do that job, there was even a minor controversy in the local newspaper covering the race. Some people wondered how I could serve on a school board when my mother was an employee of the district.

My first big political scandal! Not really.

But it was yet another time when my status was being evaluated through the prism of being "Joanne's son."

Don't get me wrong, most of the time it was an enviable credential to have.

On one occasion, an Abington police officer thought that — maybe — just maybe — I might have not fully stopped at a stop sign over in Glenside. Imagine that!

Halfway through writing the ticket the officer came back up to my car and asked — "Hold on — are you Joanne's son?"

I told him I was, and through some miraculous process, the ticket was written with the wrong date on it.

With that kind of defect, it wasn't too hard for the local judge to dismiss it. Especially when he called me back into his chambers afterward and asked me — you guessed it — "aren't you Joanne's son?"

What's interesting is that Mom, like me, grew up in the shadow of a well-known and very well-respected parent — her dad, Ken Mateer.

To be clear, her mother, Jean Mateer, was a significant influence on Joanne. But anyone who knows the whole story knows that the household where my mom grew up was dominated by the academic, athletic, and civic achievements of her dad.

And he had high expectations of my mother. Very high.

But as we reflect on my mother's life today, it can be said without qualification, that in each of those three categories — academic, athletic, and civic — she was every bit the achiever — the overachiever — my grandfather was.

Those of you who knew Mom as an adult might not know that she was an athlete in high school and a good one at that. Her dad expected his daughters to be involved in athletics to stay busy and learn teamwork. My mom did that. And her love of sports lasted a lifetime.

She was a faithful spectator at the many sporting events of her own children — Karen's field hockey games, Laurie's softball games, and my lacrosse games. She also loved the Phillies.

Next was academics. Most of you know that Mom graduated from the University of Pennsylvania. But the Mateer family had no money for tuition. And the financial aid resources available today simply weren't around in the 1940s.

But because Joanne was such an outstanding student, she earned a Pennsylvania State Senate scholarship, which paid for her tuition at Penn. And she took that university by storm, excelling at her school-work, joining a sorority, and becoming editor of the Penn Yearbook, which was considered a scholarly and difficult position to obtain.

Her co-editor was another sharp young kid with big dreams for the future: U.S. Senator Arlen Specter.

She went on to earn a master's degree at Temple, several other graduate school credits, an elementary principal's certificate and a secondary principal's certificate. She even taught graduate school at night.

Ken Mateer was alive to see all of it and I'm an eyewitness to the fact that he was bust-out-all-over proud of her academic achievements. And her academics and career in education largely mirrored his.

For those of us who believe past is prologue, that comes as no surprise.

Sports, academics, and community.

That brings us to my mom's dedication to community. I would guess that's where most of you here today came to know her.

Although she taught elsewhere early in her career, my mom spent most of her professional life in the Abington schools. Classroom teacher, reading teacher, curriculum specialist, founder of the Human Development Program, and a principal for two different elementary schools.

And despite raising three rowdy kids with little or no help, she made the time to be a positive force in her community during what little free time she had.

She was one of the founders of the Abington Police Athletic League, also known as PAL. She was also one of the founders of the Abington DARE program, aimed at warning kids about the dangers of drugs and alcohol abuse.

She loved working with the police. And — as you can see today — they loved her.

She was the first — and only — chairperson of Abington's Community Relations Commission. That group intervened to help calm tensions and defuse tempers when neighborhood conflicts boiled and roiled and threatened to turn violent.

If you remember the 1970s in Abington, you know there were at least two major racial conflagrations that could have divided our community black against white. My mother was on the front lines of those disputes and was accepted and respected by both sides. The fact that they never deteriorated into mass violence is a testament to her calm approach and caring style.

And she'd be the first to remind me to tell you that she was just one person in a larger effort.

For more than three decades, when there was a difficult neighbor dispute or racial incident, Abington police had my mother on speed dial.

She and her commission achieved real and lasting harmony in that community. That was her wish; that was her way.

Athletics, academics, and community.

My mother brought great joy and union to so many people. But her life was rent with sorrow and, too often — before she met (her second husband) Rudy — emptiness.

There were countless times when Mom longed for love and acceptance and didn't get it.

Her childhood was not one of destitution but it was one of great need and many occasions of simply going without.

While cars were becoming a common sight in middle-class neighborhoods of her youth, she and her family couldn't afford one until she was nearly grown.

So, they relied on rides from friends. Or they walked.

At Penn, she was surrounded by children of privilege. In many cases, they were the next generation of the ruling class. That wasn't her crowd and it wasn't her pedigree.

She was frugal because she had to be.

Two stories of that era stand out to me. Each time I recall them, they wash over me with bracing waves of sadness and empathy.

While she was a member of a sorority, Mom couldn't afford to pay for her room and board. Her scholarship only covered tuition.

So, after each meal served in the sorority house, her sorority sisters retired to other rooms to study or socialize. Mom would stay behind to clean up and do the dishes that her friends had left on the table. That and other cleaning jobs in the house paid for her room and board.

On another occasion, Mom had worked all summer to save money for her personal living expenses. So, at the beginning of one school year, she thought she would try to stretch her pennies a little further by buying some things in bulk.

One day, she bought a large glass bottle of shampoo. Large enough to last her a semester.

I'll never forget her sad expression when she told me how heartbroken she was when — moments after paying for the big bottle of shampoo and walking outside— she accidentally dropped it and it shattered in front of her. That sidewalk was soaked with shampoo and tears alike.

A small story about a big challenge in Joanne's early life. But her adult years were often tough, too.

In the early 1970s, not too many families experienced divorce, and Mom often felt like one of the only divorced mothers around.

So, she worked two or three jobs to support Karen, Laurie, and me. And child support of $100 a week helped a little, but not much.

Yet, she always found a way to give us a nice Christmas surprise — whether it was a piano, a ping-pong table or, once, a trip to Disney World.

It would be years later before my sisters and I learned Mom paid for it all by going into debt and choosing to save nothing for her own retirement.

But, with my mom, other people came first. Her aging parents. Her dead sister's children. My sisters and me.

And — I'm guessing — so many of you who came here today.

So, what legacy can we glean from the life of this good and decent woman? It's simple and it's complex — all at once.

When you sort through all that my mom did in 82 years looking for that one common thread, that one foundational principle that she taught us, it's this: Treat other people the way you want to be treated.

She taught that to parents and students in the "magic circles" she moderated as the Human Development Program coordinator for Abington Schools.

Her message to the people in the magic circles: *"We all like to be listened to, so let's all listen."*

She also taught the golden rule to neighbors who were so angry at each other over relations so brittle that they teetered on the edge of violence, sometimes even racial violence.

Her message to the neighbors in an uproar: *"We all like to be understood, so let's all try to understand."*

She even taught that message in our own family.

Like when she said: *"Mark, you don't like to be handcuffed to a tree so why don't you go un-handcuff your little sister from that tree?"*

Mom was funny that way.

Treat others the way you want to be treated.

It was her mantra, but it wasn't original to her.

Jesus taught us that the second greatest commandment is *"love your neighbor as yourself."* That's the legacy of Joanne Weaver.

That's what she wanted us to remember.

So easy to say it; so hard to live it. But we can do it. If it matters to us, we can do it. If *she* matters to us, we should do it.

A great lesson. A great life. A great woman.

Which leaves me where I began.

A lot of people call me by a lot of different names. My law students call me "professor." The defendants in the court where I'm a magistrate call me "Your Honor." Jamieson and Robbie call me "Dad."

But the title that will endlessly humble me; the term that will always swell my chest; the identity that's become so familiar; so descriptive; yet such a challenge to deserve...

I'm Joanne Weaver's son.

A wordsmith's toolbox

A SUMMARY OF MY TECHNIQUES AND STRATEGIES TO HELP YOU IN YOUR NEXT WRITING ENDEAVOR

CHAPTER 71

Use these tools to sharpen your writing

This book is meant to be much more than a collection of some of my best-written work. I'm hopeful you can use these chapters as a regular resource to help you improve and sharpen your own writing skills. What I may lack in intellect I make up in experience. I've learned much of what I know from that cruel teaching pair: trial and error. I also know good writing when I read it. That's why, when I find a good writer, someone who wrangles words the way J.S. Bach melded musical notes, I usually carefully look for things I can learn. This chapter contains some of my best recommendations on what strategies, theories, and tactics I use to write essays and speeches that (as in the subtitle of this book) persuade, inform, and amuse.

People are easily distracted. Write with that in mind.

Remember every piece of writing competes for a readers' time. Only the best headlines placed in the right places will consistently attract readers in today's constant whirl of texts, tweets, and alerts. The quality of your writing and persuasiveness of your arguments will determine how long someone is willing to ignore distractions and focus on your work.

Good writers constantly keep their target audience in mind. Writing for readers of an industry journal vs. your local small-town newspaper requires a much different approach, structure, and vocabulary. Who are you trying to influence today? Dads trying to read while dodging a toddler whining for a snack will need a different writing approach than mothers helping a daughter plan her wedding. A businessperson with a never-silent phone and a cascade of emails will only linger long enough for you to make your point quickly and in a memorable fashion, while a senior citizen with a diminishing pool of friends and children who rarely call may be willing to endure a bit more exposition from you. Think these audience issues through before you write. Envision the end product and how it might be consumed.

No matter the format, shorter sentences and punchier phrases will draw in your reader. *Trust me.*

Where possible and appropriate, so will bolded headlines and sub headlines. ***I mean it.***

Look at the way a modern newspaper is laid out and you'll get some ideas for what you can do to make the piece more graphically approachable. Good newspaper editors care as much about layout as content.

Fewer words will almost always do the job better than more words. Here's a case study on that precise point.

Two politicians spoke at the dedication of a Pennsylvania cemetery on Nov. 19, 1863. The keynote speaker, one of the most respected orators in the nation, gave his listeners 13,607 words to ponder. His skill as a wordsmith was not in doubt. In fact, the opening sentence of U.S. Senator Edward Everett's remarks was best in class for the speeches of the day:

> *"Standing beneath this serene sky, overlooking these broad fields now reposing from the labors of the waning year, the mighty Alleghenies dimly towering before us, the graves of our brethren beneath our feet, it is with hesitation that I raise my poor voice to break the eloquent silence of God and Nature."*

You'd think that such a great American wordsmith would be some-one you learned about in history class with the likes of Daniel Web-ster, William Jennings Bryant, or Martin Luther King. But Sen. Everett was eclipsed that day. The second speaker spoke many fewer words than Everett— 271 to be exact. And the quality of the rhetoric was similarly stellar.

Yet by saying so much in such a short amount of time, President Abraham Lincoln's address to those gathered that day in Gettysburg became the greatest speech in our nation's history. His voice was, by most accounts, high pitched and a bit off-key. But his words were pitch perfect.

This great exposition of the American founding, the American re-sponse to adversity, and the American devotion to honor is short enough to include here and important enough for you to luxuriate over the deftness and economy of Lincoln's word choices:

> "Four score and seven years ago our fathers brought forth on this continent, a new nation, conceived in Liberty, and dedicated to the proposition that all men are created equal.
>
> Now we are engaged in a great civil war, testing whether that nation, or any nation so conceived and so dedicated, can long endure. We are met on a great battlefield of that war. We have come to dedicate a portion of that field, as a final resting place for those who here gave their lives that that nation might live. It is altogether fitting and proper that we should do this.
>
> But, in a larger sense, we cannot dedicate — we cannot consecrate — we cannot hallow — this ground. The brave men, living and dead, who struggled here, have consecrated it, far above our poor power to add or detract. The world will little note, nor long remember what we say here, but it can never forget what they did here.
>
> It is for us the living, rather, to be dedicated here to the unfinished work which they who fought here have thus far so nobly advanced. It is rather for us to be here dedicated to the great task remaining be-fore us — that from these honored dead we take increased devotion to that cause for which they gave the last full measure of devotion — that we here highly resolve that these dead shall not have died in vain — that this nation, under God, shall have a new birth of freedom — and that government of the people, by the people, for the people, shall not perish from the earth."

While we're thinking about the Gettysburg Address, I'll make a short observation. People who write speeches for politicians fall into two categories: those who acknowledge having tried to capture Lincoln's style here and those who've done so and won't admit it. Count me in the first group.

It's easy to write a long speech or column. But it takes work — difficult and uncomfortable effort — to make it work in a shorter format. Another great wordsmith, British philosopher John Locke, made this point well when he apologized for the length of an essay he published in 1690, saying: *"I am now too lazy, or too busy to make it shorter."* I like an honest man. Someone should write a constitution or something with his work in mind!

Multiple editing sessions (done with respite and change of activity in between) will help you mold and sharpen your words to those that are most needed to convey your thoughts.

Persuasion works when the target is open to it.

Those who desire to persuade others would be wise to recall and embrace the serenity prayer:

> *"God, grant me the serenity to accept what I cannot change; the courage to change the things I can; and the wisdom to know the difference."*

There are some minds you cannot change. Be serene about that. There are many others open to your endeavor. With those people, have the courage to try.

You're highly unlikely to convert liberals into conservatives in the time it takes to read 750 words. It may be enough to just plant a seed — get people to pause and think about an issue in a new way. You might be able to build — or reinforce — support for your cause or issue, especially if you win the primacy battle and make your side of the argument before others make a contrary appeal.

In your quest to persuade — and in the hope of getting published — here are a few tactics you might consider.

- **Take a bold stance:** There are times when the boldness of your main point will generate sufficient interest from readers to hook them. Boldness should be used carefully and somewhat sparingly with the understanding it could repel some people. My op-ed on kids left to die in hot cars (Chapter 34) falls into this category, because I made a point that many people are afraid to say publicly. "Cases like this are negligence, perhaps criminal negligence," I wrote.

- **Be the contrarian:** There are days when public opinion seems to be securely onboard a one-way express train where dissenting viewpoints are run over or forgotten. With the right timing, a thoughtful piece can raise questions or points left out of the debate and give readers pause to reconsider the issue at hand. My columns on the 2017 "Women's March" (Chapter 2) and a different op-ed on how presidents are not alone in their responsibility to appoint a Supreme Court justice (Chapter 11) are good examples of this approach. Such columns are more likely to be published than pieces from those already advancing the most commonly-heard viewpoints.

- **Offer your expertise:** If you have an expert perspective, use it. Just remember your audience and write in a way your readers can understand. I used this approach on my op-eds that talked about the legal system, drawing on my work as a prosecutor, magistrate, and U.S. Justice Department spokesman. Readers are more likely to side with experts, much in the same way expert witnesses can carry weight with a jury. (Chapters 5, 6, 12, 16, 21, 28)

- **Make it personal:** A newspaper editor once told me that features with personal stories on addicts fighting for their lives will generate more engaged minutes of reading from online readers than "straight news" stories on the same topic. Personal anecdotes such as my reflections on seeing killer Robert Buell on Ohio's Death Row (Chapter 32) can be among the most powerful form of op-eds. This approach humanizes the writer and allows for a better connection with readers who may empathize with your position. Columnists also can make their subjects highly personal by using strong imagery and focusing on character development.

- **Support your argument:** It's easy to make a claim and much harder to prove it. You may hope that the merit of your premise will stand on its own. But advancing three convincing and thoughtful underlying arguments to persuade will make that hope much more secure. Simple fact-based arguments can persuade powerfully. Many of my op-eds fall into this category.

- **Tell your own bad news:** While it can go against human nature, proactively releasing any information — especially negative news — before your critics reveal it, helps you win the battle for "primacy." This is the scientifically-proven notion that people most believe the argument they hear first. Remember the Tylenol example in this book. After a tampering scare, consumers saw Tylenol putting safety over profits and they stuck with the product. (Chapter 27) Now, imagine if VW had proactively told people they had mistakenly built cars to trick emissions tests and were fixing the issue. Instead, federal regulators released its version of the story first, nearly breaking the VW brand.

- **Compare to the past:** You've heard that history repeats itself. It can and often does. That's why I often use history to draw parallels to current events. Often, readers have never thought about the connection I make. Looking back at past events — especially old stories that readers will remember — can be an effective way to make a point on today's issues. You'll see how I did this in my op-ed contrasting George Zimmerman (on trial in 2013 for killing Trayvon Martin) with Sam Sheppard (on trial in 1954 for allegedly killing his wife). (Chapter 19) I also did this in the column where I compared the over-reassurances from city leaders in Philadelphia during the 1917-18 Great Influenza pandemic with similar over-reassurance from national leaders during the 2014 Ebola scare. (Chapter 17)

- **Address objections:** There are often good people and good arguments on both sides of a controversial issue. Calling names is rarely the right response and can undermine your integrity. Yet identifying and addressing some of the most pertinent objections raised by opponents of your own position can increase the credibility of your arguments. My column on former New York Mayor Rudy Giuliani shows what can happen when you don't address such objections from opponents. However, when seeking to address what your opposition is saying about your policy position, it's crucial to avoid repeating particularly damaging phrases or buzz words that they regularly use. When President Richard Nixon famously said, "I am not a crook," he wasn't really rebuffing his critics, he was reinforcing them. There's a fine line between addressing issues and giving certain terminology or concepts undeserved credibility. (Chapter 24)

- **Switch perspectives:** Find an argument or example that stretches the reader's mind to see a broader perspective. Imagine a lawsuit between downtrodden person and a large corporation. Instead of the company necessarily being the bad actor in a lawsuit, point out that companies are owned by shareholders and run by humans often trying to do their best job. If the facts fit, the person suing could be a vexatious litigator, represented by a greedy over-eager personal injury lawyer. The best example of switching perspectives is my op-ed on former President Obama and judicial empathy. (Chapter 23)

- **Apply your logic to their cause:** This is a powerful and effective way to force your opponent into acknowledging your point. Select a rule or issue opposed by the other side and apply that logic in a new context. Examine how their position could negatively impact a business or group your adversary normally supports. In my op-ed on outrage over Indiana's law allowing service businesses to not participate in gay weddings or situations that violated an owner's sincerely held religious beliefs, I closed with two strong examples using this technique. (Chapter 15)

- **Parallel construction:** Like comparing historical events with current affairs, this strategy involves connecting two seemingly random events that have much in common. This allows you to offer a lesson that obviously applied in the well-known example as one that also exists in the more recent example.

- **Triangulation:** As seen in my op-ed on the 2017 "Women's March," this technique identifies the common ground between two competing viewpoints as a place of common sense — a starting point for conversation. While this concept can be cynically employed to pit political factions against each other, I prefer to use it to bring people together. Finding common ground is often the first step to resolving conflicts or at least exposing two differing sides to a place of moderation. (Chapter 2)

Terms and tools

- **Primacy:** The idea that the first thing an unbiased listener hears is the most credible. Telling your side of the story first will allow people to adopt your view of a situation. Once they see things your way, they are less likely to change that opinion. That's largely because of a concept called "confirmation bias," as well as the next key term, cognitive dissonance.

- **Cognitive dissonance:** The mind likes things to be neat and in agreement. That's why new information that's in line with a someone's previous belief is likely to be accepted, while contrary new information is rejected as unharmonious or dissonant. Attitudes are a lot like blocks of cement, once hardened, it's hard to change them.

- **Alliteration:** This simply means starting a few keywords with the same letter, typically a consonant. When done sparingly, alliteration can make a powerful passage positively persuasive. If you know what I mean. You'll see this style used in many of my columns and speeches.

- **Metaphor:** Metaphor comes from the Latin word metaphora and roughly means "carrying over." It helps you explain a new concept by comparing it to an already-understood idea. The information carries over. A well-chosen metaphor can add punch to an essay or speech. Think back to my column on former President Bill Clinton's nominations for attorney general where I wrote: "Clinton's political flip-flops have made the "Flying Wallendas" look like amateurs." (Chapter 38) You may also recall my use of "Rock, Paper, Scissors" to help third-graders understand the separation of powers in our government. These are examples of metaphors. (Chapter 47)

- **Power words:** Use strong verbs and adjectives whenever possible. Avoid using "is" and "was" too frequently and use action words instead of passive tense. Word choice can make a real difference in the argument. Was the BP incident in the Gulf of Mexico involving oil a "leak" or a "spill." Was what happened at the bar an "accident" or an "incident." Is the government agency undertaking an "investigation" or a "review?" Choosing the right words can make a big difference.

- **Simile:** Use similes to help strengthen your persuasion effort. For my column about the Attorney General of Pennsylvania who disgraced her office, I used the simile of a driver heading down a dead-end road to describe what was happening in a way that might resonate well with readers. (Chapter 14)

- **Word imagery:** Highly descriptive words can draw readers into your stirring symphony of thoughts. "The liquid hiss of sprinklers quenching lawns and gardens" from my column about kids left to die in hot cars is one example of such language. (Chapter 34)

Final thoughts

A wordsmith's work is never done.

This book began in fits and starts. I started a different book, one intended for business leaders, but a data blip sent it to the graveyard of good efforts. I will resurrect it someday.

Now that this book is complete, I hope to devote my non-professional writing to a novel I outlined in my head many years ago. Here and there I've written chapters and snips and snaps of dialogue. To say it's half-finished would be too charitable. I've shared the storyline with a few dozen people over the years, and nearly all of them express great interest in reading it. Such is the reaction of overly-generous friends and colleagues. Once complete, we shall see what the larger book-buying public thinks of it.

To be fully honest, I doubt I'll make much money in books. I've earned a good living cobbling together speeches, op-eds, legal briefs, and scripts for clients. That enterprise has fed my family and sent my kids to college. This book, and those to come, are more avocation than vocation and that suits me just fine.

So, whether my phone buzzes with a client in crisis or my email inbox blinks with another request to draft a speech, one thing is clear to me: God willing, there will always be work for this wordsmith.

About the Author

Mark R. Weaver is an author, attorney, and media expert with decades of experience. He regularly works with public and private sector clients on crisis communications, executive speech coaching, and news media relations and has counseled clients in 18 states. NBC News in Charlotte, North Carolina, called Mr. Weaver "one of the nation's foremost experts in crisis communications."

Before founding his own company, Communications Counsel, Inc., Mr. Weaver was the Deputy Attorney General of Ohio, where he was responsible for crisis management, strategic counseling, and all communications for an agency with 1,400 employees and 50,000 cases. He also served on the Attorney General's four-member Executive Staff and acted as a senior policy advisor and chief spokesman.

His past professional assignments include serving as the Assistant Director of Public Affairs for the U.S Department of Justice, Public Information Director for a large Pennsylvania municipality, and Vice President of a national communications firm in Washington, D.C.

His teaching experience includes work as an Adjunct Professor at The Ohio State University Moritz College of Law, the School of Government at the University of North Carolina Chapel Hill, and the Bliss Institute of Applied Politics at the University of Akron.

Mr. Weaver has provided media advice to thousands of government officials. He's written hundreds of PR plans, conducted media coaching, and supervised countless polls and focus groups. His media production skills have earned him more than a dozen national awards for excellence in advertising. In 1993, as a young media professional, he wrote, produced, and directed the TV special "An American Story," hosted by former President Ronald Reagan.

Early in his career, Mr. Weaver was a Communications Director with the Pennsylvania House of Representatives. He also ran a Philadelphia-area communications consulting firm serving more than 100 clients.

Mr. Weaver earned bachelors and masters degrees in Public Administration from Kutztown University in Pennsylvania, where he has received more alumni awards than any other graduate of that institution. He also pursued graduate studies at the University of Delaware.

He earned his Juris Doctorate from the Delaware Law School of Widener University, where he graduated in the top 15 percent of his class. In 2004, the University of Akron awarded Mr. Weaver an honorary degree in Applied Politics. In 2012, Mr. Weaver was named Distinguished Chair of that university's Bliss Institute of Applied Politics.

His op-ed writing has been featured in major U.S. newspapers and he has been interviewed by every major national media outlet in America including 60 Minutes, Nightline, ABC News, CBS News, NBC News, MSNBC, CNN, FOX News, NPR, USA Today, Newsweek, Time, the *New York Times, the Washington Post, the Los Angeles Times*, and the Associated Press.

Mr. Weaver and his wife, Lori are the proud parents of two children: Jamieson and Mark Robert Weaver, Jr. (Robbie). The Weaver family resides in Central Ohio.

Their red Labrador retriever Gracie wants to say "hi."

Woof.